More superb collections in
DELL LAUREL EDITIONS

SHORT STORY MASTERPIECES
Edited by Robert Penn Warren
and Albert Erskine.
The finest collection of modern short stories available by such masters as Hemingway, Faulkner, Fitzgerald, Steinbeck, Maugham, Joyce, Conrad, Thurber and 26 others.   *75c*

GREAT AMERICAN SHORT STORIES
Edited by Wallace and Mary Stegner
A century and a quarter of the finest American short stories from Washington Irving to John O'Hara. *75c*

SIX GREAT MODERN SHORT NOVELS
A collection acclaimed by schools and colleges. James Joyce: *The Dead*; Melville: *Billy Budd, Foretopman*; Katherine Anne Porter: *Noon Wine*; Gogol: *The Overcoat*; Glenway Wescott: *The Pilgrim Hawk*; Faulkner: *The Bear*.   *60c*

CONTENTS

Introduction

This is a seaman's selection of sea stories. I am not sure that they are the best in all the vast collection of sea writings down the centuries, and I am not certain of greatness except as it makes a personal impact upon me. I set myself up in no way as a judge of literature. But I have served in a few different types of ships when I could, and maybe, over the past forty years, I have learned something about seafaring—enough, I trust, to distinguish the falsehood of the non-maritime yarn-gatherer spinning too much from too little; the too personal reflections of the misfit ashore who far too often becomes a misfit at sea, temporarily sailing in ships manned by types I have never met, to write there-after of a sea he never knew and no one else may recognize.

There are plenty of good seamen writers and have been since the Rev. Hakluyt first thought of collecting their stories over three hundred years ago. Most of the great sailing discoverers left remarkably good accounts of their voyages. Dampier (who was as often a pirate as he was a discoverer), the illustrious Yorkshireman James Cook, the too little known Carteret, for instance, have left us excellent narrations of their voyages, and the Hakluyt Society publishes some new-old account of great voyagings each year to this day. Marryat for the Navy, Dana for the merchant service, Melville for whalers and whaling, all knew their subject at first hand, and not from any mere dogwatch of experience sought for the sake of writing about it either. At least one truly great novelist and one of the greatest living poets were professional seamen before they were writers, and served ships for years before putting pen to paper. And so it seems to me that, for real portrayal of ships and the sea as seamen know them, we have no need to look past the seamen-writers themselves.

Not that I mean to be dogmatic about it. A few others have written excellent sea books. But for the authentic movement of the true sea, the shriek of the real gale, the sound of the wind in the rigging, the throb of power down below and all the rest that goes with the service of ships which ply the sea, I prefer to go to the writings of those who have gone down to the sea themselves, as a profession, in the service of ships and not editors. When it comes to the sea and ships, I readily admit to bias. I go along with Captain Conrad. "No adventure ever came to one for the asking," writes that master of ships and writing, in *The Mirror of the Sea*. "He who starts on a deliberate quest of adventure goes forth but to gather dead-sea fruit, unless, indeed, he be beloved of the gods and great among heroes. . . ."

I have made my selection of what I considered memorable, and I put it forward hoping that it may form a book of some value which anyone may pick up and read, realizing that, whatever their literary shortcomings, these are stories of ships the way they are, of the sea the way that seamen have learned to know it down the years.

ALAN VILLIERS

Oxford
June, 1959

CAPTAIN JOSEPH CONRAD

"The few sailors who do write, *can* write!" as a literary Don said to me with enthusiasm the other day. Of such sailors, Captain Joseph Conrad is Number One. He is the beginning and the end. When I read him, I give up. He has said it all—said it brilliantly, profoundly, in compelling and perfect English, said it to last forever. He was born a Pole, an aristocrat, brought up inland. He did not go to sea until his late teens, at a time when youth usually set out on that arduous profession nearer the age of twelve, and his first ships were French. He spoke English with an accent all his life, and did not know the language at all until he sailed in British ships, where he first learned it in the forecastle. He saw service in tough ships, and rose to command. Chance seems to have played an important part alike in his seafaring and his writing—or call it fate if you wish. An error in calculating the ship's probable stability when he was mate of the ship *Highland Forest* and, as such, responsible for loading her outward cargo, caused the ship to throw a spar adrift one day, on passage toward Samarang. She was stiff and she rolled very badly. The spar hit Conrad who had to go to hospital to recover. His ship sailed without him, and he had to take a berth as chief officer in an old steamer called the *Virdar,* trading out of Singapore round the islands to earn his living. Here he met the trader who later was immortalized as Almayer.

"If I had not got to know Almayer pretty well it is almost certain there never would have been a line of mine in print," he wrote in *A Personal Record*. Conrad began writing *Almayer's Folly* while temporarily ashore in London in 1889. He was still working on it when, years later, John Galsworthy came as passenger in the famous wool clipper *Torrens* on a run to Australia. The great novelist en couraged the young mate of the Limejuice clipper; he found Conrad scribbling away at a masterpiece when he should have been asleep, during brief watches below.

Much of Conrad's writing is based on his experiences as a professional seaman. Command of the barque *Otago* brought *The Secret Sharer* and *The Shadow Line*. (I knew that lovely little barque well in her last days, when she was a coal hulk at Hobart. Even as a blackened and semi-mechanized hulk, her grace of line and thoroughbred proportions shone through the grime. She must have been a stirring command.) An appointment in a West African river steamer led to the *Heart of Darkness*. The schooner *Saint-Antoine,* whose mate was a gun-running Corsican named Dominic, gave him the material for *Nostromo*.

The story chosen, "Youth," arose directly from Conrad's first berth as second mate. This was in an old-timer named *Palestine*, a deepwaterman of scarce four hundred tons, in which he loaded a cargo of coal on the Tyne toward Bangkok in 1881. The *Palestine* never delivered that cargo at Bangkok. She was old and leaky and, after being forced twice to go back to Falmouth to mend leaks in her poor but graceful old hull, she had finally to be abandoned in the Banka Straits with her coal cargo hopelessly afire. It had been under hatches for too long. Seventeen years after that abandonment "Youth" first saw print in 1898. Conrad took his time.

I get a little tired of high-brows and others who regard Teodor Jozef Konrad Korzeniowski as a writer who just more or less happened to drift to sea. Captain Conrad was a professional seaman who chose to go to sea and served there, mainly under sail, for twenty years. As a master mariner, a naturalized Britisher, he did things with square-rigged ships which few other masters dared to try. Once, for example, when bound from Melbourne toward Mauritius (a passage in which the first part is a slog against westerly gales) he sought and gained his owners' permission to sail their barque by way of the Coral Sea and Torres Straits, as dangerous a reef-littered and treacherous spot as a square-rigger might fear to find. Conrad *chose* to go that way, and made a fine passage of it.

He writes of what he knows, and he uses the sea and sailors as only a real sailorman could. It was scarcity of berths that drove him ashore. At the age of nearly forty, like many others who had elected to stay with sail, he found berths hard to come by and it was late then to join a steamship company and "work up," even if he had wished. He knew that he could write though, at first at any rate, he did not seem to have thought much of his prospects in that profession. "The only existence remaining to me is writing," he said in March, 1896. "It is just a matter of earning money, which is something quite distinct from literary merit."

Yet he went on to become the greatest writer of the sea. He died in August, 1924, and is buried at Canterbury in Kent in England. I was still a working seaman then and I never met him. It was ten years afterward before I met his widow, whose permission I was seeking to rename in honor of her husband the beautiful little full-rigged ship *Georg Stage,* which I had just bought and by the terms of the contract had to give another name. Mrs. Conrad received me graciously and the matter was soon arranged. But to me, something of the great brooding spirit of that adventurous and extraordinarily gifted Polish seaman still could be felt in his Canterbury house, so typical a piece of England. It was Captain Conrad's permission I had really come for, though he was then a decade dead. I went away feeling that, well, perhaps I had that, too.

Youth

by CAPTAIN JOSEPH CONRAD

This could have occurred nowhere but in England, where men and sea interpenetrate, so to speak—the sea entering into the life of most men, and the men knowing something or everything about the sea, in the way of amusement, of travel, or of bread-winning.

We were sitting round a mahogany table that reflected the bottle, the claret-glasses, and our faces as we leaned on our elbows. There was a director of companies, an accountant, a lawyer, Marlow, and myself. The director had been a *Conway* boy, the accountant had served four years at sea, the lawyer—a fine crusted Tory, High Churchman, the best of old fellows, the soul of honor—had been chief officer in the P. & O. service in the good old days when mail-boats were square-rigged at least on two masts, and used to come down the China Sea before a fair monsoon with stun'-sails set alow and aloft. We all began life in the merchant service. Between the five of us there was the strong bond of the sea, and also the fellowship of the craft, which no amount of enthusiasm for yachting, cruising, and so on can give, since one is only the amusement of life and the other is life itself.

Marlow (at least I think that is how he spelt his name) told the story, or rather the chronicle, of a voyage:—

"Yes, I have seen a little of the Eastern seas; but what I remember best is my first voyage there. You fellows know there are those voyages that seem ordered for the illustration of life, that might stand for a symbol of existence. You fight, work, sweat, nearly kill yourself, sometimes do kill yourself, trying to accomplish something—and you can't. Not from any fault of yours. You simply can do nothing, neither great nor little—not a thing in the world—not even marry an old maid, or get a wretched 600-ton cargo of coal to its port of destination.

"It was altogether a memorable affair. It was my first voyage to the East, and my first voyage as second mate; it was also my skipper's first command. You'll admit it was time. He was sixty if a day; a little man, with a broad, not very straight back, with bowed shoulders and one leg more bandy than the other, he had that queer twisted-about appearance you see so often in men who work in the fields. He had a nut-cracker face—chin and nose trying to come together over a sunken mouth—and it was framed in iron-gray fluffy hair, that looked like a chin-strap of cotton-wool sprinkled with coal-dust. And he had blue eyes in that old face of his, which were amazingly like a boy's, with that candid expression some quite common men preserve to the end of their days by a rare internal gift of simplicity of heart and rectitude of soul. What induced him to accept me was a wonder. I had come out of a crack Australian clipper, where I had been third officer, and he seemed to have a prejudice against crack clippers as aristocratic and high-toned. He said to me, 'You know, in this ship you will have to work.' I said I had to work in every ship I had ever been in. 'Ah, but this is different, and you gentlemen out of them big ships; . . . but there! I dare say you will do. Join tomorrow.'

"I joined tomorrow. It was twenty-two years ago; and I was just twenty. How time passes! It was one of the happiest days of my life. Fancy! Second mate for the first time—a really responsible officer! I wouldn't have thrown up my new billet for a fortune. The mate looked me over carefully. He was also an old chap, but of another stamp. He had a Roman nose, a snow-white, long beard, and his name was Mahon, but he insisted that it should be pronounced Mann. He was well connected; yet there was something wrong with his luck, and he had never got on.

"As to the captain, he had been for years in coasters, then in the Mediterranean, and last in the West Indian trade. He had never been round the Capes. He could just write a kind of sketchy hand, and didn't care for writing at all. Both were thorough good seamen of course, and between those two old chaps I felt like a small boy between two grandfathers.

"The ship also was old. Her name was the *Judea*. Queer name, isn't it? She belonged to a man Wilmer, Wilcox—some name like that; but he has been bankrupt and dead these twenty years or more, and his name don't matter. She had been laid up in Shadwell basin for ever so long. You may imagine her state. She was all rust, dust, grime—soot aloft, dirt on deck. To me it was like coming out of a palace into a ruined cottage. She was about 400 tons, had a primitive windlass, wooden latches to the doors, not a bit of brass about her, and a big square stern. There was on it, below her name in big letters, a lot of scrollwork, with the gilt off, and some sort of a coat of arms, with the motto 'Do or Die' underneath. I remember it took my fancy immensely. There was a touch of romance in it, something that made me love the old thing—something that appealed to my youth!

"We left London in ballast—sand ballast—to load a cargo of coal in a northern port for Bankok. Bankok! I thrilled. I had been six years at sea, but had only seen Melbourne and Sydney, very good places, charming places in their way—but Bankok!

"We worked out of the Thames under canvas, with a North Sea pilot on board. His name was Jermyn, and he dodged all day long about the galley drying his handkerchief before the stove. Apparently he never slept. He was a dismal man, with a perpetual tear sparkling at the end of his nose, who either had been in trouble, or was in trouble, or expected to be in trouble—couldn't be happy unless something went wrong. He mistrusted my youth, my common-sense, and my seamanship, and made a point of showing it in a hundred little ways. I dare say he was right. It seems to me I knew very little then, and I know not much more now; but I cherish a hate for that Jermyn to this day.

"We were a week working up as far as Yarmouth Roads, and then we got into a gale—the famous October gale of twenty-two years ago. It was wind, lightning, sleet, snow, and a terrific sea. We were flying light, and you may imagine how bad it was when I tell you we had smashed bulwarks and a flooded deck. On the second night she shifted her ballast into the lee bow, and by that time we had been blown off somewhere on the Dogger Bank. There was nothing for it but go below with shovels and try to right her, and there we were in that vast hold, gloomy like a cavern, the tallow dips stuck and flickering on the beams, the gale howling above, the ship tossing about like mad on her side; there we all were, Jermyn, the captain, everyone, hardly able to keep our feet, engaged on that gravedigger's work, and trying to toss shovelfuls of wet sand up to windward. At every tumble of the ship you could see vaguely in the dim light men falling down with a great flourish of shovels. One of the ship's boys (we had two), impressed by the weirdness of the scene, wept as if his heart would break. We could hear him blubbering somewhere in the shadows.

"On the third day the gale died out, and by and by a north-country tug picked us up. We took sixteen days in all to get from London to the Tyne! When we got into dock we had lost our turn for loading, and they hauled us off to a pier where we remained for a month. Mrs. Beard (the captain's name was Beard) came from Colchester to see the old man. She lived on board. The crew of runners had left, and there remained only the officers, one boy and the steward, a mulatto who answered to the name of Abraham. Mrs. Beard was an old woman, with a face all wrinkled and ruddy like a winter apple, and the figure of a young girl. She caught sight of me once, sewing on a button, and insisted on having my shirts to repair. This was something different from the captains' wives I had known on board crack clippers. When I brought her the shirts, she said: 'And the socks? They want mending, I am sure, and John's—Captain Beard's—things are all in order now. I would be glad of something to do.' Bless the old woman. She overhauled my outfit for me, and meantime I read for the first time *Sartor Resartus* and Burnaby's *Ride to Khiva*. I didn't understand much of the first then; but I remember I preferred the soldier to the philosopher at the time; a preference which life has only confirmed. One was a man, and the other was either more—or less. However, they are both dead and Mrs. Beard is dead, and youth, strength, genius, thoughts, achievements, simple hearts—all die. . . . No matter.

"They loaded us at last. We shipped a crew. Eight able seamen and two boys. We hauled off one evening to the buoys at the dock-gates, ready to go out, and with a fair prospect of beginning the voyage next day. Mrs. Beard was to start for home by a late train. When the ship was fast we went to tea. We sat rather silent through the meal—Mahon, the old couple, and I. I finished first, and slipped away for a smoke, my cabin being in a deck-house just against the poop. It was high water, blowing fresh with a drizzle; the double dock-gates were opened, and the steam-colliers were going in and out in the darkness with their lights burning bright, a great plashing of propellers, rattling of winches, and a lot of hailing on the pier heads. I watched the procession of head-lights, gliding high and of green lights gliding low in the night, when suddenly a red gleam flashed at me, vanished, came into view again, and remained. The fore-end of a steamer loomed up close. I shouted down the cabin, 'Come up, quick!' and then heard a startled voice saying afar in the dark, 'Stop her, sir.' A bell jingled. Another voice cried warningly, 'We are going right into that barque, sir.' The answer to this was a gruff 'All right,' and the next thing was a heavy crash as the steamer struck a glancing blow with the bluff of her bow about our fore-rigging. There was a moment of confusion, yelling, and running about. Steam roared. Then somebody was heard saying, 'All clear, sir.' . . . 'Are you all right?' asked the gruff voice. I had jumped forward to see the damage, and hailed back, 'I think so.' 'Easy astern,' said the gruff voice. A bell jingled. 'What steamer is that?' screamed Mahon. By that time she was no more to us than a bulky shadow maneuvering a little way off. They shouted at us some name—a woman's name, Miranda or Melissa—or some such thing. 'This means another month in this beastly hole,' said Mahon to me, as we peered with lamps about the splintered bulwarks and broken braces. 'But where's the captain?'

"We had not heard or seen anything of him all that time. We went aft to look. A doleful voice arose hailing somewhere in the middle of the dock, '*Judea* ahoy!' . . . How the devil did he get there? . . . 'Hallo!' we shouted. 'I am adrift in our boat without oars,' he cried. A belated water-man offered his services, and Mahon struck a bargain with him for half-a-crown to tow our skipper alongside; but it was Mrs. Beard that came up the ladder first. They had been floating about the dock in that mizzly cold rain for nearly an hour. I was never so surprised in my life.

"It appears that when he heard my shout 'Come up' he understood at once what was the matter, caught up his wife, ran on deck, and across, and down into our boat, which was fast to the ladder. Not bad for a sixty-year-old. Just imagine that old fellow saving heroically in his arms that old woman—the woman of his life. He set her down on a thwart, and was ready to climb back on board when the painter came adrift somehow, and away they went together. Of course in the confusion we did not hear him shouting. He looked abashed. She said cheerfully, 'I suppose it does not matter my losing the train now?' 'No, Jenny—you go below and get warm,' he growled. Then to us: 'A sailor has no business with a wife—I say. There I was, out of the ship. Well, no harm done this time. Let's go and look at what that fool of a steamer smashed.'

"It wasn't much, but it delayed us three weeks. At the end of that time, the captain being engaged with his agents, I carried Mrs. Beard's bag to the railway-station and put her all comfy into a third-class carriage. She lowered the window to say, 'You are a good young man. If you see John—Captain Beard—without his muffler at night, just remind him from me to keep his throat well wrapped up.' 'Certainly, Mrs. Beard,' I said. 'You are a good young man; I noticed how attentive you are to John—to Captain—' The train pulled out suddenly; I took my cap off to the old woman: I never saw her again. . . . Pass the bottle.

"We went to sea next day. When we made that start for Bankok we had been already three months out of London. We had expected to be a fortnight or so—at the outside.

"It was January, and the weather was beautiful—the beautiful sunny winter weather that has more charm than in the summertime, because it is unexpected, and crisp, and you know it won't, it can't, last long. It's like a windfall, like a godsend, like an unexpected piece of luck.

"It lasted all down the North Sea, all down Channel; and it lasted till we were three hundred miles or so to the westward of the Lizards: then the wind went round to the sou'west and began to pipe up. In two days it blew a gale. The *Judea,* hove to, wallowed on the Atlantic like an old candle-box. It blew day after day: it blew with spite, without interval, without mercy, without rest. The world was nothing but an immensity of great foaming waves rushing at us, under a sky low enough to touch with the hand and dirty like a smoked ceiling. In the stormy space surrounding us there was as much flying spray as air. Day after day and

night after night there was nothing round the ship but
the howl of the wind, the tumult of the sea, the noise
of water pouring over her deck. There was no rest for
her and no rest for us. She tossed, she pitched, she stood
on her head, she sat on her tail, she rolled, she groaned,
and we had to hold on while on deck and cling to our
bunks when below, in a constant effort of body and
worry of mind.

"One night Mahon spoke through the small window
of my berth. It opened right into my very bed, and I
was lying there sleepless, in my boots, feeling as though
I had not slept for years, and could not if I tried. He
said excitedly—

" 'You got the sounding-rod in here, Marlow? I
can't get the pumps to suck. By God! it's no child's
play.'

"I gave him the sounding-rod and lay down again,
trying to think of various things—but I thought only
of the pumps. When I came on deck they were still at
it, and my watch relieved at the pumps. By the light of
the lantern brought on deck to examine the sounding-
rod I caught a glimpse of their weary, serious faces.
We pumped all the four hours. We pumped all night,
all day, all the week—watch and watch. She was working herself loose, and leaked badly—not enough to
drown us at once, but enough to kill us with the work
at the pumps. And while we pumped the ship was going from us piecemeal: the bulwarks went, the stanchions were torn out, the ventilators smashed, the cab-
in-door burst in. There was not a dry spot in the ship.
She was being gutted bit by bit. The long-boat changed,
as if by magic, into matchwood where she stood in her
gripes. I had lashed her myself, and was rather proud
of my handiwork, which had withstood so long the
malice of the sea. And we pumped. And there was no
break in the weather. The sea was white like a sheet
of foam, like a caldron of boiling milk; there was not
a break in the clouds, no—not the size of a man's hand
—no, not for so much as ten seconds. There was for us

no sky, there were for us no stars, no sun, no universe—nothing but angry clouds and an infuriated sea. We pumped watch and watch, for dear life; and it seemed to last for months, for years, for all eternity, as though we had been dead and gone to a hell for sailors. We forgot the day of the week, the name of the month, what year it was, and whether we had ever been ashore. The sails blew away, she lay broadside on under a weather-cloth, the ocean poured over her, and we did not care. We turned those handles, and had the eyes of idiots. As soon as we had crawled on deck I used to take a round turn with a rope about the men, the pumps, and the mainmast, and we turned, we turned incessantly, with the water to our waists, to our necks, over our heads. It was all one. We had forgotten how it felt to be dry.

"And there was somewhere in me the thought: By Jove! this is the deuce of an adventure—something you read about; and it is my first voyage as second mate—and I am only twenty—and here I am lasting it out as well as any of these men, and keeping my chaps up to the mark. I was pleased. I would not have given up the experience for worlds. I had moments of exultation. Whenever the old dismantled craft pitched heavily with her counter high in the air, she seemed to me to throw up, like an appeal, like a defiance, like a cry to the clouds without mercy, the words written on her stern: '*Judea*, London. Do or Die.'

"O Youth! The strength of it, the faith of it, the imagination of it! To me she was not an old rattle-trap carting about the world a lot of coal for a freight—to me she was the endeavor, the test, the trial of life. I think of her with pleasure, with affection, with regret—as you would think of someone dead you have loved. I shall never forget her. . . . Pass the bottle.

"One night when tied to the mast, as I explained, we were pumping on, deafened with the wind, and without spirit enough in us to wish ourselves dead, a heavy sea crashed aboard and swept clean over us. As soon as I got my breath I shouted, as in duty bound, 'Keep on, boys!' when suddenly I felt something hard floating on deck strike the calf of my leg. I made a grab at it and missed. It was so dark we could not see each other's faces within a foot—you understand.

"After that thump the ship kept quiet for a while, and the thing, whatever it was, struck my leg again. This time I caught it—and it was a saucepan. At first, being stupid with fatigue and thinking of nothing but the pumps, I did not understand what I had in my hand. Suddenly it dawned upon me, and I shouted, 'Boys, the house on deck is gone. Leave this, and let's look for the cook.'

"There was a deck-house forward, which contained the galley, the cook's berth, and the quarters of the crew. As we had expected for days to see it swept away, the hands had been ordered to sleep in the cabin—the only safe place in the ship. The steward, Abraham, however, persisted in clinging to his berth, stupidly, like a mule—from sheer fright I believe, like an animal that won't leave a stable falling in an earthquake. So we went to look for him. It was chancing death, since once out of our lashings we were as exposed as if on a raft. But we went. The house was shattered as if a shell had exploded inside. Most of it had gone overboard—stove, men's quarters, and their property, all was gone; but two posts, holding a portion of the bulkhead to which Abraham's bunk was attached, remained as if by a miracle. We groped in the ruins and came upon this, and there he was, sitting in his bunk, surrounded by foam and wreckage, jabbering cheerfully to himself. He was out of his mind; completely and forever mad, with this sudden shock coming upon the fag-end of his endurance. We snatched him up, lugged him aft, and pitched him head-first down the cabin companion. You understand there was no time to carry him down with infinite precautions and wait to see how he got on. Those below would pick him up at the bottom of the stairs all right. We were in a hurry to go back to the pumps. That business could not wait. A bad leak is an inhuman thing.

"One would think that the sole purpose of that fiendish gale had been to make a lunatic of that poor devil of a mulatto. It eased before morning, and next day the sky cleared, and as the sea went down the leak took up. When it came to bending a fresh set of sails the crew demanded to put back—and really there was nothing else to do. Boats gone, decks swept clean, cabin gutted, men without a stitch but what they stood in, stores spoiled, ship strained. We put her head for home, and—would you believe it? The wind came east right in our teeth. It blew fresh, it blew continuously. We had to beat up every inch of the way, but she did not leak so badly, the water keeping comparatively smooth. Two hours' pumping in every four is no joke —but it kept her afloat as far as Falmouth.

"The good people there live on casualties of the sea, and no doubt were glad to see us. A hungry crowd of shipwrights sharpened their chisels at the sight of that carcass of a ship. And, by Jove! they had pretty pickings off us before they were done. I fancy the owner was already in a tight place. There were delays. Then it was decided to take part of the cargo out and caulk her topsides. This was done, the repairs finished, cargo reshipped; a new crew came on board, and we went out—for Bankok. At the end of a week we were back again. The crew said they weren't going to Bankok— a hundred and fifty days' passage—in a something hooker that wanted pumping eight hours out of the twenty-four; and the nautical papers inserted again the little paragraph: '*Judea*. Barque. Tyne to Bankok; coals; put back to Falmouth leaky and with crew refusing duty.'

"There were more delays—more tinkering. The owner came down for a day, and said she was as right as a little fiddle. Poor old Captain Beard looked like the ghost of a Geordie skipper—through the worry and humiliation of it. Remember he was sixty, and it was

his first command. Mahon said it was a foolish business, and would end badly. I loved the ship more than
ever, and wanted awfully to get to Bankok. To Bankok! Magic name, blessed name. Mesopotamia wasn't
a patch on it. Remember I was twenty, and it was my
first second-mate's billet, and the East was waiting for
me.

"We went out and anchored in the outer roads with
a fresh crew—the third. She leaked worse than ever. It
was as if those confounded shipwrights had actually
made a hole in her. This time we did not even go outside. The crew simply refused to man the windlass.

"They towed us back to the inner harbor, and we
became a fixture, a feature, an institution of the place.
People pointed us out to visitors as 'That 'ere barque
that's going to Bankok—has been here six months—put
back three times.' On holidays the small boys pulling
about in boats would hail, '*Judea,* ahoy!' and if a head
showed above the rail shouted, 'Where you bound to?
—Bankok?' and jeered. We were only three on board.
The poor old skipper mooned in the cabin. Mahon
undertook the cooking, and unexpectedly developed
all a Frenchman's genius for preparing nice little
messes. I looked languidly after the rigging. We became
citizens of Falmouth. Every shopkeeper knew us. At
the barber's or tobacconist's they asked familiarly, 'Do
you think you will ever get to Bankok?' Meantime the
owner, the underwriters, and the charterers squabbled
amongst themselves in London, and our pay went on.
. . . Pass the bottle.

"It was horrid. Morally it was worse than pumping
for life. It seemed as though we had been forgotten
by the world, belonged to nobody, would get nowhere;
it seemed that, as if bewitched, we would have to live
forever and ever in that inner harbor, a derision and
a byword to generations of long-shore loafers and dis-
honest boatmen. I obtained three months' pay and a
five days' leave, and made a rush for London. It took
me a day to get there and pretty well another to come

back—but three months' pay went all the same. I don't know what I did with it. I went to a music-hall, I believe, lunched, dined, and supped in a swell place in Regent Street, and was back to time, with nothing but a complete set of Byron's works and a new railway rug to show for three months' work. The boatman who pulled me off to the ship said: 'Hallo! I thought you had left the old thing. *She* will never get to Bankok.' 'That's all *you* know about it,' I said scornfully—but I didn't like that prophecy at all.

"Suddenly a man, some kind of agent to somebody, appeared with full powers. He had grog-blossoms all over his face, an indomitable energy, and was a jolly soul. We leaped into life again. A hulk came alongside, took our cargo, and then we went into dry dock to get our copper stripped. No wonder she leaked. The poor thing, strained beyond endurance by the gale, had, as if in disgust, spat out all the oakum of her lower seams. She was recaulked, new coppered, and made as tight as a bottle. We went back to the hulk and reshipped our cargo.

"Then, on a fine moonlight night, all the rats left the ship.

"We had been infested with them. They had destroyed our sails, consumed more stores than the crew, affably shared our beds and our dangers, and now, when the ship was made seaworthy, concluded to clear out. I called Mahon to enjoy the spectacle. Rat after rat appeared on our rail, took a last look over his shoulder, and leaped with a hollow thud into the empty hulk. We tried to count them, but soon lost the tale. Mahon said: 'Well, well! don't talk to me about the intelligence of rats. They ought to have left before, when we had that narrow squeak from foundering. There you have the proof how silly is the superstition about them. They leave a good ship for an old rotten hulk, where there is nothing to eat, too, the fools! . . . I don't believe they know what is safe or what is good for them, any more than you or I.'

"And after some more talk we agreed that the wisdom of rats had been grossly overrated, being in fact no greater than that of men.

"The story of the ship was known, by this, all up the Channel from Land's End to the Forelands, and we could get no crew on the south coast. They sent us one all complete from Liverpool, and we left once more—for Bankok.

"We had fair breezes, smooth water right into the tropics, and the old *Judea* lumbered along in the sunshine. When she went eight knots everything cracked aloft, and we tied our caps to our heads; but mostly she strolled on at the rate of three miles an hour. What could you expect? She was tired—that old ship. Her youth was where mine is—where yours is—you fellows who listen to this yarn; and what friend would throw your years and your weariness in your face? We didn't grumble at her. To us aft, at least, it seemed as though we had been born in her, reared in her, had lived in her for ages, had never known any other ship. I would just as soon have abused the old village church at home for not being a cathedral.

"And for me there was also my youth to make me patient. There was all the East before me, and all life, and the thought that I had been tried in that ship and had come out pretty well. And I thought of men of old who, centuries ago, went that road in ships that sailed no better, to the land of palms, and spices, and yellow sands, and of brown nations ruled by kings more cruel than Nero the Roman, and more splendid than Solomon the Jew. The old bark lumbered on, heavy with her age and the burden of her cargo, while I lived the life of youth in ignorance and hope. She lumbered on through an interminable procession of days; and the fresh gilding flashed back at the setting sun, seemed to cry out over the darkening sea the words painted on her stern, '*Judea*, London. Do or Die.'

"Then we entered the Indian Ocean and steered

northerly for Java Head. The winds were light. Weeks slipped by. She crawled on, do or die, and people at home began to think of posting us as overdue.

"One Saturday evening, I being off duty, the men asked me to give them an extra bucket of water or so— for washing clothes. As I did not wish to screw on the fresh-water pump so late, I went forward whistling, and with a key in my hand to unlock the forepeak scuttle, intending to serve the water out of a spare tank we kept there.

"The smell down below was as unexpected as it was frightful. One would have thought hundreds of paraffin-lamps had been flaring and smoking in that hole for days. I was glad to get out. The man with me coughed and said, 'Funny smell, sir.' I answered negligently, 'It's good for the health they say,' and walked aft.

"The first thing I did was to put my head down the square of the midship ventilator. As I lifted the lid a visible breath, something like a thin fog, a puff of faint haze, rose from the opening. The ascending air was hot, and had a heavy, sooty, paraffiny smell. I gave one sniff, and put down the lid gently. It was no use choking myself. The cargo was on fire.

"Next day she began to smoke in earnest. You see it was to be expected, for though the coal was of a safe kind, that cargo had been so handled, so broken up with handling, that it looked more like smithy coal than anything else. Then it had been wetted—more than once. It rained all the time we were taking it back from the hulk, and now with this long passage it got heated, and there was another case of spontaneous combustion.

"The captain called us into the cabin. He had a chart spread on the table, and looked unhappy. He said, 'The coast of West Australia is near, but I mean to proceed to our destination. It is the hurricane month, too; but we will just keep her head for Bankok, and fight the fire. No more putting back anywhere, if we all get roasted. We will try first to stifle this 'ere damned combustion by want of air.'

"We tried. We battened down everything, and still she smoked. The smoke kept coming out through imperceptible crevices; it forced itself through bulkheads and covers; it oozed here and there and everywhere in slender threads, in an invisible film, in an incomprehensible manner. It made its way into the cabin, into the forecastle; it poisoned the sheltered places on the deck, it could be sniffed as high as the mainyard. It was clear that if the smoke came out the air came in. This was disheartening. This combustion refused to be stifled.

"We resolved to try water, and took the hatches off. Enormous volumes of smoke, whitish, yellowish, thick, greasy, misty, choking, ascended as high as the trucks. All hands cleared out aft. Then the poisonous cloud blew away, and we went back to work in a smoke that was no thicker now than that of an ordinary factory chimney.

"We rigged the force-pump, got the hose along, and by and by it burst. Well, it was as old as the ship—a prehistoric hose, and past repair. Then we pumped with the feeble head-pump, drew water with buckets, and in this way managed in time to pour lots of Indian Ocean into the main hatch. The bright stream flashed in sunshine, fell into a layer of white crawling smoke, and vanished on the black surface of coal. Steam ascended mingling with the smoke. We poured salt water as into a barrel without a bottom. It was our fate to pump in that ship, to pump out of her, to pump into her; and after keeping water out of her to save ourselves from being drowned, we frantically poured water into her to save ourselves from being burnt.

"And she crawled on, do or die, in the serene weather. The sky was a miracle of purity, a miracle of azure. The sea was polished, was blue, was pellucid, was sparkling like a precious stone, extending on all sides, all round to the horizon—as if the whole terrestrial globe had been one jewel, one colossal sapphire, a single gem fashioned into a planet. And on the luster of the great calm waters the *Judea* glided imperceptibly, enveloped in languid and unclean vapors, in a lazy cloud that drifted to leeward, light and slow; a pestiferous cloud defiling the splendor of sea and sky.

"All this time of course we saw no fire. The cargo smoldered at the bottom somewhere. Once Mahon, as we were working side by side, said to me with a queer smile: 'Now, if she only would spring a tidy leak—like that time when we first left the Channel—it would put a stopper on this fire. Wouldn't it?' I remarked irrelevantly, 'Do you remember the rats?'

"We fought the fire and sailed the ship too as carefully as though nothing had been the matter. The steward cooked and attended on us. Of the other twelve men, eight worked while four rested. Everyone took his turn, captain included. There was equality, and if not exactly fraternity, then a deal of good feeling. Sometimes a man, as he dashed a bucketful of water down the hatchway, would yell out, 'Hurrah for Bankok!' and the rest laughed. But generally we were taciturn and serious—and thirsty. Oh! how thirsty! And we had to be careful with the water. Strict allowance. The ship smoked, the sun blazed. . . . Pass the bottle.

"We tried everything. We even made an attempt to dig down to the fire. No good, of course. No man could remain more than a minute below. Mahon, who went first, fainted there, and the man who went to fetch him out did likewise. We lugged them out on deck. Then I leaped down to show how easily it could be done. They had learned wisdom by that time, and contented themselves by fishing for me with a chain-hook tied to a broom-handle, I believe. I did not offer to go and fetch up my shovel, which was left down below.

"Things began to look bad. We put the long-boat into the water. The second boat was ready to swing out. We had also another, a 14-foot thing, on davits aft, where it was quite safe.

"Then, behold, the smoke suddenly decreased. We redoubled our efforts to flood the bottom of the ship. In two days there was no smoke at all. Everybody was on the broad grin. This was on a Friday. On Saturday no work, but sailing the ship of course, was done. The men washed their clothes and their faces for the first time in a fortnight, and had a special dinner given them. They spoke of spontaneous combustion with contempt, and implied *they* were the boys to put out combustions. Somehow we all felt as though we each had inherited a large fortune. But a beastly smell of burning hung about the ship. Captain Beard had hollow eyes and sunken cheeks. I had never noticed so much before how twisted and bowed he was. He and Mahon prowled soberly about hatches and ventilators, sniffing. It struck me suddenly poor Mahon was a very, very old chap. As to me, I was as pleased and proud as though I had helped to win a great naval battle. O Youth!

"The night was fine. In the morning a homeward-bound ship passed us hull down—the first we had seen for months; but we were nearing the land at last, Java Head being about 190 miles off, and nearly due north.

"Next day it was my watch on deck from eight to twelve. At breakfast the captain observed, 'It's wonderful how that smell hangs about the cabin.' About ten, the mate being on the poop, I stepped down on the main-deck for a moment. The carpenter's bench stood abaft the mainmast: I leaned against it sucking at my pipe, and the carpenter, a young chap, came to talk to me. He remarked, 'I think we have done very well, haven't we? and then I perceived with annoyance the fool was trying to tilt the bench. I said curtly, 'Don't, Chips,' and immediately became aware of a queer sensation, of an absurd delusion,—I seemed somehow to be in the air. I heard all round me like a pent-up breath released—as if a thousand giants simultaneously had said Phoo!—and felt a dull concussion which made my ribs ache suddenly. No doubt about it—I was in the air, and my body was describing a short parabola. But short as it was, I had the time to think several thoughts in, as far as I can remember, the following order: 'This can't be the carpenter—What is it?—Some accident—Submarine volcano?—Coals, gas!—By Jove! we are being blown up—Everybody's dead—I am falling into the after-hatch—I see fire in it.'

"The coal-dust suspended in the air of the hold had glowed dull-red at the moment of the explosion. In the twinkling of an eye, in an infinitesimal fraction of a second since the first tilt of the bench, I was sprawling full length on the cargo. I picked myself up and scrambled out. It was quick like a rebound. The deck was a wilderness of smashed timber, lying crosswise like trees in a wood after a hurricane; an immense curtain of soiled rags waved gently before me—it was the mainsail blown to strips. I thought, The masts will be toppling over directly; and to get out of the way bolted on all-fours toward the poop-ladder. The first person I saw was Mahon, with eyes like saucers, his mouth open, and the long white hair standing straight on end round his head like a silver halo. He was just about to go down when the sight of the main-deck stirring, heaving up, and changing into splinters before his eyes, petrified him on the top step. I stared at him in unbelief, and he stared at me with a queer kind of shocked curiosity. I did not know that I had no hair, no eyebrows, no eyelashes, that my young mustache was burnt off, that my face was black, one cheek laid open, my nose cut, and my chin bleeding. I had lost my cap, one of my slippers, and my shirt was torn to rags. Of all this I was not aware. I was amazed to see the ship still afloat, the poop-deck whole—and, most of all, to see anybody alive. Also the peace of the sky and the serenity of the sea were distinctly surprising. I suppose I expected to see them convulsed with horror. . . . Pass the bottle.

"There was a voice hailing the ship from somewhere—in the air, in the sky—I couldn't tell. Presently

I saw the captain—and he was mad. He asked me eagerly, 'Where's the cabin-table?' and to hear such a question was a frightful shock. I had just been blown up, you understand, and vibrated with that experience, —I wasn't quite sure whether I was alive. Mahon began to stamp with both feet and yelled at him, 'Good God! don't you see the deck's blown out of her?' I found my voice, and stammered out as if conscious of some gross neglect of duty, 'I don't know where the cabin-table is.' It was like an absurd dream.

"Do you know what he wanted next? Well, he wanted to trim the yards. Very placidly, and as if lost in thought, he insisted on having the foreyard squared. 'I don't know if there's anybody alive,' said Mahon, almost tearfully. 'Surely,' he said, gently, 'there will be enough left to square the foreyard.'

"The old chap, it seems, was in his own berth winding up the chronometers, when the shock sent him spinning. Immediately it occurred to him—as he said afterward—that the ship had struck something, and he ran out into the cabin. There, he saw, the cabin-table had vanished somewhere. The deck being blown up, it had fallen down into the lazarette of course. Where we had our breakfast that morning he saw only a great hole in the floor. This appeared to him so awfully mysterious, and impressed him so immensely, that what he saw and heard after he got on deck were mere trifles in comparison. And, mark, he noticed directly the wheel deserted and his barque off her course—and his only thought was to get that miserable, stripped, undecked, smoldering shell of a ship back again with her head pointing at her port of destination. Bankok! That's what he was after. I tell you this quiet, bowed, bandy-legged, almost deformed little man was immense in the singleness of his idea and in his placid ignorance of our agitation. He motioned us forward with a commanding gesture, and went to take the wheel himself.

"Yes; that was the first thing we did—trim the yards

of that wreck! No one was killed, or even disabled, but everyone was more or less hurt. You should have seen them! Some were in rags, with black faces, like coal-heavers, like sweeps, and had bullet heads that seemed closely cropped, but were in fact singed to the skin. Others, of the watch below, awakened by being shot out from their collapsing bunks, shivered incessantly, and kept on groaning even as we went about our work. But they all worked. That crew of Liverpool hard cases had in them the right stuff. It's my experience they always have. It is the sea that gives it—the vastness, the loneliness surrounding their dark stolid souls. Ah! Well! we stumbled, we crept, we fell, we barked our shins on the wreckage, we hauled. The masts stood, but we did not know how much they might be charred down below. It was nearly calm, but a long swell ran from the west and made her roll. They might go at any moment. We looked at them with apprehension. One could not foresee which way they would fall.

"Then we retreated aft and looked about us. The deck was a tangle of planks on edge, of planks on end, of splinters, of ruined woodwork. The masts rose from that chaos like big trees above a matted undergrowth. The interstices of that mass of wreckage were full of something whitish, sluggish, stirring—of something that was like a greasy fog. The smoke of the invisible fire was coming up again, was trailing, like a poisonous thick mist in some valley choked with dead wood. Already lazy wisps were beginning to curl upward amongst the mass of splinters. Here and there a piece of timber, stuck upright, resembled a post. Half of a fife-rail had been shot through the foresail, and the sky made a patch of glorious blue in the ignobly soiled canvas. A portion of several boards holding together had fallen across the rail, and one end protruded overboard, like a gangway leading upon nothing, like a gangway leading over the deep sea, leading to death—as if inviting us to walk the plank at once and be done with our ridiculous troubles. And still the air, the sky —a ghost, something invisible was hailing the ship.

"Someone had the sense to look over, and there was the helmsman, who had impulsively jumped overboard, anxious to come back. He yelled and swam lustily like a merman, keeping up with the ship. We threw him a rope, and presently he stood amongst us streaming with water and very crestfallen. The captain had surrendered the wheel, and apart, elbow on rail and chin in hand, gazed at the sea wistfully. We asked ourselves, What next? I thought, Now, this is something like. This is great. I wonder what will happen. O Youth!

"Suddenly Mahon sighted a steamer far astern. Captain Beard said, 'We may do something with her yet.' We hoisted two flags, which said in the international language of the sea, 'On fire. Want immediate assistance.' The steamer grew bigger rapidly, and by and by spoke with two flags on her foremast, 'I am coming to your assistance.'

"In half an hour she was abreast, to windward within hail, and rolling slightly, with her engines stopped. We lost our composure, and yelled all together with excitement, 'We've been blown up.' A man in a white helmet, on the bridge, cried, 'Yes! All right! all right!' and he nodded his head, and smiled, and made soothing motions with his hand as though at a lot of frightened children. One of the boats dropped in the water, and walked toward us upon the sea with her long oars. Four Calashes pulled a swinging stroke. This was my first sight of Malay seamen. I've known them since, but what struck me then was their unconcern: they came alongside, and even the bowman standing up and holding to our main-chains with the boat-hook did not deign to lift his head for a glance. I thought people who had been blown up deserved more attention.

"A little man, dry like a chip and agile like a monkey, clambered up. It was the mate of the steamer. He gave one look, and cried, 'O boys—you had better quit.'

"We were silent. He talked apart with the captain for a time,—seemed to argue with him. Then they went away together to the steamer.

"When our skipper came back we learned that the steamer was the *Somerville,* Captain Nash, from West Australia to Singapore *via* Batavia with mails, and that the agreement was she should tow us to Anjer or Batavia, if possible, where we could extinguish the fire by scuttling, and then proceed on our voyage—to Bankok! The old man seemed excited. 'We will do it yet,' he said to Mahon, fiercely. He shook his fist at the sky. Nobody else said a word.

"At noon the steamer began to tow. She went ahead slim and high, and what was left of the *Judea* followed at the end of seventy fathom of tow-rope,—followed her swiftly like a cloud of smoke with mast-heads protruding above. We went aloft to furl the sails. We coughed on the yards, and were careful about the bunts. Do you see the lot of us there, putting a neat furl on the sails of that ship doomed to arrive nowhere? There was not a man who didn't think that at any moment the masts would topple over. From aloft we could not see the ship for smoke, and they worked carefully, passing the gaskets with even turns. 'Harbor furl—aloft there!' cried Mahon from below.

"You understand this? I don't think one of those chaps expected to get down in the usual way. When we did I heard them saying to each other, 'Well, I thought we would come down overboard, in a lump—sticks and all—blame me if I didn't.' 'That's what I was thinking to myself,' would answer wearily another battered and bandaged scarecrow. And, mind, these were men without the drilled-in habit of obedience. To an onlooker they would be a lot of profane scallywags without a redeeming point. What made them do it—what made them obey me when I, thinking consciously how fine it was, made them drop the bunt of the foresail twice to try and do it better? What? They had no professional reputation—no examples, no praise. It wasn't a sense of duty; they all knew well enough how to shirk, and laze, and dodge—when they had a mind to it—and mostly they had. Was it the two pounds ten a month that sent them there? They didn't think their pay half good enough. No; it was something in them, something inborn and subtle and everlasting. I don't say positively that the crew of a French or German merchantman wouldn't have done it, but I doubt whether it would have been done in the same way. There was a completeness in it, something solid like a principle, and masterful like an instinct—a disclosure of something secret—of that hidden something, that gift of good or evil that makes racial difference, that shapes the fate of nations.

"It was that night at ten that, for the first time since we had been fighting it, we saw the fire. The speed of the towing had fanned the smoldering destruction. A blue gleam appeared forward, shining below the wreck of the deck. It wavered in patches, it seemed to stir and creep like the light of a glowworm. I saw it first, and told Mahon. 'Then the game's up,' he said. 'We had better stop this towing, or she will burst out suddenly fore and aft before we can clear out.' We set up a yell; rang bells to attract their attention; they towed on. At last Mahon and I had to crawl forward and cut the rope with an ax. There was no time to cast off the lashings. Red tongues could be seen licking the wilderness of splinters under our feet as we made our way back to the poop.

"Of course they very soon found out in the steamer that the rope was gone. She gave a loud blast of her whistle, her lights were seen sweeping in a wide circle, she came up ranging close alongside, and stopped. We were all in a tight group on the poop looking at her. Every man had saved a little bundle or a bag. Suddenly a conical flame with a twisted top shot up forward and threw upon the black sea a circle of light, with the two vessels side by side and heaving gently in its center. Captain Beard had been sitting on the gratings still and mute for hours, but now he rose slowly and advanced in front of us, to the mizzen-shrouds. Captain Nash hailed: 'Come along! Look sharp. I have mail-bags on board. I will take you and your boats to Singapore.'

" 'Thank you! No!' said our skipper. 'We must see the last of the ship.'

" 'I can't stand by any longer,' shouted the other. 'Mails—you know.'

" 'Ay! ay! We are all right.'

" 'Very well! I'll report you in Singapore. . . . Good-by!'

"He waved his hand. Our men dropped their bundles quietly. The steamer moved ahead, and passing out of the circle of light, vanished at once from our sight, dazzled by the fire which burned fiercely. And then I knew that I would see the East first as commander of a small boat. I thought it fine; and the fidelity to the old ship was fine. We should see the last of her. Oh, the glamour of youth! Oh, the fire of it, more dazzling than the flames of the burning ship, throwing a magic light on the wide earth, leaping audaciously to the sky, presently to be quenched by time, more cruel, more pitiless, more bitter than the sea—and like the flames of the burning ship surrounded by an impenetrable night.

"The old man warned us in his gentle and inflexible way that it was part of our duty to save for the underwriters as much as we could of the ship's gear. Accordingly we went to work aft, while she blazed forward to give us plenty of light. We lugged out a lot of rubbish. What didn't we save? An old barometer fixed with an absurd quantity of screws nearly cost me my life: a sudden rush of smoke came upon me, and I just got away in time. There were various stores, bolts of canvas, coils of rope; the poop looked like a marine bazaar, and the boats were lumbered to the gunwales. One would have thought the old man wanted to take as much as he could of his first command with him. He was very, very quiet, but off his balance evidently. Would you believe it? He wanted to take a length of old stream-cable and a kedge-anchor with him in the long-boat. We said, 'Ay, ay, sir,' deferentially, and on the quiet let the things slip overboard. The heavy medicine-chest went that way, two bags of green coffee, tins of paint—fancy, paint!—a whole lot of things. Then I was ordered with two hands into the boats to make a stowage and get them ready against the time it would be proper for us to leave the ship.

"We put everything straight, stepped the long-boat's mast for our skipper, who was to take charge of her, and I was not sorry to sit down for a moment. My face felt raw, every limb ached as if broken, I was aware of all my ribs, and would have sworn to a twist in the backbone. The boats, fast astern, lay in a deep shadow, and all around I could see the circle of the sea lighted by the fire. A gigantic flame arose forward straight and clear. It flared fierce, with noises like the whirr of wings, with rumbles as of thunder. There were cracks, detonations, and from the cone of flame the sparks flew upward, as man is born to trouble, to leaky ships, and to ships that burn.

"What bothered me was that the ship, lying broadside to the swell and to such wind as there was—a mere breath—the boats would not keep astern where they were safe, but persisted, in a pig-headed way boats have, in getting under the counter and then swinging alongside. They were knocking about dangerously and coming near the flame, while the ship rolled on them, and, of course, there was always the danger of the masts going over the side at any moment. I and my two boat-keepers kept them off as best we could, with oars and boat-hooks; but to be constantly at it became exasperating, since there was no reason why we should not leave at once. We could not see those on board, nor could we imagine what caused the delay. The boat-keepers were swearing feebly, and I had not only my share of the work but also had to keep at it two men who showed a constant inclination to lay themselves down and let things slide.

"At last I hailed, 'On deck there,' and someone looked over. 'We're ready here,' I said. The head disappeared, and very soon popped up again. 'The captain says, All right, sir, and to keep the boats well clear of the ship.'

"Half an hour passed. Suddenly there was a frightful racket, rattle, clanking of chain, hiss of water, and millions of sparks flew up into the shivering column of smoke that stood leaning slightly above the ship. The cat-heads had burned away, and the two red-hot anchors had gone to the bottom, tearing out after them two hundred fathom of red-hot chain. The ship trembled, the mass of flame swayed as if ready to collapse, and the fore top-gallant-mast fell. It darted down like an arrow of fire, shot under, and instantly leaping up within an oar's-length of the boats, floated quietly, very black on the luminous sea. I hailed the deck again. After some time a man in an unexpectedly cheerful but also muffled tone, as though he had been trying to speak with his mouth shut, informed me, 'Coming directly, sir,' and vanished. For a long time I heard nothing but the whirr and roar of the fire. There were also whistling sounds. The boats jumped, tugged at the painters, ran at each other playfully, knocked their sides together, or, do what we would, swung in a bunch against the ship's side. I couldn't stand it any longer, and swarming up a rope, clambered aboard over the stern.

"It was as bright as day. Coming up like this, the sheet of fire facing me was a terrifying sight, and the heat seemed hardly bearable at first. On a settee cushion dragged out of the cabin Captain Beard, his legs drawn up and one arm under his head, slept with the light playing on him. Do you know what the rest were busy about? They were sitting on deck right aft, round

an open case, eating bread and cheese and drinking
bottled stout.

"On the background of flames twisting in fierce
tongues above their heads they seemed at home like
salamanders, and looked like a band of desperate pi-
rates. The fire sparkled in the whites of their eyes,
gleamed on patches of white skin seen through the torn
shirts. Each had the marks as of a battle about him—
bandaged heads, tied-up arms, a strip of dirty rag
round a knee—and each man had a bottle between his
legs and a chunk of cheese in his hand. Mahon got up.
With his handsome and disreputable head, his hooked
profile, his long white beard, and with an uncorked
bottle in his hand, he resembled one of those reckless
sea-robbers of old making merry amidst violence and
disaster. 'The last meal on board,' he explained sol-
emnly. 'We had nothing to eat all day, and it was no
use leaving all this.' He flourished the bottle and indicated the sleeping skipper. 'He said he couldn't swallow anything, so I got him to lie down,' he went on;
and as I stared, 'I don't know whether you are aware,
young fellow, the man had no sleep to speak of for
days—and there will be dam' little sleep in the boats.'
'There will be no boats by-and-by if you fool about
much longer,' I said, indignantly. I walked up to the
skipper and shook him by the shoulder. At last he
opened his eyes, but did not move. 'Time to leave her,
sir,' I said quietly.

"He got up painfully, looked at the flames, at the
sea sparkling round the ship, and black, black as ink
farther away; he looked at the stars shining dim
through a thin veil of smoke in a sky black, black as
Erebus.

" 'Youngest first,' he said.

"And the ordinary seaman, wiping his mouth with
the back of his hand, got up, clambered over the taffrail, and vanished. Others followed. One, on the point
of going over, stopped short to drain his bottle, and

with a great swing of his arm flung it at the fire. 'Take this!' he cried.

"The skipper lingered disconsolately, and we left him to commune alone for a while with his first command. Then I went up again and brought him away at last. It was time. The ironwork on the poop was hot to the touch.

"Then the painter of the long-boat was cut, and the three boats, tied together, drifted clear of the ship. It was just sixteen hours after the explosion when we abandoned her. Mahon had charge of the second boat, and I had the smallest—the 14-foot thing. The long-boat would have taken the lot of us; but the skipper said we must save as much property as we could—for the underwriters—and so I got my first command. I had two men with me, a bag of biscuits, a few tins of meat, and a breaker of water. I was ordered to keep close to the long-boat, that in case of bad weather we might be taken into her.

"And do you know what I thought? I thought I would part company as soon as I could. I wanted to have my first command all to myself. I wasn't going to sail in a squadron if there were a chance for independent cruising. I would make land by myself. I would beat the other boats. Youth! All youth! The silly, charming, beautiful youth.

"But we did not make a start at once. We must see the last of the ship. And so the boats drifted about that night, heaving and setting on the swell. The men dozed, waked, sighed, groaned. I looked at the burning ship.

"Between the darkness of earth and heaven she was burning fiercely upon a disc of purple sea shot by the blood-red play of gleams; upon a disc of water glittering and sinister. A high, clear flame, an immense and lonely flame, ascended from the ocean, and from its summit the black smoke poured continuously at the sky. She burned furiously; mournful and imposing like a funeral pile kindled in the night, surrounded by the sea, watched over by the stars. A magnificent death had come like a grace, like a gift, like a reward to that old ship at the end of her laborious days. The surrender of her weary ghost to the keeping of stars and sea was stirring like the sight of a glorious triumph. The masts fell just before daybreak, and for a moment there was a burst and turmoil of sparks that seemed to fill with flying fire the night patient and watchful, the vast night lying silent upon the sea. At daylight she was only a charred shell, floating still under a cloud of smoke and bearing a glowing mass of coal within.

"Then the oars were got out, and the boats forming in a line moved round her remains as if in procession —the long-boat leading. As we pulled across her stern a slim dart of fire shot out viciously at us, and suddenly she went down, head first, in a great hiss of steam. The unconsumed stern was the last to sink; but the paint had gone, had cracked, had peeled off, and there were no letters, there was no word, no stubborn device that was like her soul, to flash at the rising sun her creed and her name.

"We made our way north. A breeze sprang up, and about noon all the boats came together for the last time. I had no mast or sail in mine, but I made a mast out of a spare oar and hoisted a boat-awning for a sail, with a boat-hook for a yard. She was certainly over-masted, but I had the satisfaction of knowing that with the wind aft I could beat the other two. I had to wait for them. Then we all had a look at the captain's chart, and, after a sociable meal of hard bread and water, got our last instructions. These were simple: steer north, and keep together as much as possible. 'Be careful with that jury-rig, Marlow,' said the captain; and Mahon, as I sailed proudly past his boat, wrinkled his curved nose and hailed, 'You will sail that ship of yours under water, if you don't look out, young fellow.' He was a malicious old man—and may the deep sea where he sleeps now rock him gently, rock him tenderly to the end of time!

"Before sunset a thick rain-squall passed over the two boats, which were far astern, and that was the last I saw of them for a time. Next day I sat steering my cockle-shell—my first command—with nothing but water and sky around me. I did sight in the afternoon the upper sails of a ship far away, but said nothing, and my men did not notice her. You see I was afraid she might be homeward bound, and I had no mind to turn back from the portals of the East. I was steering for Java—another blessed name—like Bankok, you know. I steered many days.

"I need not tell you what it is to be knocking about in an open boat. I remember nights and days of calm, when we pulled, we pulled, and the boat seemed to stand still, as if bewitched within the circle of the sea horizon. I remember the heat, the deluge of rain-squalls that kept us bailing for dear life (but filled our water-cask), and I remember sixteen hours on end with a mouth dry as a cinder and a steering-oar over the stern to keep my first command head on to a breaking sea. I did not know how good a man I was till then. I remember the drawn faces, the dejected figures of my two men, and I remember my youth and the feeling that will never come back any more—the feeling that I could last forever, outlast the sea, the earth, and all men; the deceitful feeling that lures us on to joys, to perils, to love, to vain effort—to death; the triumphant conviction of strength, the heat of life in the handful of dust, the glow in the heart that with every year grows dim, grows cold, grows small, and expires—and expires, too soon, too soon—before life itself.

"And this is how I see the East. I have seen its secret places and have looked into its very soul; but now I see it always from a small boat, a high outline of mountains, blue and afar in the morning; like faint mist at noon; a jagged wall of purple at sunset. I have the feel of the oar in my hand, the vision of a scorching blue sea in my eyes. And I see a bay, a wide bay, smooth as glass and polished like ice, shimmering in the dark. A red light burns far off upon the gloom of the land, and the night is soft and warm. We drag at the oars with aching arms, and suddenly a puff of wind, a puff faint and tepid and laden with strange odors of blossoms, of aromatic wood, comes out of the still night the first sigh of the East on my face. That I can never forget. It was impalpable and enslaving, like a charm, like a whispered promise of mysterious delight.

"We had been pulling this finishing spell for eleven hours. Two pulled, and he whose turn it was to rest sat at the tiller. We had made out the red light in that bay and steered for it, guessing it must mark some small coasting port. We passed two vessels, outlandish and high-sterned, sleeping at anchor, and, approaching the light, now very dim, ran the boat's nose against the end of a jutting wharf. We were blind with fatigue. My men dropped the oars and fell off the thwarts as if dead. I made fast to a pile. A current rippled softly. The scented obscurity of the shore was grouped into vast masses, a density of colossal clumps of vegetation, probably—mute and fantastic shapes. And at their foot the semicircle of a beach gleamed faintly, like an illusion. There was not a light, not a stir, not a sound. The mysterious East faced me, perfumed like a flower, silent like death, dark like a grave.

"And I sat weary beyond expression, exulting like a conqueror, sleepless and entranced as if before a profound, a fateful enigma.

"A splashing of oars, a measured dip reverberating on the level of water, intensified by the silence of the shore into loud claps, made me jump up. A boat, a European boat, was coming in. I invoked the name of the dead; I hailed: *Judea* ahoy! A thin shout answered.

"It was the captain. I had beaten the flagship by three hours, and I was glad to hear the old man's voice again, tremulous and tired. 'Is it you, Marlow?' 'Mind the end of that jetty, sir,' I cried.

"He approached cautiously, and brought up with the deep-sea lead-line which we had saved—for the underwriters. I eased my painter and fell alongside. He sat, a broken figure at the stern, wet with dew, his hands clasped in his lap. His men were asleep already. 'I had a terrible time of it,' he murmured. 'Mahon is behind—not very far.' We conversed in whispers, in low whispers, as if afraid to wake up the land. Guns, thunder, earthquakes would not have awakened the men just then.

"Looking round as we talked, I saw away at sea a bright light traveling in the night. 'There's a steamer passing the bay,' I said. She was not passing, she was entering, and she even came close and anchored. 'I wish,' said the old man, 'you would find out whether she is English. Perhaps they could give us a passage somewhere.' He seemed nervously anxious. So by dint of punching and kicking I started one of my men into a state of somnambulism, and giving him an oar, took another and pulled toward the lights of the steamer.

"There was a murmur of voices in her, metallic hollow clangs of the engine-room, footsteps on the deck. Her ports shone, round like dilated eyes. Shapes moved about, and there was a shadowy man high up on the bridge. He heard my oars.

"And then, before I could open my lips, the East spoke to me, but it was in a Western voice. A torrent of words was poured into the enigmatical, the fateful silence; outlandish, angry words, mixed with words and even whole sentences of good English, less strange but even more surprising. The voice swore and cursed violently; it riddled the solemn peace of the bay by a volley of abuse. It began by calling me Pig, and from that went crescendo into unmentionable adjectives—in English. The man up there raged aloud in two languages, and with a sincerity in his fury that almost convinced me I had, in some way, sinned against the harmony of the universe. I could hardly see him, but began to think he would work himself into a fit.

"Suddenly he ceased, and I could hear him snorting and blowing like a porpoise. I said—

" 'What steamer is this, pray?'

" 'Eh? What's this? And who are you?'

" 'Castaway crew of an English barque burnt at sea. We came here tonight. I am the second mate. The captain is in the long-boat, and wishes to know if you would give us a passage somewhere.'

" 'Oh, my goodness! I say. . . . This is the *Celestial* from Singapore on her return trip. I'll arrange with your captain in the morning, . . . and, . . . I say, . . . did you hear me just now?'

" 'I should think the whole bay heard you.'

" 'I thought you were a shore-boat. Now, look here —this infernal lazy scoundrel of a caretaker has gone to sleep again—curse him. The light is out, and I nearly ran foul of the end of this damned jetty. This is the third time he plays me this trick. Now, I ask you, can anybody stand this kind of thing? It's enough to drive a man out of his mind. I'll report him. . . . I'll get the Assistant Resident to give him the sack, by . . . ! See— there's no light. It's out, isn't it? I take you to witness the light's out. There should be a light, you know. A red light on the—'

" 'There was a light,' I said, mildly.

" 'But it's out, man! What's the use of talking like this? You can see for yourself it's out—don't you? If you had to take a valuable steamer along this God-forsaken coast you would want a light, too. I'll kick him from end to end of his miserable wharf. You'll see if I don't. I will—'

" 'So I may tell my captain you'll take us?' I broke in.

" 'Yes, I'll take you. Good night,' he said, brusquely.

"I pulled back, made fast again to the jetty, and then went to sleep at last. I had faced the silence of the East. I had heard some of its language. But when I opened my eyes again the silence was as complete as though it had never been broken. I was lying in a flood of light, and the sky had never looked so far, so high, before. I opened my eyes and lay without moving.

"And then I saw the men of the East—they were looking at me. The whole length of the jetty was full of people. I saw brown, bronze, yellow faces, the black eyes, the glitter, the color of an Eastern crowd. And all these beings stared without a murmur, without a sigh, without a movement. They stared down at the boats, at the sleeping men who at night had come to them from the sea. Nothing moved. The fronds of palms stood still against the sky. Not a branch stirred along the shore, and the brown roofs of hidden houses peeped through the green foliage, through the big leaves that hung shining and still like leaves forged of heavy metal. This was the East of the ancient navigators, so old, so mysterious, resplendent and somber, living and unchanged, full of danger and promise. And these were the men. I sat up suddenly. A wave of movement passed through the crowd from end to end, passed along the heads, swayed the bodies, ran along the jetty like a ripple on the water, like a breath of wind on a field—and all was still again. I see it now —the wide sweep of the bay, the glittering sands, the wealth of green infinite and varied, the sea blue like the sea of a dream, the crowd of attentive faces, the blaze of vivid color—the water reflecting it all, the curve of the shore, the jetty, the high-sterned outlandish craft floating still, and the three boats with the tired men from the West sleeping, unconscious of the land and the people and of the violence of sunshine. They slept thrown across the thwarts, curled on bottom-boards, in the careless attitudes of death. The head of the old skipper, leaning back in the stern of the long-boat, had fallen on his breast, and he looked as though he would never wake. Farther out old Mahon's face was upturned to the sky, with the long white beard spread out on his breast, as though he had been shot where he sat at the tiller; and a man, all in a heap in the bows of the boat, slept with both arms embracing the stem-head and with his cheek laid on the gunwale. The East looked at them without a sound.

"I have known its fascination since; I have seen the mysterious shores, the still water, the lands of brown nations, where a stealthy Nemesis lies in wait, pursues, overtakes so many of the conquering race, who are proud of their wisdom, of their knowledge, of their strength. But for me all the East is contained in that vision of my youth. It is all in that moment when I opened my young eyes on it. I came upon it from a tussle with the sea—and I was young—and I saw it looking at me. And this is all that is left of it! Only a moment; a moment of strength, of romance, of glamour—of youth! . . . A flick of sunshine upon a strange shore, the time to remember, the time for a sigh, and—good-by!—Night—Good-by. . . !"

He drank.

"Ah! The good old time—the good old time. Youth and the sea. Glamour and the sea! The good, strong sea, the salt, bitter sea, that could whisper to you and roar at you and knock your breath out of you."

He drank again.

"By all that's wonderful it is the sea, I believe, the sea itself—or is it youth alone? Who can tell? But you here—you all had something out of life: money, love—whatever one gets on shore—and, tell me, wasn't that the best time, that time when we were young at sea; young and had nothing, on the sea that gives nothing, except hard knocks—and sometimes a chance to feel your strength—that only—what you all regret?"

And we all nodded at him: the man of finance, the man of accounts, the man of law, we all nodded at him over the polished table that like a still sheet of brown water reflected our faces, lined, wrinkled; our faces marked by toil, by deceptions, by success, by love; our weary eyes looking still, looking always, looking anxiously for something out of life, that while it is expected is already gone—has passed unseen, in a sigh, in a flash—together with the youth, with the strength, with the romance of illusions.

WILLIAM McFEE

William McFee, Londoner with a Scots name (and ancestry), former chief engineer of American ships, later farmer in Connecticut and, briefly, Master's Clerk under Captain Sir David Bone in the Transatlantic liner *Tuscania,* is a professional seaman who became—and is—an outstanding writer. Unlike most others in this anthology, he chose to serve in the engine-room, after rather more than the usual preparation ashore; he was in ships' engine-rooms from 1906, more or less, until 1922. He was a British Royal Naval Reserve engineer-lieutenant of the first World War, and an American chief engineer with the good-looking ships of the United Fruit Company not long afterward. He took up writing professionally, working in America, in 1922, and a long succession of classics has come from his pen: *Casuals of the Sea, Aliens, An Ocean Tramp, Harbors of Memory, The Harbor-Master, Watch Below, Spenlove in Arcady,* and many more. The reference books nowadays list him as "novelist," and that indeed he is; but his first profession was the sea.

The story of Captain Carlsen of the Isbrandtsen cargoship *Flying Enterprise* caught the imagination of the world, when the Danish-American sea captain chose to stay aboard to try single-handed to save his sinking and all but capsized ship in an Atlantic gale eight years ago. Carlsen himself wrote nothing, as far as I am aware, of that or any other incident in his career, regarding such an episode as no more than doing his duty as he saw it. It was irrelevant, in his view, that in this particular instance, doing that duty brought grave risk of death, and he was astonished at the public enthusiasm which acclaimed the deed. Carlsen refused steadfastly to have anything to do with the exploitation of a courageous piece of seafaring which he took for granted. In this matter, too, he gave a notable example of good, seamanlike conduct which is infrequently followed. Many wrote about the *Flying Enterprise* affair, if he did not. It deserved to be recorded permanently and well, and this McFee has done.

Here in this piece then, two good seamen are recognized: the Carlsen who wouldn't write, McFee, who does, superbly. I take off my cap to them both.

The Reluctant Hero

by WILLIAM McFEE

December, 1951, was ending in Europe with a series of phenomenal gales. Sunday, the thirtieth, winds of hurricane force were reported, and the Irish airport at Shannon was closed. "*Seas Lash Europe*," the New York headlines ran, in moderate type. Sixty-three were dead and seventeen persons were missing in Great Britain and Ireland. *Queen Mary,* the great Cunarder, was seventy-two hours late, after buffeting what were described as sixty-foot waves. Who measured them we are not informed. We will come across that figure, sixty, more than once in this story.

Captain Harry Grattidge, commander of *Queen Mary,* was content to say that it had been "terrific," while an official recalled the scenes in the dining saloons as "a nightmare." A German freighter, *Irene Ollendorf,* went down off Borkum in the North Sea. A Dutch and a Norwegian tanker were wrecked in the Bay of Biscay. Another Norwegian tanker lost her master and her third mate when her bridge was swept away in a huge wave. A six-thousand-ton British tanker, *Mactra*, was disabled off the Cornish coast, and was being towed in by "the most powerful tug in the world," *Turmoil*.

On the last day of the year the *New York Times* carried the headline, *"EUROPEAN STORM TOLL GROWS. CAPTAIN ALONE ON LISTING SHIP. New Jersey Man Is Trying to Save Battered Craft off Irish Coast."* The paper went on to describe the scene:

> A lone figure was reported last night to be clinging to the bridge of the battered *Flying Enterprise* as the U.S. cargo ship was tossed about in the stormy waters of the North Atlantic some 300 miles S.W. of Ireland. He was Kurt Henrik Carlsen, 37-year-old skipper of the 6,711 ton vessel, a veteran shipmaster. He lives with his wife and two children in Woodbridge, New Jersey.

Biographical data on the lonely figure clinging to his ship is no more than adequate. Born at Hilleroed, Denmark, in 1914, Kurt Henrik Carlsen went to sea at fourteen in Danish vessels, and we may assume, from his recent record, that he was a good example of the industrious apprentice and lost no opportunity to improve his education and his professional skills. We know he is a ready radio operator, which many shipmasters are not, and the little-publicized achievement on board a sister ship of the *Enterprise* in 1948, when he was thirty-four, marks him as a fellow of unusual character and manual dexterity. One of his engineers, in a quarrel with a crew-man, was stabbed in a dozen places, and was bleeding to death. Captain Carlsen carried out "an extremely delicate operation," in the middle of the Indian Ocean, and saved his officer's life. Some seagoing engineers would be willing to maintain that any shipmaster who saves an engineer's life is already marked out for greatness.

Nine years before the storm we are now dealing with

in 1951 (1942, that is), Captain Carlsen entered the service of Hans Isbrandtsen, a Danish shipowner operating a round-the-world freight and passenger service, a gentleman of great enterprise and vigorous independence in what he regarded as international free trade. Apart from the surgical exploit in the Indian Ocean in 1948, Captain Carlsen rejoiced in the obscurity he considers proper to the dignity of a shipmaster.

About the time the captain entered Isbrandtsen's service, something occurred which profoundly affected not only him and his owner but the state of Denmark, something so rotten that the author of *Hamlet* had never dreamed of it. This was the Nazi onslaught. Ships of Danish, Dutch, and Norwegian registry which were at sea took refuge in Allied harbors. Hans Isbrandtsen, who had had offices for years on Lower Broadway, eventually established his reconstructed business under American registry. In due course the personnel became American citizens.

It is generally conceded that hurricanes do not usually invade the Narrow Seas around the British Isles, but in December of 1951 there was no other word to describe what was going on when Captain Carlsen took *Flying Enterprise* out of the Elbe on the twenty-first. Part of his cargo consisted of pig iron. Just why an American ship was bringing pig iron to America nobody seems to have inquired. There it was, however, properly stowed. The subsequent inquiry made a great deal of this pig iron, arguing that it might have been improperly stowed, thus causing the frightful list which forced the captain to send everybody away except himself. The cargo, he insisted, was properly stowed. If he had to load the ship again, he would stow it as it was on that occasion. A shipmaster of his quality was undoubtedly able to load his ship correctly for a voyage across "Winter North Atlantic," which officially implies the worst possible conditions.

Ships were foundering in the North Sea, and the weather recalls Kipling's "Ballad of the Bolivar":

We put out from Sunderland, loaded down with rails,
  We put back to Sunderland 'cause our cargo shifted,
We put out from Sunderland, met the winter gales,
  Seven days and seven nights to the Start we drifted.

For Sunderland and rails read Hamburg and pig iron, and you have the situation Captain Carlsen coped with from December twenty-second to thirtieth. His cargo did not shift, however, until he had worked his ship some four hundred miles west of Brest and a hundred miles southwest of Ireland. It was when he was facing the full onslaught of the Western Ocean that his steering gear carried away. Out of control, *Flying Enterprise* swung broadside to titanic seas which threw her on her beam ends, and she began to open up.

She began to split. We have Captain Carlsen's word for it that she developed two vertical three-foot fractures and a horizontal crack across the front of number three hatch, which is abaft the engine-room structure and bridge deck. One of the crew, an engine-room wiper, Louis Rodock, who wears glasses and has been at sea for twenty-five years, told of "a roaring explosion," and a sixty-foot fissure.

Here we may revert to what we can call the psychological byproducts of the adventure, its effect on the minds of men. The people of Europe and America were suffering from the frustration of the Korean business. They were unhappy because international tensions, the shadow of atomic war, and the apparent impossibility of any understanding of the Asiatic enigma which is the Kremlin, were producing a mental fatigue which made them search for something relatively human and warm, some evidence that the old heroic virtues still existed somewhere in the world. They were ready for miracles, for great deeds which would uplift their hearts, show them man making a clean fight against odds, and winning gloriously. They were ready to magnify everything connected with such an episode. They wanted something bigger than themselves.

It is shyly suggested here that this feeling, so to speak, was "in the air" and inspired everyone, from engine wiper to journalist, to speak or write in superlatives. All, that is, except the star actor in the play, the actor cast in the role of hero. And so we have waves sixty feet high; we have nightmares in *Queen Mary's* dining saloons; we have the wiper with his "roaring explosion" and his sixty-foot fissures in the ship's hull; we have the ship lying over at sixty degrees. And we hear presently that "the most powerful tug in the world" would be on hand to render succor when she had rescued *S.S. Mactra*. We were in a wonderful world. Did not Captain Carlsen report that one of his passengers, Mr. Nikola Bundjakowsky, had expired?

The tired public, nauseated with denunciations, countercharges, international double-talk, and the ringing emptiness of political oratory, turned with pleasure and excitement to watch one man against the sea. Ships gathered around the stricken vessel to save life. Captain Carlsen, making his decisions promptly, ordered his crew of forty and his ten passengers to leave at once. S.S. *Southland* took off fifteen, and on Sunday, December thirtieth, the U.S. troop carrier *General A. W. Greeley* reported that all on board had been transferred except Captain Carlsen, who not only refused to abandon his ship, but expressed confidence that she could be towed to safety.

When it was learned that he lived in a small place, Woodbridge in New Jersey, with his Danish-born wife and two little girls, Sonja and Karen, the public was charmed and took him to its bosom. The idea of that lonely figure clinging to his ship in such a position that the bulkhead became a deck, put everything else out of mind for a few days. An American navy ship, the *Weeks*, was standing by, and in addition to a fine portrait of the captain himself, a handsome man if there ever was one, we had in the papers pictures of

Captain Parker of the *General Greeley* and Captain Thompson of the *Weeks*. Soon these three were holding three-way conversations over the radio. Carlsen had a small emergency apparatus and was using it to tell us how things were going with him and how he proposed to have the tow made. He was still in command. This was on January fourth.

On December twenty-seventh, he said, there was a wind of Force 12 on the Beaufort Scale, which is hurricane weather, sixty-five miles an hour. On the twenty-eighth he was in another cyclonic storm, in which one wave knocked the ship off her course, and she split across number three hatch. Number three hatch, remember, is abaft the engine-room. That hold was full of water. Which is what you get when a welded ship meets with Force 12 in a disabled condition. One of the features of a welded hull is that when a crack starts it cannot stop. Rivets hold on, each of them giving a little, but holding on. With a welded joint there is no give. Once a weld breaks, the ship is in danger of opening up like a wet paper bag.

Some of his personnel, two of the engineers and one or two seamen, wanted to stay with the captain, but he wouldn't have it. This was not captiousness or vainglory, the noble captain going down with his ship and all the rest of it. It was plain common sense. There was almost no food and no sanitation. They would have been in each other's road on that steeply sloping deck. He had not foreseen getting food and flasks of hot coffee by line from the other ships, and it might have been wisdom to have kept his mate with him. That is hindsight. When the towline first came aboard, he was unable to hold it single-handed and it fell away. As for going down with his ship, he proposed to save her. He nearly did, too. Old Man Western Ocean beat him, but he nearly did.

On January fourth, hopes were high. "The most powerful tug in the world", *Turmoil*, 1,136 tons, 4,000 horsepower, came surging upon the scene. Captain

Carlsen had an anxiety. Would the tremendous pull of such a tug make his ship turn turtle? Great care would be needed. She was precarious. Her reserve buoyancy had been diminishing daily. The wind had risen again; another storm was coming. This was the sixth day of Carlsen's solitary vigil. The public was almost holding its breath. The papers were now loaded with "fillers," odds and ends of news about the Carlsens, about salvage and insurance. Prayers were being offered for the captain's safety and success. Pictures of Mrs. Carlsen in her Woodbridge home with Sonja and Karen appeared, and the captain's parents, Mr. and Mrs. Martin Carlsen in their cottage in Bagovaerd, Denmark, waiting for news of their son. Salvage experts, suddenly and unexpectedly popular, had to dispel some romantic nonsense newspapermen and the public had picked up from fiction read in youth. It was true, of course, that so long as the captain remained on board, *Flying Enterprise* was not technically a derelict. She could not be salvaged by any passing ship, supposing a passing ship had no business of her own, no schedule to keep, no cargo rating demurrage, no passengers who wanted to reach their destination. The owners were employing *Turmoil,* and a French tug, *Abeille,* was also standing by now. The position was very much as when a car has broken down and the owner has telephoned for a tow. The old romantic conditions of the sea existed now only in the minds of landsmen and fiction writers who do not read technical journals.

The pictures of *Flying Enterprise* now being printed in the papers (on January fourth) give us a vivid impression of Carlsen's predicament. The text refers constantly to a list of sixty degrees. Not fifty-nine degrees; sixty. Careful study of the pictures puts the actual list at forty-five, which is enough to bring one's heart into the mouth, surely. But the public appetite had been whetted and it was sixty. We read of sixty-foot waves (an impossibility), sixty-mile-an-hour winds, sixty-foot cracks in the hull, and a sixty-degree list. Events are inevitably shaped to moods, so everything had to go like sixty. . . .

Except, we may venture, on the *Flying Enterprise,* where "the New Jersey man," moving slowly, carefully, and painfully, half on the deck, half on the bulkhead of his stricken vessel, or wedging himself into a corner of the charthouse settee for an hour or so of uneasy slumber, waited through the long days and longer nights for the weather to make a tow possible. The strain, bodily and mental, must have been heavy. After the great decision, and he had seen the last of his passengers and crew safe into the boats, there would be a reaction. He had accepted the burden. He had time, ample time, to reflect on what it meant for himself. He might be outwardly confident, but he must have entertained some doubts of the outcome.

He had thought of the lives of others, he had assumed responsibility for his ship and her owners. As the nights closed around him, and the weather, instead of moderating, worsened, as though sunshine and calm blue seas had left the Atlantic forever, he would think of the anxiety imposed on his wife at home in New Jersey. Mrs. Carlsen, of course, had long been adjusted and disciplined to the long absences which are the lot of sailors' wives everywhere. She had confidence in her husband's judgment. But she was not in the position of the old-time women of Salem and Martha's Vineyard. She could not, like them, cultivate stoicism and leave the future in the hands of God. She was getting the news every day over the radio and in the newspapers. She was sharing in thought his weary vigil on a ship which was on the point of foundering. She was answering the telephone, receiving curious newspapermen and photographers, meeting questions which must have kept her nerves jumping. Captain Carlsen would be a very unimaginative man if he had not sensed what his family was enduring while he clung to his heaving, rolling charge on the gray Atlantic. It would step up his own anxiety a hundredfold. And he would suffer many a twinge, too, when he thought of Sonja and Karen, and what might happen to them if he did not pull it off.

There was another thing. It is impossible to maintain an imperturbable demeanor when a ship lists more than a few degrees. When she is lying literally on her beam ends, when, instead of rolling buoyantly, she just lies there and never comes up, a feeling of dread and exasperation saps a man's courage when he needs it most. And he is assailed by minor annoyances. He is sodden with sea water, he is bruised and worn out by incessant collisions with metal fittings and the struggle to keep his balance in the sloping surfaces. He cannot wash, he cannot bathe or shave. He cannot perform the most ordinary functions of hygiene in any comfort. As for sleeping, although we have his word for it that he did sleep, it was more likely an unrestful drowse. To quote an ancient English writer, "he slumbered rather than slept."

He becomes an affront to his normal, decent self. He is outwardly a pariah who would be arrested as a vagrant in his home town. Yet all the while he has to steel his mind and heart, to be alert to the weather and the ships standing by.

So far as one may judge, Captain Carlsen remained in full command of himself as well as his ship. There must have been excitement and alarm when he realized the noise he was making in the world. It would be something of which he not only had no experience, but for which he had no guiding lights, no previous warning. He passed some of the time, as we shall see, reading a book, a useful professional volume, *The Seaman and the Law*. But what about the seaman and the public? No one seems to have written a book about that. Shipowners supply instructions to their masters for use in special circumstances. But no shipowner sends out instructions on what to do in case of sudden fame. He would have to rely on himself. He must have felt appallingly inadequate, as he contemplated himself, an unshaven, shabby limpet clinging to a plunging, waterlogged derelict in a wintry sea. But he need have had no fear. He had reserves of character and nerve even for this.

Suddenly, on January fifth, there was a new thrill. Enter, by a violent leap from the most powerful tug in the world, which had gotten alongside, Mr. Kenneth R. Dancy, age twenty-seven, mate of *Turmoil,* who had become mysteriously identified in the public mind as a lover of classical music and an amateur knitter. There is nothing unusual in a seaman knitting his own socks. I have had shipmates, generally Scotchmen, who were very good at it. It fascinates the public, though, to find one of the mariners of England affecting such a lady-like hobby. It was gratifying and augmented the interest. Captain Carlsen would be able to get the towline fast next time, surely. The public could hardly wait. Promoters, advertising men, publishers, radio men, refused to wait. Obviously Captain Carlsen was their meat. Fantastic offers to endorse deodorants, soaps, and other goods poured into the line's offices, offers for radio and television broadcasts and appearances, to lecture to women's clubs, to write articles and books piled up, while the object of their pursuit, the Danish-born shipmaster and his new colleague, who liked classical music, were finally getting a towline made fast to the forecastle bitts. Asked what he thought of the situation, the captain who hadn't had a dry stitch on him for a week, and who was living on cake, sandwiches, and coffee, still refused to leave his ship and gave his chances as seventy-five per cent good. They were moving at three knots toward Falmouth.

By January eighth, they had made two-thirds of the distance and speed was increased to three and a half knots. More prayers at Woodbridge, New Jersey. Next day the towline parted fifty miles from port. To make matters worse, the shackle, which had held the broken steel wire, had jammed. Carlsen and Dancy had to release it with a hacksaw, almost plunging overboard as they clung to the upended forecastle. On January tenth, the bridge of *Flying Enterprise* was under water. Naval vessels signaled that night that they must wait for daylight to have another go. *Flying Enterprise* was drifting, helpless, off Falmouth.

By January eleventh, it was plain that neither prayers nor tugs could do much for her. The list was now sixty-five degrees, which meant she was about to go. Carlsen and Dancy were perched perilously on the practically horizontal funnel of the ship. The other ships closed in on her. The two men jumped into the boiling sea and swam for the *Weeks*. Dancy, ten years younger and much fresher physically and mentally, gave the captain some assistance. They were hauled on board in time to see *Flying Enterprise* plunge to the bottom of the English Channel.

Two people back home were in tears. Hans Isbrandtsen, the owner, tolling a bell in his office for the death of a fine ship, and Mrs. Carlsen, weeping for joy in Woodbridge because her husband was saved and alive. Lloyds of London did not weep, although the dénouement was a financial reverse. On the contrary, they welcomed Captain Carlsen when he reached London and gave him a citation for his plucky attempt to save his ship.

Now Falmouth, in Cornwall, population fourteen thousand, a parliamentary borough and a nice little fishing port once known as Pennycomequick, with a yacht club, a Saturday market and a tourist trade in summer, suddenly became the cynosure of the western world. Trains, cars, and planes brought in swarms of newspapermen, photographers, officials and the aforementioned promoters, who proposed to take over Captain Carlsen in the modern commercial manner. For sums aggregating over a hundred thousand dollars he was to lend his name and fame and his reputation for sanity to various undertakings which had nothing to do with *Flying Enterprise,* to lay his personal probity on the altar of Mammon.

In the midst of this uproar, having been hastily furnished with a hot bath, a room for rest, and some fresh clothing, Captain Carlsen maintained his accustomed imperturbable dignity and good humor. He declined the commercial propositions and, although he would probably have preferred to concentrate on his professional problems, he consented to face the ranks of interviewers and tell them, to the best of his ability, what they wanted to know.

Space is lacking to report all they wanted to know. Captain Carlsen confesses that he "was scared of the press business" even before he jumped from his ship into a raging sea of publicity. One of the first legends he promptly disposed of was that Mrs. Carlsen had sent a message begging him to leave the ship. He knew nothing of any such message. He thought it extremely unlikely that Mrs. Carlsen would have done anything so out of character. Then, would he now quit going to sea to go lecturing and broadcasting? "No," he said, "I have no intention of changing my profession." Questions veered to what he did while alone on the ship. What did he live on? Mostly, he said, he lived on cake. Cake? Yes, pound cake. This was almost as sensational as Mr. Dancy's knitting and classical music. What else? they wanted to know. Well, he read a book. What book? He said he was reading *The Seaman and the Law.* He handled their occasionally inappropriate interrogations with such cool skill that he might have been studying a treatise on the psychology of newspapermen and women.

No doubt his reply to the questions of what he had been reading was a dead end. Nobody had ever heard of the book. An inspired questioner, who sounds feminine, but we have no information about that, shot out the query: "Captain, are you a religious man?" Some men, driven beyond endurance, might have said it was

none of their business. Not Carlsen. He had an answer
to that one, too. "I am not exactly a heathen," he said
pleasantly. It was the perfect answer. It covered everything.

But to the insistent curiosity of inquirers, knowing
of those rich, juicy offers of pecuniary reward, he re-
sponded with an unmistakable negative. "The thought
of commercial or financial advantage has never entered
my mind at all." That was that. Period.

Looking back nostalgically at some of the sea adventures in recent years, the barnstorming "heroes" of the
burning *Morro Castle* and the rescuers of a ship-
wrecked crew gallantly smoking "Luckies" while pulling oars in a gale of wind, this behavior of Carlsen must
have appeared very peculiar. The man seemed clad in
an impenetrable armor of honesty and sober common
sense. Cynics might doubt its permanence. They might
wonder whether it would not melt when the roar of
New York crowds hailed the returning hero to the land
of his adoption. Very few celebrities were able to keep
their heads when they moved up the canyon of Broadway under descending clouds of ticker tape.

Even when he realized that the public, the many-
headed monster, was not to be denied its human sacri-
fice, Captain Carlsen introduced an original, revolutionary notion into the traditional ceremony. He
would, he said, *walk* up Broadway to City Hall. He
had often walked up Broadway and knew how to do
it. To sit on the rear end of an open car, to grin and
wave vacuously while thousands cheered, was repug-
nant to him. He knew his own value all right, but it
was not that kind of value.

But it was not to be. He who had faced the peril of
the storm unflinching could not alter the great tradition. He could not induce Mr. Grover Whalen, the
celebrated greeter of celebrities, to walk up Broadway.
This was perhaps the most serious test of all. He had
brushed off the offers of commercial promoters. He had

yet to run the gantlet of the luncheons, the tributes, the plaques, and the anonymous gate crashers with their expensive presents.

It is a pleasure to report that he survived them all. Not even the unexpected appearance of an extravagantly costly wrist watch from a total stranger could catch the captain unaware. Grover Whalen was even on the point of making the presentation when, in a whisper, the captain explained that he could not accept material rewards for doing his duty. So the watch returned to its obscure and generous donor. It was a matter of principle.

Citations, plaques, scrolls, and so on, symbols of public appreciation, the reluctant hero took in his stride. He even posed kissing his wife, although we may be confident that they both regarded such an antic as kissing before a camera as exquisite torture, an invasion of domestic privacy. It was something to be endured, put behind them, before they could resume their roles as private citizens. Some sure instinct told the captain that the quickest way out of the intolerable limelight was to accede to anything compatible with honor and probity. But he never deviated from what he deemed honorable and honest by a fraction of an inch. He had done his duty, and if it was now his duty to answer thousands of letters pouring in from admirers all over the world, he would read them and, so far as he could, he would acknowledge them. He may have had a suspicion that the writers would soon be activated by other emotions and be taken up with some fresh sensation. By January nineteenth, he had vanished temporarily from the news columns. The Right Honourable Winston Churchill, Britain's Prime Minister, was leaving the country. This was news. Then, on January twenty-third, a plane crashed into Elizabeth, New Jersey, killing an ex-secretary of war, and deflected attention from Woodbridge, where Captain Carlsen was coping heroically with "ten thousand letters" and reading a highly emotional account of how he came home from sea. "The two had been apart for a long time," chanted one reporter, a person of exquisite sensibility, but not prone to read his, or her, own paper on the marine page. According to schedule, Captain Carlsen had sailed from New York in November, forty-six days before. To a man accustomed to the sea from the age of fourteen, as the captain was, this would appear overwrought.

He had said: "I don't want my attempt cheapened. It is a matter of principle." There he had them. It was a matter of principle. We used to have a phrase in the British Merchant Navy. We would say of a dependable shipmate that he had principle. "Good principle," a chief would say of a good junior. It was an accolade much prized. So Captain Carlsen had his principle. But someone, a master of diplomacy in the Produce Exchange, when they had Captain Carlsen to luncheon to present him with a scroll, produced two one-thousand dollar bonds, one each for Sonja and Karen. Would the captain accept *them*? This was the Achilles heel of the hero. He couldn't refuse those two kids. His flawless conception of principle detected no sinister commercialism in this gracious and delicate tribute to a father's courage. And when the Propeller Club gave him a ship's clock with an inscription, with a citation from the Maritime Commission; when the Seamen's Church Mission came along with a sextant and the inevitable scroll (you will remember he described himself as "not exactly a heathen"), he accepted them in the spirit in which they were offered. They were in the tradition he understood.

This is a success story because Captain Carlsen, having kept his honor and principle untarnished, finally achieved his ambition, which was to get another ship and go to sea. Far away on the oceans, accompanied, we like to think, by his sextant and his ship's clock, by the scrolls and citations and the pictures of his wife and Sonja and Karen, he is free once again to live the life he prefers. Free also to contemplate, from a safe distance, that fantastic world of promoters, photographers, sob sisters and flashlight bulbs, from which he had escaped. Is not this success? To have principle, which is a start, and to follow it? To be shown the kingdoms of the bright lights of flashy financial notoriety, and to reject them with firmness? How can we grudge him his peace of mind, his professional ethics, his personal record, his unbroken home life? He has given us something intangible in return, something of great value, the inspiration of a noble career.

CAPTAIN JOSHUA SLOCUM

Captain Joshua Slocum is another sailor who really can write, and who gave himself something to write about. He was a Nova Scotian square-rigged seaman of the old school, the tough, hard-bitten Blue-Nose school, now dead. He went to sea, by choice at the age of twelve, to make sailing a lifetime profession, and the obvious lack of education which goes with such a beginning shows in such of his papers as have survived apart from his few books. He served in fishermen, and in deepsea tramp square-riggers, large and small, over the oceans of the world. His native abilities and capacity for leadership brought him a second mate's berth at eighteen. At twenty-five he had his first command, a coastwise schooner trading between San Francisco and Seattle. Next he was appointed to command the barque *Washington,* which went pioneering after salmon in Alaskan waters very soon after the forty-ninth state had been acquired from the Russians.

Slocum was an adventurous character at a time when red-blooded adventure came readily to those who were unafraid of it. The *Washington* was driven ashore and wrecked, through no fault of his. So he built a thirty-five-footer to sail to the nearest civilized port, leaving a valuable cache of salmon salted down in barrels to be picked up later. Like many a Yankee venturer of those times, Captain Slocum engaged in seafaring enterprises of his own. He helped a merchant build a steamer in the Philippines and accepted a ninety-ton schooner called the *Pato* in part-payment for his work. The *Pato* was small, grim, and comfortless, but Slocum made a hard living out of her over the blue Pacific—salvaging, fishing, trading. He was able to sell the *Pato* in Hawaii at a good profit after demonstrating her speed by sailing rings around a well-known mail schooner which had, until then, a reputation as a fast ship. Larger and better ships followed, but he was wrecked out of the best of them, the barque *Aquidneck,* on the coast of Brazil.

Again he built himself a thirty-five-footer, and sailed away. But the day of the individualist Yankee (or Blue-Nose) venturer was at an end. There were no more *Aquidnecks,* and few *Patos.* Slocum was broke. His first wife had died. Shrewd, enterprising, a competent and well-proven sailing-ship seaman of long and varied experience, in the prime of life—he was in his early forties when the *Aquidneck* was lost—he could find no berth. Almost in derision, a brother shipmaster offered him the wreck of a thirty-five-foot sloop called the *Spray,* lying at Fairhaven. Slocum had hoped to take this gift-ship fishing, to make a living out of her somehow. But she was unfit to fish in those hard waters. So he rebuilt her himself and sailed her alone around the world.

It was a remarkable feat, copied by many since but by none on his route. There was no Panama Canal then. Slocum used the Capes—westward through Magellan's Straits and homeward round Good Hope, with plenty of hard passages of months at sea in between. He sailed in 1895 and was gone thirty-eight months. He had tried writing before with an account of his escape after the *Aquidneck* wreck, self-published and a failure. This time he sat down and wrote a classic.

How this Blue-Nose seadog, self-taught and no author by ordinary standards, managed to excel as navigator, seaman, and (at least with his *Sailing Alone Around the World*) as writer is astonishing; before the *Spray* sailed, he could not write a grammatical letter. He had a little literary help, I have been told, from some editorial chap in Boston, to lick *Sailing Alone* into shape. It was only help, not ghosting—the book was his, as were the adventures. There were no "ghosts," literary or maritime. The old captain could still find no berth as a deepsea sailing-shipmaster, and he continued to knock about in the *Spray.* He had a home, a second wife, and children, but generally he was alone aboard the *Spray.*

He was still alone when the little *Spray* sailed from Bristol, Rhode Island, in the fall of 1907, touched at Miami, and disappeared. Nothing of the famous ship or her redoubtable master was ever found. The *Spray* was a ripe old wagon by that time, and she never had been a really stout ship since Slocum had her. He was without a spare cent when he made her over in 1895, with whatever material came cheaply to hand, and he had had to make his way around the world by his wits. By 1908 the *Spray* could hardly have been fit to ride out much of a blow, even with all Slocum's skill to help her. She might have been knocked down at night by a steamer which would never have known that she had been in collision. But she would have disintegrated then. Something should have drifted ashore, some time, somewhere. Nothing ever did. More likely, she quietly opened up and went to the bottom, taking the old Blue-Nose at last where he could find no thirty-five-footer to replace her.

"Captain," President Theodore Roosevelt is reported to have said when Slocum presented himself at the White House, "our adventures have been a little different."

"That is true, Mr. President," replied the master of the *Spray,* "but you got here first."

Well, old Josh was first around the world single-handed, anyway, and he wrote not only the first book on that subject; he wrote the best.

"Seventy-two days without a port"

by CAPTAIN JOSHUA SLOCUM

To be alone forty-three days would seem a long time, but in reality, even here, winged moments flew lightly by, and instead of my hauling in for Nukahiva, which I could have made as well as not, I kept on for Samoa, where I wished to make my next landing. This occupied twenty-nine days more, making seventy-two days in all. I was not distressed in any way during that time. There was no end of companionship; the very coral reefs kept me company, or gave me no time to feel lonely, which is the same thing, and there were many of them now in my course to Samoa.

First among the incidents of the voyage from Juan Fernandez to Samoa (which were not many) was a narrow escape from collision with a great whale that was absent-mindedly plowing the ocean at night while I was below. The noise from his startled snort and the commotion he made in the sea, as he turned to clear my vessel, brought me on deck in time to catch a wetting from the water he threw up with his flukes. The monster was apparently frightened. He headed quickly for the east; I kept on going west. Soon another whale passed, evidently a companion, following in its wake. I saw no more on this part of the voyage, nor did I wish to.

Hungry sharks came about the vessel often when she

From *Sailing Alone Around the World* by Captain Joshua Slocum.

neared islands or coral reefs. I own to a satisfaction in shooting them as one would a tiger. Sharks, after all, are the tigers of the sea. Nothing is more dreadful to the mind of a sailor, I think, than a possible encounter with a hungry shark.

A number of birds were always about; occasionally one poised on the mast to look the *Spray* over, wondering, perhaps, at her odd wings, for she now wore her Fuego mainsail, which, like Joseph's coat, was made of many pieces. Ships are less common on the southern seas than formerly. I saw not one in the many days crossing the Pacific.

My diet on these long passages usually consisted of potatoes and salt cod and biscuits, which I made two or three times a week. I had always plenty of coffee, tea, sugar, and flour. I carried usually a good supply of potatoes, but before reaching Samoa I had a mishap which left me destitute of this highly prized sailors' luxury. Through meeting at Juan Fernandez the Yankee Portuguese named Manuel Carroza, who nearly traded me out of my boots, I ran out of potatoes in mid-ocean, and was wretched thereafter. I prided myself on being something of a trader; but this Portuguese from the Azores by way of New Bedford, who gave me new potatoes for older ones I had got from the *Colombia,* a bushel or more of the best, left me no ground for boasting. He wanted mine, he said, "for changee the seed." When I got to sea I found that his tubers were rank and unedible, and full of fine yellow streaks of repulsive appearance. I tied the sack up and returned to the few left of my old stock, thinking that maybe when I got right hungry the island potatoes would improve in flavor. Three weeks later I opened the bag again, and out flew millions of winged insects! Manuel's potatoes had all turned to moths. I tied them up quickly and threw all into the sea.

Manuel had a large crop of potatoes on hand, and as a hint to whalemen, who are always eager to buy vegetables, he wished me to report whales off the island of Juan Fernandez, which I have already done, and big ones at that, but they were a long way off.

Taking things by and large, as sailors say, I got on fairly well in the matter of provisions even on the long voyage across the Pacific. I found always some small stores to help the fare of luxuries; what I lacked of fresh meat was made up in fresh fish, at least while in the trade-winds, where flying-fish crossing on the wing at night would hit the sails and fall on deck, sometimes two or three of them, sometimes a dozen. Every morning except when the moon was large I got a bountiful supply by merely picking them up from the lee scuppers. All tinned meats went begging.

On the 16th of July, after considerable care and some skill and hard work, the *Spray* cast anchor at Apia, in the kingdom of Samoa, about noon. My vessel being moored, I spread an awning, and instead of going at once on shore I sat under it till late in the evening, listening with delight to the musical voices of the Samoan men and women.

A canoe coming down the harbor, with three young women in it, rested her paddles abreast the sloop. One of the fair crew, hailing with the naïve salutation, "Talofa lee" ("Love to you, chief"), asked:

"Schoon come Melike?"

"Love to you," I answered, and said, "Yes."

"You man come 'lone?"

Again I answered, "Yes."

"I don't believe that. You had other mans, and you eat 'em."

At this sally the others laughed. "What for you come long way?" they asked.

"To hear you ladies sing," I replied.

"Oh, talofa lee!" they all cried, and sang on. Their voices filled the air with music that rolled across to the grove of tall palms on the other side of the harbor and back. Soon after this six young men came down in the United States consul-general's boat, singing in parts and beating time with their oars. In my interview with them I came off better than with the damsels in the canoe. They bore an invitation from General Churchill for me to come and dine at the consulate. There was a lady's hand in things about the consulate at Samoa. Mrs. Churchill picked the crew for the general's boat, and saw to it that they wore a smart uniform and that they could sing the Samoan boatsong, which in the first week Mrs. Churchill herself could sing like a native girl.

Next morning bright and early Mrs. Robert Louis Stevenson came to the *Spray* and invited me to Vailima the following day. I was of course thrilled when I found myself, after so many days of adventure, face to face with this bright woman, so lately the companion of the author who had delighted me on the voyage. The kindly eyes, that looked me through and through, sparkled when we compared notes of adventure. I marveled at some of her experiences and escapes. She told me that, along with her husband, she had voyaged in all manner of rickety craft among the islands of the Pacific, reflectively adding, "Our tastes were similar."

Following the subject of voyages, she gave me the four beautiful volumes of sailing directories for the Mediterranean, writing on the fly-leaf of the first:

> To CAPTAIN SLOCUM. These volumes have been read and re-read many times by my husband, and I am very sure that he would be pleased that they should be passed on to the sort of seafaring man that he liked above all others.
> FANNY V. DE G. STEVENSON.

Mrs. Stevenson also gave me a great directory of the Indian Ocean. It was not without a feeling of reverential awe that I received the books so nearly direct from the hand of Tusitala, "who sleeps in the forest." Aolele, the *Spray* will cherish your gift.

The novelist's stepson, Mr. Lloyd Osbourne, walked

through the Vailima mansion with me and bade me write my letters at the old desk. I thought it would be presumptuous to do that; it was sufficient for me to enter the hall on the floor of which the "Writer of Tales," according to the Samoan custom, was wont to sit.

Coming through the main street of Apia one day, with my hosts, all bound for the *Spray*, Mrs. Stevenson on horseback, I walking by her side, and Mr. and Mrs. Osbourne close in our wake on bicycles, at a sudden turn in the road we found ourselves mixed with a remarkable native procession, with a somewhat primitive band of music, in front of us, while behind was a festival or a funeral, we could not tell which. Several of the stoutest men carried bales and bundles on poles. Some were evidently bales of tapa-cloth. The burden of one set of poles, heavier than the rest, however, was not so easily made out. My curiosity was whetted to know whether it was a roast pig or something of a gruesome nature, and I inquired about it. "I don't know," said Mrs. Stevenson, "whether this is a wedding or a funeral. Whatever it is, though, captain, our place seems to be at the head of it."

The *Spray* being in the stream, we boarded her from the beach abreast, in the little razeed Gloucester dory, which had been painted a smart green. Our combined weight loaded it gunwale to the water, and I was obliged to steer with great care to avoid swamping. The adventure pleased Mrs. Stevenson greatly, and as we paddled along she sang, "They went to sea in a pea-green boat." I could understand her saying of her husband and herself, "Our tastes were similar."

As I sailed farther from the center of civilization I heard less and less of what would and what would not pay. Mrs. Stevenson, in speaking of my voyage, did not once ask me what I would make out of it. When I came to a Samoan village, the chief did not ask the price of gin, or say, "How much will you pay for roast pig?"

but, "Dollar, dollar," said he; "white man know only dollar."

"Never mind dollar. The *tapo* has prepared ava; let us drink and rejoice." The tapo is the virgin hostess of the village; in this instance it was Taloa, daughter of the chief. "Our taro is good; let us eat. On the tree there is fruit. Let the day go by; why should we mourn over that? There are millions of days coming. The breadfruit is yellow in the sun, and from the cloth-tree is Taloa's gown. Our house, which is good, cost but the labor of building it, and there is no lock on the door."

While the days go thus in these Southern islands we at the North are struggling for the bare necessities of life.

For food the islanders have only to put out their hand and take what nature has provided for them; if they plant a banana-tree, their only care afterward is to see that too many trees do not grow. They have great reason to love their country and to fear the white man's yoke, for once harnessed to the plow, their life would no longer be a poem.

The chief of the village of Caini, who was a tall and dignified Tonga man, could be approached only through an interpreter and talking man. It was perfectly natural for him to inquire the object of my visit, and I was sincere when I told him that my reason for casting anchor in Samoa was to see their fine men, and fine women, too. After a considerable pause the chief said: "The captain has come a long way to see so little; but," he added, "the tapo must sit nearer the captain." "Yack," said Taloa, who had so nearly learned to say yes in English, and suiting the action to the word, she hitched a peg nearer, all hands sitting in a circle upon mats. I was no less taken with the chief's eloquence than delighted with the simplicity of all he said. About him there was nothing pompous; he might have been taken for a great scholar or statesman, the least assuming of the men I met on the voyage. As for Taloa, a sort of Queen of the May, and the other tapo girls, well, it is wise to learn as soon as possible the manners and customs of these hospitable people, and meanwhile not to mistake for overfamiliarity that which is intended as honor to a guest. I was fortunate in my travels in the islands, and saw nothing to shake one's faith in native virtue.

To the unconventional mind the punctilious etiquette of Samoa is perhaps a little painful. For instance, I found that in partaking of ava, the social bowl, I was supposed to toss a little of the beverage over my shoulder, or pretend to do so, and say, "Let the gods drink," and then drink it all myself; and the dish, invariably a coconut-shell, being empty, I might not pass it politely as we would do, but politely throw it twirling across the mats at the tapo.

My most grievous mistake while at the islands was made on a nag, which, inspired by a bit of good road, must needs break into a smart trot through a village. I was instantly hailed by the chief's deputy, who in an angry voice brought me to a halt. Perceiving that I was in trouble, I made signs for pardon, the safest thing to do, though I did not know what offense I had committed. My interpreter coming up, however, put me right, but not until a long palaver had ensued. The deputy's hail, liberally translated, was: "Ahoy, there, on the frantic steed! Know you not that it is against the law to ride thus through the village of our fathers?" I made what apologies I could, and offered to dismount and, like my servant, lead my nag by the bridle. This, the interpreter told me, would also be a grievous wrong, and so I again begged for pardon. I was summoned to appear before a chief; but my interpreter, being a wit as well as a bit of a rogue, explained that I was myself something of a chief, and should not be detained, being on a most important mission. In my own behalf I could only say that I was a stranger, but, pleading all this, I knew I still deserved to be roasted, at which the chief showed a fine row of teeth and seemed pleased, but allowed me to pass on.

The chief of the Tongas and his family at Caini, returning my visit, brought presents of tapa-cloth and fruits. Taloa, the princess, brought a bottle of coconut-oil for my hair, which another man might have regarded as coming late.

It was impossible to entertain on the *Spray* after the royal manner in which I had been received by the chief. His fare had included all that the land could afford, fruits, fowl, fishes, and flesh, a hog having been roasted whole. I set before them boiled salt pork and salt beef, with which I was well supplied, and in the evening took them all to a new amusement in the town, a rocking-horse merry-go-round, which they called a "kee-kee," meaning theater; and in a spirit of justice they pulled off the horses' tails, for the proprietors of the show, two hard-fisted countrymen of mine, I grieve to say, unceremoniously hustled them off for a new set, almost at the first spin. I was not a little proud of my Tonga friends; the chief, finest of them all, carried a portentous club. As for the theater, through the greed of the proprietors it was becoming unpopular, and the representatives of the three great powers, in want of laws which they could enforce, adopted a vigorous foreign policy, taxing it twenty-five per cent on the gate-money. This was considered a great stroke of legislative reform!

It was the fashion of the native visitors to the *Spray* to come over the bows, where they could reach the head-gear and climb aboard with ease, and on going ashore to jump off the stern and swim away; nothing could have been more delightfully simple. The modest natives wore *lava-lava* bathing-dresses, a native cloth from the bark of the mulberry-tree, and they did no harm to the *Spray*. In summer-land Samoa their coming and going was only a merry everyday scene.

One day the head teachers of Papauta College, Miss Schultze and Miss Moore, came on board with their ninety-seven young women students. They were all dressed in white, and each wore a red rose, and of course came in boats or canoes in the cold-climate style. A merrier bevy of girls it would be difficult to find. As soon as they got on deck, by request of one of the teachers, they sang "The Watch on the Rhine," which I had never heard before. "And now," said they all, "let's up anchor and away." But I had no inclination to sail from Samoa so soon. On leaving the *Spray* these accomplished young women each seized a palm-branch or paddle, or whatever else would serve the purpose, and literally paddled her own canoe. Each could have swum as readily, and would have done so, I dare say, had it not been for the holiday muslin.

It was not uncommon at Apia to see a young woman swimming alongside a small canoe with a passenger for the *Spray*. Mr. Trood, an old Eton boy, came in this manner to see me, and he exclaimed, "Was ever king ferried in such state?" Then, suiting his action to the sentiment, he gave the damsel pieces of silver till the natives watching on shore yelled with envy. My own canoe, a small dugout, one day when it had rolled over with me, was seized by a party of fair bathers, and before I could get my breath, almost, was towed around and around the *Spray*, while I sat in the bottom of it, wondering what they would do next. But in this case there were six of them, three on a side, and I could not help myself. One of the sprites, I remember, was a young English lady, who made more sport of it than any of the others.

CAPTAIN F. C. HENDRY

(''SHALIMAR'')

Captain F. C. Hendry, Officer of the Order of the British Empire, holder of the Military Cross, former merchant seaman, Rangoon River pilot, war-time army captain, walked into a store in Grantown-on-Spey in Scotland, bought himself a sixpenny school exercise book, went home and wrote a story. He was retired then, and he needed something to do. This was the first such attempt he had ever made. The story finished, he sent it to the famous *Blackwood's Magazine*, in Edinburgh. They published it, paid for it with many good sixpences, and asked for more stories. From that day, Captain Hendry the writer never looked back.

Captain Hendry chose the pen-name of Shalimar—why, I don't know, or indeed why any pen-name at all, except that it seemed to be a *Blackwood's* tradition, for a good many high-placed civil servants, former and serving officers and the like, chose to write for *Blackwood's*. I knew him as Captain Hendry, a Scots professional seaman who had served his apprenticeship in a big and beautiful Cape Horner called the *Routenburn,* and had earned his first command within seven years of going to sea. I knew the *Routenburn* well, in her later days. Renamed *Beatrice* out of Gothenburg and cut down to a bald-headed four-mast barque, she raced against us from Australia to Falmouth for orders, in the famous *Herzogin Cecilie*. That ex-German was a splendid ship but, cut-down in rig or not, the ex-*Routenburn* had an excellent chance of winning. She was well manned and well sailed. Yet we beat her by three weeks. Captain Hendry wrote to ask how this had come about, and the acquaintanceship begun that way lasted through the years.

The *Routenburn* was the last wool clipper, and Hendry was one of her last Scots apprentices. After that he was a long time in Eastern waters serving in a little ship like Conrad's (and for the same Singapore owner, who retained outstanding memories of the Polish-British mate he had hired from hospital as the "most conscientious chief officer he had ever had, who had learned to speak Malay fluently, though with a strange guttural accent, in an incredibly short time"). Years in the Rangoon Pilot Service for the Government of Burma followed, at a time when these great Asian pilotage services—on the Hooghly, the Irrawaddy, and at Singapore—were considered the plums of the merchant service. In the first World War, Hendry became first an officer in the Indian Army serving on the North-West Frontier, and later in command of unorthodox river gunboats and other mysterious vessels on the Tigris and Euphrates. He came home to his beloved Scotland to retire in 1922. Thirty years later, he was still producing yarns of the sea, all with the ring of authenticity which none but the true seaman can achieve so effortlessly and convincingly.

Shalimar is dead now, and buried in Scotland. He was a good sailor, and he could write.

Easting Down

by CAPTAIN F. C. HENDRY

The *Knightley*, a tramp steamer of about 5,000 tons gross, was lying in Victoria Basin, Cape Town. Breakfast in the saloon was nearly over. It had been eaten in comparative silence, for the *Knightley* was not a particularly happy ship; the captain and the chief officer thought very little of each other, the captain's thoughts being distinctly the less charitable. Toward the end of the meal there had been some talk about the ship's work, which encouraged the chief officer to get on to his favorite subject—cleanliness, and the slapping on of paint.

"The bulwarks on the fore-deck require chipping very badly, but we'll get that done during the next week or so," he said. "Luckily we're in for a fine weather passage."

"Indeed, Mr. Wilkins," the captain remarked loftily.

He rose and left the saloon. The other officers drained their coffee cups and also prepared to go.

"What's he getting at now?" the chief officer growled.

His officers never knew what Captain Hartnell was getting at, and he certainly never took the trouble to enlighten them. He conveyed the impression that he was much too superior to reach down to their meager intellects, and the impression was probably a correct one; for if ever a man suffered from the reverse of what, in modern jargon, is termed a complex of inferiority, that man was Captain Hartnell. With one exception not a man in the ship could ignore his own inferiority when in the captain's presence—the exception being the young third officer, a Scotsman from the Buchan district of Aberdeenshire, who, placid and laconic, had never discovered any reason why he should be either intimidated or unduly impressed even by a successful shipmaster like his captain who had never suffered the slightest check to his meteoric career and was, without doubt, an outstanding seaman.

Still only thirty-two, Captain Hartnell had got command of a barque when he was twenty-four—a great, modern slab-sided barque that sailormen declared was too slow to get out of her own way. He had been chock-full of confidence from the moment he boarded her. Her code number in the International Book of Signals was M.N.B.S., and on the first night out, bowling down-channel before a fresh breeze, he was heard reciting a rhyme of his own composing:

"M.N.B.S.,
My name brings success,
Go, you flat-bottomed scow, go."

The "flat-bottomed scow" went so well that he drove her out to Australia in twenty days less than his predecessor had taken on the previous voyage, and since that first successful passage he had never tired of proving to his owners that he was the smartest man in their employ. Because of that, and the fact that he was at all times acutely aware of his own merits, he was far from being a favorite with his brother shipmasters. Tall and muscular, he carried himself with a swagger, and when he passed over the gangway that forenoon even the independent stevedores on the quay wall greeted him with respect. He was hardly three yards away from the ship, however, when an able seaman named Kelly brushed against him, then lurched unsteadily up the gangway. Kelly had evidently been ashore all night and looked the worse for wear. It was strange, the captain thought, that the miserable chief officer had not reported one of the men absent without leave. Perhaps the chief officer did not even know. Pah!

Captain Hartnell walked on toward the town. The *Knightley* would be ready for sea in a couple of days and he had some preliminary clearing to do at the agent's office. The work done, he strolled along to the Grand Hotel and entered the lounge, where he found an acquaintance, a much older man who commanded another tramp steamer lying in the same dock. Both vessels were bound for Port Pirie, South Australia, in ballast, to load zinc concentrates, and over their drinks the two masters discussed their coming passages.

"I'm a couple of knots faster than you, so I'll probably pick you up somewhere to the nor'a'd of New Amsterdam, even if I sail a week later," the older man chaffed.

"You won't pick me up at all, and certainly not on

that route," Captain Hartnell retorted. "I'm going to run the easting down!"

"You're going to do *what?*"

"Run the easting down!"

"You'll regret it," the other man said seriously.

"Why? I've done it in a barque not a quarter the size of the *Knightley*."

"Oh, certainly; but the barque hadn't got a racing propeller under her counter," the other said dryly. "What's the idea?"

"To make a quicker passage. Lots of steamers used to do it—the Aberdeen White Star, Shaw Savill, the New Zealand Shipping Company."

"Yes, they *used* to, Hartnell; they don't now." The other man sat back comfortably in his chair. "Anyhow, a fine weather passage along the edge of the southeast trades as far as the hundredth meridian, then southeastward toward the Australian coast will do me," he declared. "I'll probably get all the bad weather I want off the Leeuwin at this time of the year, and I'm not hankering after any more. By the way, didn't you have wireless that time I met you in New York?"

"Yes, but they took it out of her after the war. Hard times, couldn't afford it, the owners said."

"H'm! false economy on these long voyages!"

Two days later, on a bright, calm morning, the *Knightley* hauled out of the docks, rounded Green Point, and stood down the shore of the Cape Peninsula. When the chief officer relieved the second on the bridge at four o'clock in the afternoon the faint outline of Cape Point was astern, and no land was visible along the port beam.

"Sou'-sou'east is the course by the steering compass; south-twenty-east by the standard," the second officer said.

"Sou'-sou'east! Here, what the ——?" the puzzled chief demanded.

"We're going off to do some exploring in the ruddy

Antarctic," the second answered bitterly. "Now you know what he was getting at."

Running the easting down! Sweeping along the troubled four-thousand-mile track that leads from the south of the Cape of Good Hope to the Leeuwin at the southwest corner of Australia, before the furious west winds and the rushing seas that sweep without let or hindrance halfway round the globe. Away down in that trackless waste of waters that lie beyond the parallel of 45° south latitude a succession of beautiful clippers outward bound for Australia to load the wool clip used to storm along under every stitch of canvas they could safely carry. It was there that day after day, week after week, they did the grand sailing that made their wonderful passages possible; today it is deserted except for the fluttering Cape pigeon and the hovering albatross. It was of that gale-swept tract of the great Southern Ocean that Kipling's immortal engineer said if you failed you had time to mend your shaft, even eat it, ere you were spoken, or "Make Kerguelen under sail, three trysails burned with smoke."

The *Knightley* had reached a position too far east even for the latter expedient; for the Crozets and Kerguelen were well to windward, and, in any case, she had not got a single sail on board. But failure was, of course, impossible for Captain Hartnell! M.N.B.S.! He was the only happy man on board, as Mr. Birnie, the third officer, was the only one who was indifferent. The weather was bitterly cold; squall after squall of hurricane force, and laden with sleet, shrieked out of the northwest, and icy spray lashed the after-deck, even though the vessel was in ballast trim and standing high out of the water. Lurching and pitching wildly, she swept to the eastward, throwing her bows high toward the dark flying scud of the squalls, dipping them till she tossed three-quarters of her rudder out of the sea. She was never still for a single moment, night or day; for the liquid ridges that rushed at her port quarter were of an almost incredible steepness, and the valleys between them were cavernous.

Captain Hartnell was happy because his vessel's progress was even swifter than he imagined it would be when he abandoned the fine weather route farther north and stood down into the wild westerlies. The terrific thrust of the favoring wind and waves more than made up for the power wasted by a propeller, the blades of which beat the air almost as much as they churned the sea. He got considerable pleasure from picturing the astonished face of the captain who was going to overhaul the *Knightley* somewhere about New Amsterdam, when he arrived at Port Pirie and found her already half loaded. Mr. Birnie, the third officer, was indifferent because, in spite of his placidity and apparent laziness, he was cast in an iron mold; neither cold, wet, nor discomfort worried him in the least. The other two officers were miserable and disgruntled; they felt that life was being incommensurately aggravated by this entirely unnecessary attempt to save a few days on the passage. The chief officer, a much older man than the captain, felt the cold and discomfort particularly; he could not get warm, even in his bunk, and when keeping his watch on the bridge he was weary of staying on his feet. The deck-hands had reached a state bordering on passive insubordination which might easily have deteriorated into something worse, and the chief officer, possessed of a fellow-feeling, did little to check them.

If the discomfort on deck was acute, it was worse in the engine room and stokehold. The engineer on watch had no difficulty about keeping warm; the propeller, with little more solid than air and spray to bite on half the time, would have sent the engines racing so wildly that they must have shaken themselves to pieces but for his unremitting attention to the throttle. Sweat ran in rivulets through the grime on his face, and every limb ached before the four long hours of his watch had passed. In the stokehold the boilers rocked in their saddles with every plunge; coal aimed at an open fire-door rattled against the boiler plates and rebounded; in the bunkers, trimmers were bruised by coal rumbling down on top of them. The chief engineer, stout-hearted in normal times but now feeling for his men, was sullen and resentful—and sufferance, as a rule, is not the badge of the tribe of seagoing engineers. By that time every man on board knew that there was an easier way to Port Pirie farther north.

Just after breakfast one day, the hands of the watch below, weary after four hours of buffeting, were about to turn into their bunks for a short spell of uneasy sleep. Mr. Birnie was on the bridge, pacing unsteadily to and fro, occasionally grabbing a rail to steady himself against a lurch, but keeping a keen lookout. That was Mr. Birnie's way, though there was really nothing to look out for; they had not seen a vessel since they left Cape Point and did not expect to see one; Australia was still two thousand miles away. The *Knightley*, her hull sloping upward toward the bows like the roof of a house, climbed to the crest of a huge, foaming roller, wriggled and dropped heavily into the succeeding trough. There followed a violent thud that shook her fore and aft as if she had thumped on a rock. Men and officers, certain that she had struck wreckage, for there were no rocks about in an ocean that was hundreds of fathoms deep, streamed out on deck. Captain Hartnell staggered up to the bridge.

"Put her slow!" he shouted from the top of the ladder.

Mr. Birnie rang the telegraph to slow and waited for a reply from the engine room.

"Get the carpenter along to sound the bilges and peaks," the captain ordered.

Bewildered men were staring aft striving to get a view of the wake when the stern dipped, but no extraneous object appeared on the crest of the rollers running up behind. The more pessimistic suggested low-lying ice which would be difficult to see but stout enough to damage the vessel. The captain turned on the third officer.

"Were you keeping a good look-out?" he demanded.

Mr. Birnie stared him straight in the face and hesitated as if deliberating whether he was keeping a good look-out or not. He was always deliberate and, if possible, his speech was monosyllabic; the "sir" he had to use when answering the captain seemed to come out reluctantly, as an extra effort, and always after a distinct pause.

"Yes . . . sir," he replied at last.

"And you saw no wreckage—nor anything else?"

"No . . . sir."

Even by Captain Hartnell's exacting standard Mr. Birnie was a first-class officer and one to be trusted, so there must be another reason for the thud. The chief engineer came up to the bridge with it. He said the young engineer on watch, who was the only person in authority close to the bottom of the ship, considered that the bump was due to the stern plunging into the trough of the sea more violently than usual. The carpenter reported the bilges and peaks dry.

"Put her on full speed again," the captain said.

For the next seven hours the *Knightley* kept on her tortured eastward way, climbing wind-swept ridges, swooping down into dark, half-sheltered valleys; then, shortly after four o'clock, she again shook fore and aft. The second engineer, who had just relieved the third at the throttle, was startled and badly shaken by a continuous racing of the engines; they jarred and rattled and created a resounding pandemonium in the comparatively restricted space of the engine room; the maze of glimmering brass and steel—of pistons, connecting rods, and cross-heads—danced and whirled in a frenzy. The second engineer throttled right down, then signaled to the bridge by ringing the engine-room telegraph to stop. The chief engineer discarded the cup of tea he was sipping and dashed down the iron ladder into the engine room. The engineers off duty followed.

They had an idea that the heavy thump of the morning must have fractured the shaft, and made their way into the tunnel. They worked their way aft as far as the stern-gland, but found the shaft intact. The wooden floor was slippery with oil and grease, and they had great difficulty in keeping their feet; for the ship, robbed of her steerage-way and under the influence of her high forecastle-head, had brought the wind and sea dead aft and was pitching very heavily. As it is almost impossible for a tail-shaft to break inside the stern-tube, they came to the conclusion that it had broken just outside—and that, in fact, was what had happened, as Mr. Birnie had just discovered. Getting up from his settee, on which he had been trying to sleep, he had made his way aft, got over the taffrail, leaned out as far as he could over the sea, and looked down. The steamer's stern had just dipped downward and over to port; it flew up again with a dizzy lift that exposed the greater part of the arched propeller aperture. It was empty; the propeller had gone.

Darkness was coming down. The two red lights which indicated the vessel was not under command were hoisted. Well down by the stern, she continued to lie with the wind and towering seas almost right aft—pitching heavily but lazily. Captain Hartnell retired to his cabin, shut himself in and pondered, while all over the ship, in cabins and in sailors' and firemen's forecastles, officers and men discussed the awful thing that had happened. They discussed it with voices that were almost reduced to whispering, for the prospect was indeed appalling. The accident which had robbed the ship of her mobility had in it a specially heart-rending quality because of her extreme isolation. The shock to the imagination was cruel. To present discomfort had been added an immediate future that was black and an ultimate future that would not bear thinking about.

On the bridge the chief officer, tired of keeping a useless look-out and with no helmsman to supervise, went into the chart room and pored over the outspread general chart of the South Indian Ocean. The captain had penciled a neat cross at the estimated position where the propeller was lost, but beyond that there was little on the chart but parallels of latitude and meridians of longitude. Yes, there *was* something else; much nearer than any land was an irregular dotted line marking the extreme northern limit of icebergs. The chief officer shivered. In that watery abomination of desolation the ship might drift for months without being sighted, unless the drift was suddenly checked by what the irregular dotted line indicated; and if the wind remained in the northwest, that would probably be the result of their drifting. If they got that far! Before then they might starve to death! For reasons connected with the Australian customs laws, the captain, a keen business man, had only taken sufficient provisions for the direct passage in Cape Town. He had not thought to allow for unforeseen delays. Total disablement had certainly not been allowed for, and the chief officer doubted if there was sufficient food on board to give full rations for another fortnight. Again he shivered. The silence —broken only by the wind that howled outside and the splash of the waves—and the total lack of vibration were depressing in the extreme. Tears came into his eyes. The weird feeling that he had a dead thing under him almost overwhelmed him; and a black resentment against the captain, who, in the first place, had been given command of the vessel over his head and who had now got her into this plight, surged up in his heart. The supper bell went, and the third officer came on the bridge to relieve him.

Supper was eaten in silence. The captain sat like a sphinx at the head of the table, and as soon as he had finished his meal he retired to his cabin again. The chief officer and the second—a somewhat colorless individual—would have liked to know what thoughts were working in that self-reliant brain, what pangs of remorse were tugging at the usually unresponsive heart-strings. They were left in ignorance as far as the pangs were concerned, but the thoughts were soon disclosed. At eight o'clock the captain summoned all the officers and engineers to the saloon. The boatswain was sent on the bridge to allow the third officer to attend; the don-key-man relieved the fourth engineer in the silent engine room. Very soon those assembled discovered that they had not been called to a conference, or a council of war, or even a discussion of ways and means of carrying out a plan. They had come to be told what the captain proposed to do, and to receive instructions—and what the captain proposed to do was to fit the square propeller and tail shaft! Blank incredulity showed on every face but one, and the chief engineer voiced it.

"But . . . but you can't do that at sea," he spluttered indignantly.

"*Can't!*" the captain repeated with apparent surprise.

"If you knew the trouble it is to fit a propeller and shaft in a sheltered harbor you wouldn't talk like that. With this sea running it's impossible. To begin with, you would have to tip her down by the head till the stern-tube is out of the water."

"Quite right," the captain answered calmly. "We'll make a start at that tomorrow morning. We'll pump out the after-peak and ballast tanks, and flood No. 1 hold."

"Flood No. 1 hold!" the chief officer shouted hysterically. "You'll wreck the ship! You'll lose her! What bulkheads would stand hundreds of tons of water washing against them? If they do, she'll roll over with us!"

"We'll have to chance that—unless you can suggest anything else, Mr. Wilkins."

The chief officer did not reply. There was a silent, puzzled pause and a shuffling of feet. Nobody *could* suggest anything else, and all knew it. The chief engineer broke the silence.

"Look here, Captain Hartnell, I'm as keen as you are to try something; God knows I don't want to end my life down here," he said soberly. "But I tell you it's quite impossible, especially with this sea running. If you would wait for a calm, even."

"Calms are scarce in this latitude and we might wait a month," the captain replied. "By that time we should be so weak with starvation that we could do nothing."

"And you propose to have men working under the counter with a ship jumping like this! It's murder! They'll either drown or have their brains bashed out! I tell you straight, none of *my* men will go over the stern!"

"They had better wait till they're asked," the captain said dryly. "I'm going over the stern myself."

"So am I!"

The assembled men looked round in astonishment. The speaker was the young third officer who up till then had remained unobtrusively in the background, apparently studying, with an absent mind, the rivets in the beams overhead.

"Thank you, Mr. Birnie," said the captain.

The third officer's prompt offer had a definite, and remedying, effect. It dropped the seeds of doubt, in some cases of shame, into men's minds; it stirred something in their souls and made an appeal for a more robust attitude toward the crisis that had overtaken them. In a flash it was realized by most of them that resentment, no matter how much it may have been justified, would get them nowhere; that their present attitude was unworthy of British seamen. They shuffled their feet and looked at each other, trying to read each other's minds, as if they were strikers afraid of being suspected of blacklegging. The captain quickly sensed their hesitation.

"Gentlemen, this is the crux of the matter," he said. "Are we to remain inactive while the ship drifts helplessly toward the icefields, or are we prepared to make an effort to save ourselves?"

The engineers nodded in apparent agreement, but the chief officer remained obdurate.

"I tell you it's madness to try and flood the for'a'd hold," he moaned.

"That's enough," Captain Hartnell said curtly. "At six o'clock tomorrow morning get all your hands on to lifting the ceiling in No. 1 lower hold, and stowing the boards securely in the 'tween-decks. The loose water in the hold *might* damage the bulkheads; if those heavy boards were washing about in it they certainly *would*. Perhaps you didn't think of *that*. Chief, as soon as Mr. Wilkins reports to you that the manhole doors have been taken off No. 1 ballast tank top, open the sea-cocks and get the hold flooded. At the same time start the pumps on the after-peak and tanks."

"Very good, sir," said the chief engineer.

A quarter of an hour later Captain Hartnell went on the bridge, and after some difficulty, for there was no light even in the useless binnacle, found the third officer leaning against the rail behind the canvas dodger, against which sleet was pattering.

"Mr. Birnie, I won't forget this," he said, "but there's something else I want you to do. I've been thinking things out, and have come to the conclusion that we shall require another hand under the counter; we can't manage the job by ourselves. Now, I won't want to *order* any man to do the job because the chief engineer certainly didn't exaggerate when he spoke of the dangers of drowning and bashing. We are in for a hell of a time, and if any man refused to take his share in it, he might well be upheld in a court of law. That would place me, as a shipmaster, in a very awkward position—but I don't want to *plead* with any man. Will you look around, pick out a suitable man, and broach him on the quiet?"

"Yes . . . sir," said Mr. Birnie.

A wild, wintry dawn was ushered in by the chattering of the winch for No. 1 hold. It was being used for sending a derrick aloft. Down in the bottom of the hold the carpenter, and some of the seamen, were lifting the heavy three-inch ceiling boards. Those were slung and hove up level with the 'tween-decks, where they were stowed and securely lashed. The ballast tank top was exposed along its full length, and the carpenter took off the manhole doors. All was ready for flooding the hold. The engineers opened the sea-cocks for the tank, which was already full, and the water overflowed into the hold. The pumping out of the after ballast tanks and after-peak began. The *Knightley* was drifting with half a gale dead aft, and still pitching heavily; the seas running up astern were rising right up to the counter as her stern dipped, and falling to the middle pintle of the rudder as it rose. It was about noon before the alteration of the trim took effect and she came on to an even keel. Her bow dipped lower in the water, and, no longer holding the wind, came up to windward, bringing the wind and the sea abeam so that the steamer lay in the trough and wallowed.

The afternoon watch will long be remembered by every soul on board. The steamer rolled as she had never rolled before, and created a panic. She put a severe strain on the arm and body muscles of men hanging on grimly to keep their footing on the decks; the only reason why those of the watch below were not pitched out of their bunks was that they did not attempt to get into them. They were, however, lucky to *be* below, for there they could feel but not see; they missed the swift swoop of masts and funnel that made men dizzy and brought a sinking feeling to the stoutest heart. Even Captain Hartnell, maintaining his position by the bridge rail by intense, painful, muscular effort, became seriously alarmed, for the first time in his career at sea. From the second his vessel's masts and funnel passed the perpendicular she would lean over somewhat lazily; then, as the great and increasing mass of loose water in the hold washed across, she would fall over with a terrific jerk that almost tore the captain's arms out of their sockets. It was the heavy mass of water that constituted the danger—and absolutely nothing could be done about it; except, perhaps, pump the hold dry again and acknowledge defeat. Even that could not promise immediate relief; and in the meantime, from being almost on her beam-ends on one side, the ship would roll over till she was almost on her beam-ends on the other—and when she was lying over on her side, to men's fevered imagination her masts and funnel seemed to be horizontal.

As she crashed over till the sea lapped over the lee bulwark rail she squashed the water so that it created a smother of foam half an acre in extent; but it was during these seconds, that passed like hours, when she lay on her side as if she would never recover, that her breathless captain suffered his most acute spasms of anxiety. It was then that he cursed illogically the damned chief officer who had prophesied disaster, and assuredly if Mr. Wilkins had gone on the bridge with a hint of "I told you so" on his lips, the captain would have committed manslaughter. Always, however, just as hope had almost died, the powerful righting lever created by her low center of gravity came reluctantly into play, overcame the mass of water that was listing her and brought her upright—only to fall heavily the other way. Toward four o'clock, when human endurance had almost failed, the rolling eased. The stern rising imperceptibly out of the water was beginning to feel the force of the wind. It blew right off and the *Knightley* came head to wind and sea, and hove herself to. Instead of rolling she pitched, but was comparatively safe. To help to keep her hove-to, two tarpaulins were spread in the main rigging, one on each side, to reinforce the elevated stern which was acting like an after-sail. She was tipped sufficiently soon after dark, when the pumps were stopped and the cocks closed.

Next morning the captain ordered the construction of a sea-anchor. Now, the sea-anchor that will hold a five-thousand-ton steamer, in her ordinary trim of being down by the stern, head to the sea in such a gale as was then blowing, has yet to be constructed; but this was different. The vessel was lying head to sea naturally, and the sea-anchor would serve to steady her. It consisted of a triangular framework of stout awning spars and lifeboat oars, on which was stretched an awning. To the apex of the triangle—which would be inverted when it was in the sea—a five-fathom length of mooring chain with a kedge anchor was attached. A three-and-a-half-inch wire hawser, to which the vessel would ride, was shackled to a triple span of two-inch wire attached to the framework. The end of the hawser had been taken on the forecastle-head, passed out through a chock, and led aft outside the ship before being shackled to the span. The derrick of No. 1 hatch was already up; the end of its fall was attached to the framework by a rope strop; the sea-anchor was lifted and swung out over the sea. The strop was cut, the anchor dropped in the water, and promptly sank. Gradually, as the steamer drifted astern, the wire hawser tightened, and presently the sea-anchor appeared on the crest of a wave about fifty yards ahead. It made an efficient drogue.

Down in the tunnel the engineers had set to work to uncouple and remove the bobbin-piece—a length of shaft in the tunnel recess that connected the main- and tail-shafts. The broken tail-shaft was withdrawn and the spare one, which had been secured by chains in the tunnel, was run out through the stern-tube till it was level with the stern-post. It was much colder work than engineers usually have to do; for while they were changing the shafts the sea poured in through the stern-tube every time the stern dipped; but, working heroically, they completed the job by midnight. As far as they were concerned all was ready for shipping the spare propeller which was lying in No. 4 'tween-decks. Had the vessel been loaded it would have been lying under tons of cargo, an indication that it was intended for use only after the vessel had been towed, disabled, into a foreign port.

At daybreak next day the chief officer with his men descended into the 'tween-decks and very carefully cast adrift the chain lashings securing it. It weighed over five tons, and there was great danger that it might take charge, surge forward along the steeply sloping deck, and maim or kill any man who tried to control it. In the meantime one of the derricks for No. 4 hatch had been rigged up. A heavy chain sling was passed through the boss of the propeller, and the lower block of a stout tackle suspended from the derrick head hooked on. A winch revolved, and a sleet squall howled at the propeller and the struggling men as it swayed up through the hatchway, with guys attached to prevent it from flying forward when it cleared the coaming. It was landed on the port side of the slippery iron deck, and three more chain slings attached to it, one also through the boss, the others on opposite blades. It was ready for being transported aft. From the counter another stout tackle, with its fall leading in through the port quarter chock on the poop, was taken along outside the poop rail, passed in over the bulwarks, and made fast to the chain sling that had just been passed through the boss.

Again the winch revolved, the propeller was lifted off the deck by means of the derrick and swung out over the heaving sea. It had to be taken aft fully fifty feet. Very carefully the fall of the derrick tackle was surged away, while the tackle from the counter, led to another winch, slowly dragged the propeller aft. More and more the stern tackle took the weight, till eventually the propeller was hanging down from the stern, level with the rudder. It was then the magnitude of the task they were committed to, and its danger, became fully realized. To get the stern-tube clear of the water the vessel had been tipped till the eight feet mark was awash; but as her stern dipped, the water

was rising to the *sixteen* feet mark, and the sea boiled
and swirled under her counter. When the stern rose
again there was a violent scour through the propeller
aperture. The heavy four-bladed propeller, practically
out of control, was surging about; now banging against
the rudder, now crunching against the plating round
the stern-tube. Darkness was almost on them, yet it
could not be left to surge about all night. It was hove
up close under the counter and made more secure;
and, as there was still some daylight left, the captain
decided to complete the preliminaries, all ready for
the morning. The job took a good deal longer than he
expected, and showed him clearly how laborious the
main business was going to be.

Under the counter were two eye-bolts, one on each
side, to which lifting tackles were hooked when taking
off the propeller for inspection in dry-dock, and for
replacing it. Those were the tackles that would be used
for suspending the propeller in its correct plumb position, and Captain Hartnell thought there was just
time to get them adjusted. Hooking the upper blocks
to the eye-bolts was easy enough; the third officer was
lowered over the stern in a boatswain's chair, and
though on occasion the water rose as high as his waist,
he accomplished the job without much difficulty. The
lower block on the port side was then attached to one
of the chain slings that had been passed round opposite blades; but before the starboard one could be
hooked on, it, and the threefold purchase rove through
it, had to be passed through the propeller aperture
from starboard to port. Down went Mr. Birnie, in his
boatswain's chair, clinging to the lower block; he was
lowered till he gained a footing on the lower plate of
the aperture, but the stern dipped and he was washed
off it. He regained it with difficulty, and men gasped
with horror when the scour through the aperture
swung him yards clear. A fathom of ratline was lowered, and he lashed himself to the rudder-post. A terrific struggle followed. Every time he got the block

close to the stern-post the scour tore it from his grasp. The captain shouted to him to give it up till the morning, but he asked for the end of a heaving line, which he passed through the aperture from port to starboard and made fast to the block. By its means the group of men leaning over the taffrail were able to check the block from surging back, and to haul it upward after it had been shoved through the aperture. It was slow work, though; for the third officer had to light the six swollen ropes of the tackle round the stern-post against which it was binding. It became so dark that he could hardly be seen from the taffrail, and the captain grew impatient.

"Come up out of that, Mr. Birnie," he shouted. "Leave everything as it is till the morning."

Mr. Birnie either could not, or would not hear, for he struggled on.

"He's as full of obstinacy as a mule," the chief officer, who wanted his supper, cried irritably.

"I prefer to call it determination, and I wish you had some of it, Mr. Wilkins," Captain Hartnell snapped.

The boatswain, who had not heard the captain's order, came along with an iron bucket in which there was a lighted fire made of oakum steeped in tar. By its light the work was continued, and the block pulled up to the taffrail and secured. Mr. Birnie, sitting in his boatswain's chair—a flat board with a rope span attached to it—was hauled up on deck and stood shaking himself like a spaniel.

About nine o'clock Captain Hartnell went along to the third officer's cabin. Mr. Birnie had been relieved of watch-keeping, and the captain found him lying in his bunk, chocked off with cushions, smoking his pipe and reading a book.

"Any luck, Mr. Birnie?" the captain asked.

"Yes . . . sir."

"Who did you get?"

"Kelly . . . sir," said Mr. Birnie.

With the first streak of dawn, while the hands assembled the gear aft, the captain stood at the break of the spray-swept forecastle-head. He looked along aft, and his vessel reminded him of a pig rooting for truffles, its nose in the ground and its stern cocked up toward the sky. He looked ahead; stretching out to the invisible sea-anchor the wire hawser became bar-tight as the *Knightley's* dripping bows lifted, then slackened and splashed into the water as they dipped. The usual dawn squall howled over the gray waste of foaming ridges, but through the sleet he could see the two red lights dangling mournfully in front of the rust-streaked funnel. Even from where he stood he could hear the heavy wash of water, fore and aft, in No. 1 hold—a dismal, menacing sound. With all his self-confidence he had to admit to considerable anxiety, and he prayed that the bulkheads would stand. He was waiting for the carpenter's report, and when it came it was good. The petty officer had sounded the fore-peak and the bilges of No. 2 hold, and found them dry. The bulkheads were not even leaking. Greatly cheered, the captain went aft, prepared for a long day of arduous toil.

Among the others waiting on the poop for him he found Kelly, who prided himself on being the hardest case in the ship—a hard case descended from hard cases, indeed a lineal descendant of the Liverpool Irish packet rats who manned the notorious Western Ocean packet ships in the middle of the last century. Unlike his officers, who were going over the stern with him wearing sea-boots, oilskins well lashed at the wrists and below the knees, and with small towels tucked under the collars of their coats, Kelly was barefooted and clad only in singlet and dungaree trousers. Erect and jaunty, as if he were going for a stroll along the beach at Southport on a summer day, he stood among his blue-lipped, shivering mates whose bodies were bent to the blast; for on that high exposed afterdeck there was little shelter except two winches on which

wire hawsers were wound, a small hatchway, some ventilators, and the emergency hand-steering wheel with
its wheel-box.

"Going for a bath this morning, Kelly?" Captain
Hartnell asked pleasantly.

"I am, sir; and I hope the maid hasn't forgotten to
turn on the hot-water tap," Kelly answered with a
grin.

From the counter the propeller was lowered by the
stern-tackle till the port lifting tackle took its weight.
The other tackle was then unhooked, and the sling
removed by the third officer who had already gone over
the stern. The propeller was lowered still farther and
the starboard lifting tackle hove on to drag it into
the aperture. The captain and Kelly got into their
boatswain's chairs and were slacked down, with life-
lines round them, to the eight feet mark. After Mr.
Birnie's experience of the previous evening they secured themselves to the rudder-post at once. The water
was icy cold, and they gasped and choked as it closed
over them; from their lower level the foaming crests
of the waves seemed to tower to an enormous height.

"Ah, well, we're nice and sheltered down here, sir,"
said Kelly.

Under the lee of the counter they were certainly
sheltered from the wind, the swirling spray, and the
driving snow which swept past the vessel's sides in two
streams and united again in the wake a few yards behind them. If the sea was not so infernally cold, the
captain thought ruefully as he fingered the heavy hammer slung round his neck. With it he had arranged
to make signals by taps on the steel-plating to the
engineers in the tunnel, but he did not have occasion to use it that day. Three whole hours elapsed
before any of the men were able to lay a hand on the
propeller which was grinding and crunching against
the stern-post. At first they found the conditions almost terrifying, and all they could do was to hang on
grimly and wipe the salt water from their eyes as their

heads emerged from the sea. The terrific scour through the propeller aperture seemed as if it would choke the very life out of them. The counter above them would lift dizzily one moment, and dip the next to create a smother of foam in which their heads would be revealed, at the next lift, to the anxious watchers hanging out over the quarters on both sides. A less determined man than Captain Hartnell would have given up the job there and then; men with less powers of endurance than Mr. Birnie and Kelly possessed could not have stood it.

It was late in the day before they could get on with the job of coaxing the propeller to lie fairly in the middle of the aperture. Shouted orders were cut short on the captain's lips, but by signaling to those who were leaning out over the quarter it was possible to convey instructions to heave, or slack, on the tackles. The adjustment became delicate. As the propeller was gradually worked into position, the heaving and slacking got down to a matter of inches. Thrice they got the hole through the boss of the propeller to coincide with the outer flange of the stern-tube, but were unable to stop the winch at the exact moment. Darkness put a stop to the work, and the men had to be hauled up on to the poop—soaked, deafened, and exhausted—with the boss and the stern-tube still out of alignment.

The following daybreak brought no change in the weather. Again the suffering seamen mustered on the bleak, wind-swept poop, appropriately christened by one of them Mount Misery. The three men were lowered into the water and secured to the rudder-post. By noon the five-ton propeller was hanging at the correct height and rubbing against the stern-post, but six inches over to starboard. Mr. Birnie and Kelly got over to that side and endeavored to lever it into position. Their combined efforts, coinciding with a lucky surge of the starboard tackle, got it into the exact position. The captain yelled frantically to the watchers to hold on everything, and hammered his signal to the waiting engineers. The sea closed over him and his companions. His head was the first to emerge from the foam.

"Is it still in its place, Kelly?" he spluttered.

"Faith, sir, it's mighty contagious!" Kelly yelled.

Again the captain hammered on the plating. For moments big as days, as it seemed—at any rate for twenty minutes which passed like hours—the three men watched, and then the thimble point of the tail-shaft making its way through the round aperture in the boss of the propeller appeared. Never did the most anxious of terriers watch a rat-hole more keenly than those men watched that aperture.

"It's coming, Birnie; by God! it's coming!" Captain Hartnell cried in triumph.

"Yes . . . sir," said Mr. Birnie.

Inch by inch the tail-shaft moved outward till six inches of it projected abaft the propeller boss; then the first thread of the worming on which the nut to secure the propeller would be screwed came into view. It would take the engineers some time to put the bobbin-piece in its place and get it connected to the tail-shaft and main-shaft; so, after the propeller had been bound hard against the stern-post by ropes leading from the quarter pipes, the three men in the water were hauled up for a welcome meal. Less than an hour of daylight remained when the chief engineer reported the job complete, and Captain Hartnell decided to wait till next morning before tackling the job of screwing on the propeller nut. At twilight, with a good horizon, the second officer got stellar observations and discovered that the *Knightley* had drifted two hundred miles to the southeast since she broke down.

Dawn found the little group of watchers mustered on the poop for what they hoped would be the last time; and shortly after that the dauntless three were secured to the rudder-post, waiting for the nut to be lowered to them. It weighed three hundred pounds and had to be slung carefully; for if it had slipped out of the sling and dropped into the sea all the work they had accomplished would have been nothing but wasted effort. There was not another nut on board, and the slinging of it had given the captain food for much anxious thought, till an ingenious engineer came to the rescue by fitting two tap-bolts to it. Even a three-hundred-pound nut takes a lot of handling under the conditions in which the men over the stern worked, and it required their united strength to get it over the thimble point of the shaft and pushed home. With the sling still attached to it they managed to get a round turn of the thread of the nut on to the worm of the shaft; then they reckoned it was safe, and the sling was dispensed with. They got three more turns by hand before the key for tightening the nut was lowered to them.

The key weighed three cwt., and had slats on the rim which fitted projections on the nut. At the end of the handle was a round hole into which the lower block of a tackle from under the counter could be hooked. At first the key could be turned by those above hauling on the tackle by hand, a quarter of a turn of the nut at a time; but to the men in the water fell the almost herculean task of shifting the position of the key on the nut, ready for another quarter of a turn. To save it from dropping into the sea it was suspended by a line from the port quarter, with a smaller line attached to the rudder-post to enable the men down there to haul it toward them when it swung outward. The sea was running as high as ever; the steamer's stern rose and fell continuously. Up it flew till it brought the nut clear of the water and gave them a brief spell in which to work; down it plunged, and they held on for their lives in the seething vortex.

At times it took them half an hour to shift the grip of the key on the nut. The hours passed; the short spell of winter daylight was drawing to a close, but the soaked, exhausted, yet indomitable men worked on, determined to get the job finished. For the last few turns of the nut the fall of the tackle had to be taken to one of the steam winches. The strain on the tackle became so great that the nut must have been nearly home, but it had to be got into a position where the hole bored through it for the locking pin coincided with the hole in the tail-shaft through which the pin had to pass.

Darkness again overtook them, and once more light was obtained from flares made by burning oakum and tar in buckets. The nut was now turning an eighth of an inch at a time. With the strain on the tackle the moisture was being squeezed out of the rope fall, which on occasion surged back round the winch and was torn out of the frozen hands of the man who was holding on to it down on the main-deck. Captain Hartnell was sitting astride the propeller boss, probing the hole in the but with the pin held in fingers numb and blue with cold. To avoid losing the pin it was attached to his wrist by a length of spun-yarn. He was almost in despair, when he felt the pin entering the hole in the shaft. He drove it home with his hammer, and the completely exhausted men were hauled up on to the poop. When they reached it they could not stand on their feet.

Later in the evening the captain told the steward to take Kelly along to the saloon and give him a good stiff dram of rum. He then did a thing he had never done since he first took command of a ship. He invited an officer—Mr. Birnie—to his cabin for a whisky-and-soda. The whisky-and-soda was followed by others, and by the time Mr. Birnie said good night he was almost discursive.

Only Mr. Birnie and Kelly went over the stern next morning, and two hours' work sufficed to cover the job of securing the pin and removing the tackles and slings from the propeller. The two men were hauled up to the taffrail for the last time. The captain gave instructions to fill the after-peak and ballast tanks, and at the same time ordered a full head of steam. Gradually the steamer's stern dropped and she came on to a more even keel, but there was still the flooded hold to be pumped out. Without a doubt as her bow rose she would fall off into the trough of the sea, in spite of the pull of the sea-anchor and the tarpaulins in the main rigging, and they might lose her yet through the mass of loose water in the half-empty hold. The memory of that awful rolling was terrifying; she must be kept head on to the sea till the hold was pumped out; the engine-room telegraph on the bridge was rung to "stand-by."

It was not answered at once; the engines had to be turned over both ways. Both on deck and in the engine room there was now considerable anxiety, heart-burning, and searching of mind. Had there been any flaw in the work carried out in the tunnel, or under the counter? Had anything been left undone? Would the first movement of the engines have as a result a crunching jar that would wreck the efforts of the past week and leave them to drift and starve? Only the actual working of the engines could tell. From the bridge Captain Hartnell listened intently. He heard the first wheezings of steam; were the engines vibrating again? They were, and, unknown to him, spray was being tossed up under the counter. The telegraph from the engine room clanged its reply; the engines were ready.

The sea-anchor was tripped by a line that had been attached to the crown of the kedge, and hoisted on board. The engines were put ahead at half-speed; the *Knightley* was steering again. The captain did not want to drive her too hard into the pounding seas, nor did he wish to steam far back to the westward and lose valuable time. But she had to be kept head to sea at all costs. For most of the time half-speed sufficed; but frequently a touch of full speed was required to give her more steerage-way and straighten her up when she fell off to a dangerous angle and gave a hint that she was about to resume her rolling. The captain's hand was continually on the telegraph handle. At last the flooded hold was pumped out down to the bilges; the manhole doors on top of the ballast tanks were replaced and secured. The chief officer came on the bridge to report, and the captain banged the telegraph handle down to full speed with an air of finality.

"Course . . . sir?" the third officer inquired.

"Keep her northeast, Mr. Birnie; you and I and Kelly are due a spell of warm weather," the captain answered with a partially concealed grin.

The *Knightley* arrived at Port Pirie only a few days overdue. So well had the work been done that she steamed from that port to the United Kingdom, thence to Singapore and back, before the propeller was attended to in the ordinary way at the regular dry-docking. The rival steamer from Cape Town had got to Port Pirie before him; but, later, Captain Hartnell had his compensations. From his owners he received a gold watch, suitably inscribed; and he and his fellow-workers under the counter were awarded Lloyd's medal for meritorious service. That decoration is bestowed irrespective of rank and nationality but it is not lightly awarded. It is recognized by seafarers all over the world as a great honor, and none has earned it more worthily than those men who were lashed to the *Knightley's* rudder-post. Captain Hartnell had his placed in a frame and displayed in a prominent place in his cabin; Mr. Birnie sent his to his mother and thought little more about it; what happened to Kelly's is unknown; for—true vagabond of the sea that he was —he left the steamer at her home port and no one connected with her ever heard of him again.

MORLEY ROBERTS

Morley Roberts, 1857–1942, was a remarkably talented writer who liked to gather material the hard way, if possible, and sometimes made it hard when that perhaps was not really necessary. Born in England, he could have led a life of comfort there, for he was well connected and well educated, and his talents were outstanding. He chose instead to go off around the world at the age of nineteen (it is said that the immediate cause was a violent quarrel with his father, who was a Tax Collector) and live rough, as a working sailor in deepsea sailing-ships (and not just in one), a bushman and a cattleman in Australia, a hobo in the West and a lumberman in Canada. He was not playing at these pastimes. Roberts lived vividly. On lumbermill or tops'l yard, as railroad navvy on the C.P.R. in Canada, or down and all but out in San Francisco, he stuck at whatever sort of life it was until he felt that he had taken all it had to offer him.

Described by a contemporary as "a very singular man . . . tall, restless, brown-haired, brown-eyed, red-bearded, powerful yet neurotic, a confirmed pessimist and rationalist whose esthetic sensibilities were nevertheless abnormally developed," he must have been an odd foremast hand and an even odder hobo. Seamen of those days (and later) had generally some grounds for suspicion of those who followed their dangerous and ill-rewarded calling for reasons other than economic necessity or because they were innocents shanghaied. A man who chose hardship, knowing better, who could quit when he wished and had an assurance of an easier life to which he could return when he liked, was not usually the type who could interpret their sea, or their seafaring. It is a tribute to the unusual abilities of Morley Roberts that they did accept him, both as a seaman and a writer. He knew his work as both and, though few of us have ever met a Captain of the *Ullswater,* his sea stories bear the authentic ring of truth. There are at least half a dozen other good stories which would have served equally well here: "Jack-All-Alone," "The Rehabilitation of the *Vigia,*" among them.

The Captain of the Ullswater

by MORLEY ROBERTS

There were enemies of Captain Amos Brown who said that he was a liar. He certainly had a vivid imagination, or a memory for a more romantic career than falls to the lot of most at sea or ashore.

"By the time we make Callao, Mr. Wardle," said the skipper to his new mate, as they lay in Prince's Dock, Liverpool, "I expect to be able to tell you something of my life, which has been a very remarkable one."

"You don't say so, sir," said Mr. Wardle, who, as it happened, had heard nothing about the skipper, and was innocently prepared to swallow quite a deal. "You don't say so, sir."

"I do say so," replied the skipper. "It has been a most remarkable career from first to last. Wonders happen to me, Mr. Wardle, so that when I am at sea I just know that something will occur that is strange. I have a collection of binoculars, with inscriptions on them for saving lives at sea, that would surprise you. They have been given me by almost every Government of any importance under the sun."

"That must be very gratifyin', sir," said the mate.

"It gets monotonous," said the skipper with a yawn. "At times I wish foreign Governments had more imagination. They never seem to think two pairs of glasses enough for any man. And the silver-mounted sextants I possess are difficult to stow away in my house. If you don't mind the inscription to me on it, I'll give you a sextant presented to me by France, Mr. Wardle, if I can remember to bring it with me from home next time."

Mr. Wardle said he should be delighted to own it, and said, further, that the inscription would naturally give it an added interest. At this the skipper yawned again, and said that he was tired of inscriptions.

"The next lot I pick up I'll request not to give my name," he said. "My wife, Mr. Wardle, gets tired of keeping a servant specially to polish 'to Captain Brown,' with a lot of complimentary jaw to follow that makes her tired. She knows what I am, Mr. Wardle, and doesn't require to be reminded of it by falling over a gold-mounted sextant every time she turns round. A woman even of a greedy mind can easily get palled with sextants, and a woman sees no particular use in them when they take up room that she wants to devote to heirlooms in her family. Before we get to Callao I'll tell you all about my wife, and how I came to marry her. It is a romantic story. She belongs to a noble family. She is the most beautiful woman that you ever set eyes on. I'll tell you all about it before we get to Callao. I've always been a very attractive man to the other sex, Mr. Wardle. She's rather jealous, too, though she belongs to a noble family. I understand in noble families it isn't good taste to be jealous, but she is. However, I must write to her now, or I shall have a letter from her at Callao that would surprise you, if by that time I know you well enough to show it to you. And now, what were you saying about those three cases marked P. D., and consigned to Manuel Garcia?"

Mr. Wardle told him what he had been saying about

the cases marked P. D., and consigned to Manuel Garcia, and it was settled what was to be done with them. The skipper said that he wished they were full of his binoculars and diamond-mounted sextants, and also his gold watches with fulsome inscriptions on them, and that they were consigned to Davy Jones.

"And this is a letter for you, sir," said the mate. The skipper opened it.

"From my wife," he said, and then he swore.

"Another pair of binoculars from the Swedish Government," he groaned. "I shall write and say that I would rather have a suit of clothes, and that if there must be an inscription on them will they put it where it can't be seen. The German Government once did that for me, but they put the inscription in good English on the collar, and I found it very inconvenient, for strangers would come and breathe in my neck while they read it."

Mr. Wardle went away to ask the second mate what he thought of the skipper. He sighed, and the second mate laughed. The second mate was an unbelieving dog and a merry one. When it came six o'clock they had a wash, and put on clean clothes, and went up town together, and had a friendly drink at a well-known public-house which was a great resort for mates and second mates, though a skipper rarely put his nose inside it.

"I wonder what kind of a chap the skipper is, after all," said Humphries, the second mate. "It seems to me, sir, that he is a holy terror of a liar, and no mistake."

"Oh, I shouldn't like to say that," replied Wardle. "I do, however, think he exaggerates and puts it on a bit thick. That isn't bein' a liar. I dare say he has saved life at sea. He wouldn't have offered me a silver-mounted sextant if he hadn't several."

"I shall believe you will get it when I see you with it," said Jack Humphries. "In my opinion, Captain Amos Brown is a first-class liar."

Perhaps he spoke a little too loudly for a public place, though that public place was a billiard-room with four second mates playing a four-handed game, and making as much row over it as if they were picking up the bunt of the foresail in a gale of wind. He was overheard by the only "old man" in the room.

"Did I hear you mention someone called Amos Brown?" said the old chap sitting next to him.

"I did, sir," said the second mate of the *Ullswater.* "Do you know him?"

"I had an Amos Brown as an apprentice with me when I commanded the *Samuel Plimsoll,*" replied the old gentleman, "and he was a very remarkable lad. I think I heard you say that this one was a liar?"

"I did," said Humphries; "though perhaps I shouldn't have done so, as I'm second mate with him now, sir."

The old boy shook his head.

"I won't tell him. But it surely must be the same. The Brown I knew was an awful liar, and I've seen many in my time, gentlemen."

He asked them to drink with him, and they did it willingly. To know the one-time skipper of the old *Samuel Plimsoll* was something worth while, seeing that she had once held the record for a day's run. And if his Brown was theirs it was a chance not to be missed. They took their drinks, and asked him to tell them all about Amos Brown.

"He went overboard in a gale of wind and saved another boy who couldn't swim," said the stranger, "and when we got them back on board, and he could speak, the very first thing he said was that he had seventeen medals from the Royal Humane Society for saving other lives. Does that sound like your man?"

Wardle told him about the binoculars and gold watches and silver-mounted sextants.

"Ah, he's the man," said the old skipper. "Don't you think because he gasses that he hasn't pluck. I'd not be surprised to hear that there is some truth in what he says. I've known one man with four pairs of inscribed binoculars. I dare say Captain Brown has a pair or two. When you see him, tell him that you met Captain Gleeson, who used to command the *Samuel Plimsoll*. And as I'm goin' now, I don't mind owning that I'm the man that has the four pairs of binoculars, gentlemen."

He bade them good night, and Humphries said when he had gone that he was probably as big a liar as the skipper, and had never seen the *Samuel Plimsoll*.

"And as for Brown bein' a hero," added the second mate, "I simply don't believe it. A liar can't be brave."

This was a large and youthful saying, and Wardle, who was not so young as his subordinate, had his doubts of it.

"I rather think the captain is all right," he said. "I'll ask him tomorrow if he was ever in the *Samuel Plimsoll*."

They were at sea before he got a chance to do so.

"The *Samuel Plimsoll*? Well, I should say so!" said the skipper. "And you actually met dear old Gleeson! Why, Mr. Wardle, he was the man that set me on makin' this collection of articles. Bar myself he is the one man in the whole merchant service with more than he can do with. His native town has a department in its museum especially devoted to what he has given them in that way. His wife refused to give them house-room, and I don't blame her. I saved most of the crew of that dear old hooker at one time or another, went overboard after them in gales of wind. They got to rely on me and grew very careless. I often told them that I wouldn't go after any more, but when you see a poor chap drownin' it is difficult to stay in the dry and let him."

"Ah," said Wardle, "he did speak about your savin' one."

The skipper cast a quick look at him, and then laughed.

"One, indeed," he said contemptuously. "Why, I

saved the whole of the mate's watch, the mate included; and on three other occasions I was hauled out of my bunk to go after one of the starboard watch. The only thing I have against old Gleeson is that he was jealous when he saw I was likely to knock his collection of medals and binoculars into a cocked hat. One, indeed! I've saved seventy men, boys, and women, by goin' in after 'em myself; and somethin' like forty-five crews by skillful seamanship in the face of unparalleled difficulties. I wish I could have a talk with Gleeson."

"He said you were one of the bravest lads he ever met, sir," said Wardle.

The skipper's face softened.

"Did he now? Well, that was nice of him, but I think he might have told you about more than one I saved."

"And he said he had only four pairs of binoculars given him by foreign Governments," added Wardle.

"That is his false modesty," said Captain Brown. "He has an idea that if he told the truth he would not be believed. I don't care who doesn't believe me, Mr. Wardle. If surprisin' things occur to a man why should he not relate them? There's my wife, for instance, one of the nobility, a knight's daughter! I know men that wouldn't mention it for fear of not bein' believed they had married so far above them. She is the most beautiful woman in the three kingdoms, to say nothin' of Europe. I know men that it would seem like braggin' in to say that, but when you get to know me, and know that speakin' the truth isn't out of gear with my natural modesty, you will see why I mention it so freely."

In the course of the next few days Captain Amos Brown mentioned a good many things freely that redounded to the credit of himself and his family, and he did it so nicely, with such an engaging air of innocent and delightful candor, that poor Wardle did not know whether he was shipmates with the most wonderful man on earth or the most magnificent liar.

"I don't know where I am," he confided in his junior.

"I know where *I* am," said the graceless second greaser. "I am with a skipper with as much jaw as a sheep's head, and if he said it was raining I should take off my oilskins. He's the biggest braggart and liar I ever met, sir."

"I cannot listen to you sayin' such things," said the mate.

"I beg your pardon for doin' so," replied Humphries, "but the 'old man' is a scorcher, and I can't help seein' it."

To a less prejudiced observer it must have been obvious that there were many fine qualities in Captain Amos Brown. He inspected the cooking of the men's food at intervals, which annoyed the cook and kept him up to his work. When he went his rounds he saw that things were shipshape even in the deck-house. The men for'ard said he might be a notorious liar, as they heard from the steward, but they said he looked like a man and a seaman. Mr. Wardle found him as smart a navigator as he had ever sailed with, and before long was learning mathematics from him.

"No officer need be ashamed of takin' a wrinkle from me, Mr. Wardle," said the skipper, after giving him a lesson in star observations that made the mate sit up. "The Astronomer Royal himself owned to me that I could give him pounds and a beating at a great deal of mathematics. I love it, there is something so fine and free about it. I go sailin' over the sea of the calculus with both sheets aft. He is goin' to publish some observations of mine about the imperfections of the sextant. They were brought to my notice by my series of silver-mounted ones. I'm inventin' a new one compensated for all different temperatures."

And yet it was quite true that, as far as Wardle went with him, a better and clearer-headed teacher could not be found.

"I shall end in believing every word he says," thought the mate.

And if the mate found him his master in navigation,

Humphries found that there wasn't a trick of practical seamanship that wasn't at his finger-ends, from cutting out a jib to a double Matthew Walker on a four-stranded rope, which the skipper could almost do with his eyes shut.

"Everything is all the same to me, Mr. Humphries," said the skipper calmly. "I'm a born pilot, and I can handle every rig as easy as if I'd been born in 'em. I can sail a scow or a schooner, and every kind of sailing-boat from a catamaran to an Arab dhow. And at steam I'm just as good."

Humphries did not believe a word of it, and used to read up old-fashioned seamanship in order to pose him. He never did, and the most out-of-date sea-riddle was to the skipper as easy as slinging a nun-buoy.

"He beats me, I own," said the second mate. "He's the best at all-round sailorizin' that I ever sailed with."

The men for'ard said the same. And the bo'sun, who was a very crusty beast from Newcastle, was of opinion that what the "old man" did not know about ships was not worth knowing.

"I'm goin' to believe 'im hif so be 'e says 'e's bin to the moon," said one cockney. "But for hall we knows the 'old man' may not show up and shine as 'e does now w'en it's 'ard weather. I was ship-met wiv a skipper once that was wonderful gassy so long's it was topmast stuns'l weather, but when it blew a gale 'e crawled into 'is bunk like a sick stooard, and there 'e stayed till the sun shone."

They soon had a chance of seeing whether the skipper was a fair-weather sailor or not. They had taken an almighty time to get to the south'ard of the Bay of Biscay, for it had been almost as calm as a pond all the way from the Tuscar. Now the barometer began to fall in a steady, businesslike way that looked as if it meant work, while a heavy swell came rolling up from the south. The dawn next morning was what ladies would have called beautiful, for it was full of wonderful color which reached in a strange glory right to the zenith. It afforded no joy, artistic or otherwise, to anyone on board the *Ullswater,* as she rolled in the swell with too little wind to steady her. The watch below came out before breakfast, and looked at the scarlet and gold uneasily. There was a tremendously dark cloud on the horizon, and the high dawn above it was alone a threat of wind. The clouds that were lighted by the hidden sun, were hard and oily; they had no loose edges, the color was brilliant but opaque. To anyone who could read the book of the sky the signs were as easy as the south cone. They meant "very heavy weather from the south and west." The skipper looked a deal more happy than he had done before. His eyes were clear and bright; there was a ring in his voice which encouraged everybody; he walked the poop rubbing his hands as if he was enjoying himself, as he undoubtedly was. He shortened the *Ullswater* down in good time, but set his three topgallantsails over the reefed topsails, and hung on to them until squalls began to come out of the south which threatened to save all trouble of furling them. By noon the sun was out of sight under a heavy gray pall, and the sea got up rapidly as the wind veered into the west of south. An hour later it was blowing enough to make it hard to hear anyone speak, and he roared the most dreadful and awe-inspiring lies into the ear of his mate.

"This is going to be quite a breeze, Mr. Wardle," he shouted joyously, "but I don't think the weather nowadays is ever what it was when I was young. I've been hove to in the Bay for three weeks at a time. And once we were on our beam ends for a fortnight, and all we ate all that time was one biscuit each. I was so thin at the finish that I had to carry weights in my pockets to keep myself from bein' blown overboard. Oh, this is nothin'! We can hang on to this till the wind is sou'west, and then maybe we'll heave to."

By the middle of the afternoon watch the *Ullswater* was hanging on to a gale on the port tack with her main-hatch awash, and the crowd for'ard had come to the conclusion that for carrying sail the "old man" beat any American Scotchman they had ever heard of. When he at last condescended to heave her to, all hands, after wearing her, had a job with the fore and mizzen-topsails that almost knocked the stuffing out of them, as they phrased it. The skipper, however, saw that they had done very well, and told the steward to serve out grog. As the owners of the *Ullswater* were tee-totalers, and about as economical as owners are made, this grog was at the skipper's own expense. When they had got it down, the entire crowd said that they would believe anything the skipper said henceforth. They went for'ard and enjoyed themselves, while the old hooker lay to with a grummet on her wheel, and the great southwester howled across the Bay. If the main-topsail hadn't been as strong as the grog and the skipper's yarns, it would have been blown out of the bolt-ropes before dark, for the way the wind blew then made the "old man" own at supper-time that it reminded him of the days of his youth.

"But you never will catch me heavin' to under anythin' so measly as a tarpaulin in the rigging," said Captain Amos Brown, with his mouth full of beef and his leg round the leg of the table, as the *Ullswater* climbed the rising seas and dived again like a swooping frigate-bird. "I like to have my ship under some kind of command however it blows. One can never tell, Mr. Humphries, when one may need to make sail to save some of our fellow-creatures. As yet neither of you two gentlemen have got as much as the cheapest pair of binoculars out of our own Board of Trade or a foreign Government. With me you'll have your chance to go home to your girl and chuck somethin' of that sort into her lap, and make her cry with joy. I saved my own wife, who is the most beautiful woman in the world, and weighs eleven stone, and has for years, and I got a sextant and a nobleman's daughter at one fell swoop. Oh, I've been a lucky man."

"How did you save your wife, sir?" asked Humphries, who was almost beginning to believe what the skipper said.

"You may well ask, and I can't tell," replied the skipper proudly. "I hardly remember how it was, for when I get excited I do things which kind friends of mine say are heroic, and I can't remember 'em. But so far as I can recall it, I swam near a mile in a sea like this, and took command of a dismasted barque with most of the crew disabled through havin' their left legs broke, a most remarkable fact. There wasn't a sound left leg in the whole crowd except my wife's, and the only thing out of order was that the captain's left leg was broke in two places. I took charge of her, and put splints on their legs, and we were picked up by a tug from Queenstown and towed in there, and the doctors all said I was the neatest hand with splints they had ever seen. And I married my wife then and there with a special license, and I've never regretted it from that day to this. By Jove, though, doesn't it blow!"

How the "nobleman's" daughter came to be on board the dismasted barque he did not explain, and he shortly afterwards turned in, leaving orders to be called if it blew much harder.

"And when I say much harder, Mr. Wardle, I mean much harder. Please don't disturb me for a potty squall."

As a result of these orders he was not called till the early dawn, when it was blowing nearly hard enough to unship the main capstan. Even then Wardle would not have ventured to rouse him if he had not fancied that he saw some dismasted vessel far to leeward in the murk and smother of the gale.

"I think I saw a vessel just now down to loo'ard," screamed the mate as the skipper made a bolt for him under the weather-cloth on the mizzen rigging. "Dismasted I think, sir."

He saw the "old man's" eye brighten and snap.

"Where did you say?" he roared; and before he could hear they had to wait till a singing squall went over.

"To loo'ard," said the mate again; and the next moment the skipper saw what he looked for.

"Not dismasted, on her beam ends," he shouted. And in a few more minutes, as the gray dawn poured across the waste of howling seas, Wardle saw that the "old man" was right.

"Poor devils," he said, "it's all over with them."

The word that there was a vessel in difficulties soon brought out the watch on deck, who were taking shelter in the deck-house. As it was close on four o'clock the watch below soon joined them, and presently Humphries came up on the poop.

"Ah!" said the second mate, "they are done for, poor chaps."

This the skipper heard, and he turned round sharply and roared, "What, with me here? Oh, not much!"

He turned to Wardle.

"Here's your chance for a pair of inscribed binoculars," he said. "I believe she's French, and the French Government have generous minds in the way of fittings and inscriptions, Mr. Wardle."

"But in this sea, sir?" stammered the mate. "Why, a boat couldn't live in it for a second, even if we launched one safe, sir."

"I've launched boats in seas to which this was a mere calm," said the skipper ardently. "And if I can't get you or Humphries to go I shall go myself."

"You don't mean it, sir," said the mate; and then the skipper swore many powerful oaths that he did mean it.

"In the meantime we're drifting down to her," said Captain Brown, "though she is light and high out of the water and we are as deep as we can be."

It soon got all over the ship that the "old man" meant to attempt a rescue of those in distress, and there was a furious argument for'ard as to whether it could be done, and whether any captain was justified in asking his crew to man a boat in such a sea. The unanimous opinion of all the older men was that it couldn't be done. The equally unanimous opinion of all the younger ones was that if the skipper said it could be done he would go in the first boat himself rather than be beaten.

"Well, it will be a case for volunteers," said one old fo'c'sle man, "and when I volunteer to drown my wife's husband I'll let all you chaps know."

And that was very much the opinion of Wardle, who was a married man too. As for Humphries, he was naturally reckless, and was now ready to do almost anything the skipper asked.

"He may be a liar," said the second mate, "but I think he's all right, and I like him."

Now it was broad daylight, and the vessel was within a mile of them. Sometimes she was quite hidden, and sometimes she was flung up high on the crest of a wave. Heavy green seas broke over her as she lay with her starboard yardarms dipping. She had been running under a heavy press of canvas when she broached to and went over on her beam ends, for even yet the sheets of the upper main-topsail were out to the lower yardarm, and though the starboard half of the sail had blown out of the bolt ropes the upper and port yardarm still was sound and as tight as a drum with the wind.

"If she hasn't sunk yet she'll swim a while longer," said the skipper of the *Ullswater,* as the day grew lighter and lighter still. "Show the British ensign, Mr. Humphries, and cheer them up if they're alive. I wish I could tell them that I am here. I'll bet they know me. I'm famous with the French from Dunkirk to Toulon. At Marseilles they call me Mounseer Binoculaire, and stand in rows to see me pass."

The lies that he told now no one had any ears for. Wardle owned afterwards that he was afraid that the "old man" would ask him to go in command of a boat, and, like the old fo'c'sle man, he was thinking a good deal of his wife's husband. But all the while Captain Amos Brown was telling whackers that would have done credit to Baron Munchausen, he was really thinking of how he was to save those whose passage to a port not named in any bills of lading looked almost certain. By this time the foreigner was not far to leeward of them.

"No one could blame us if we let 'em go," shrieked the "old man" in his mate's ear as the wind lulled for one brief moment. "But I never think of what other men would do, Mr. Wardle. I remember once in a cyclone in the Formosa Channel—"

What dreadful deed of inspired heroism he had performed in a cyclone in the Formosa Channel Wardle never knew, for the wind cut the words from the skipper's lips and sent them in a howling shower of spray far to loo'ard. But his last words became audible.

"I was insensible for the best part of a month after it," screamed Amos Brown. "The usual . . . silver-mounted . . . sickened . . . wife as I said."

Then he caught the mate by the arm.

"We'll stand by 'em, Mr. Wardle. If I get another sextant, as I suspect, I must put up with it. Get the lifeboat ready, Mr. Wardle, and get all the empty small casks and oil-drums that you can and lash them under the thwarts fore and aft. Make her so that she can't sink and I'll go in her myself."

"That's my job, sir," said Wardle, for he forgot all about his wife's husband at that moment.

"I know it," said the skipper, "but with your permission I'll take it on myself, as I've had so much experience in this sort of thing and you've had none. And I tell you you'll have to handle the *Ullswater* so as to pick us up as we go to loo'ard, and it will be a job for a seaman and no fatal error."

The mate swore softly and went away and did as he was told. The men hung back a little when he told them to get the boat ready for launching, though they followed him when they saw him begin to cast off the gear by which she was made fast. But the old fo'c'sle man had something to say.

"The captain ain't goin' to put a boat over the side in a sea like this, is he, sir?"

Wardle snorted.

"You had better ask him," he replied savagely, and then there was no more talk. He went back to the poop and reported that the boat was ready. He also reported that the men were very unlikely to volunteer.

"They'll volunteer fast enough when they know I'm goin' to ask nothin' of them that I don't ask of myself," said the captain. "I really think the wind is takin' off a little, Mr. Wardle."

Perhaps it was, but if so the sea was a trifle worse. And it seemed to the skipper and the two mates that the French vessel was lower in the water than she had been. She was getting a pounding that nothing built by human hands could stand for long.

"There's not much time to lose," said the skipper.

Captain Amos Brown apparently knew his business, and knew it, as far as boats were concerned, in a way to make half the merchant skippers at sea blush for their ignorance of one of the finest points of seamanship. The skipper had the crew aft under the break of the poop, and came down to them himself. They huddled in the space between the two poop-ladders and looked very uneasy.

"Do any of you volunteer to try and save the poor fellows to loo'ard of us?" asked the "old man." And no one said a word. They looked at the sea and at each other with shifty eyes, but not at him.

"Why, sir, 'tis our opinion that no boat can't live in this sea," said the bo'sun.

"I think it can," said the captain, "and I'm goin' to try. Do any of you volunteer to come with your captain? I ask no man to do what I won't do myself."

There was something very fine about the liar of the *Ullswater* as he spoke, and everyone knew that now at least he was telling no lies.

"I'm wiv you, sir," said a young cockney, who was the foulest mouthed young ruffian in the ship, and had been talked to very severely by his mates on that very point. It is not good form for a youngster to use worse language than his elders at sea. Some of the others looked at him angrily, as if they felt that they had to go now. A red-headed Irishman followed the cockney, just as he had followed him into horrid dens down by Tiger Bay.

"I'm with ye, too, sorr," said Mike.

"I'm only askin' for six," said the skipper. Then the old fo'c'sle man, who had been so anxious about his wife's husband, hooked a black quid out of his black teeth and threw it overboard.

"I'll come, sir."

But now all the other young men spoke together. The skipper had his choice, and he took the unmarried ones.

He gave his orders to the mate without a touch of braggadocio.

"We'll run her off before the wind, Mr. Wardle, and then quarter the sea and lower away on the lee quarter. See that there is a man on the weather quarter with oil, so as to give us all the smooth you can. When we are safe afloat give us your lee to work in all you can, and hang her up in the wind to windward of the wreck all you know. While you are there don't spare oil; let it come down to her and us. It is possible that we may not be able to get a line to the wreck, but we'll go under her stern and try. With all her yards and gear in the sea it won't be possible to get right in her lee, so we may have to call to them to jump. My reckonin' is that we may pick up some that way before we get too far to loo'ard. When we get down close to her, fire the signal-gun to rouse them up to try and help us. When you see us well to loo'ard of the wreck, put your helm up, and run down and give us your lee again. If we miss her and have to try again, we must beat to windward once more. But that's anticipatin', ain't it? You can put your helm up now, Mr. Wardle. Shake hands."

And they shook hands. Then the skipper and his men took to the boat, which was ready to lower in patent gear, with Humphries in charge of it, and the *Ullswater* went off before the wind. Then at a nod from the captain she came up a little, till she quartered the sea with very little way on her.

"Now, Mr. Humphries," said the skipper. In ten seconds they hit the water fair and the hooks disengaged. The oil that was being poured over on the weather quarter helped them for a moment, and even when they got beyond its immediate influence they kept some of the lee of the ship. They drifted down upon the wreck, and rode the seas by pulling ahead or giving her sternway till they were within half a cable's length of the doomed vessel. At that moment they fired the signal-gun on board the *Ullswater*, and they saw some of the poor chaps to loo'ard of them show their heads above the rail. Then the full sweep of the gale struck them. But the liar of the *Ullswater*, who had saved more crews in worse circumstances than he could count, actually whistled as he sat in the stern-sheets with a steering oar in his hands.

To handle a boat in a heavy sea, with the wind blowing a real gale, is a thing that mighty few deepwater seamen are good at. But the skipper of the *Ullswater* knew his business even then as if he had been a Deal puntman, a North Sea trawler, or a Grand Bank fisherman all his life. The boat in which he made his desperate and humane venture was double-ended like a whale-boat, and she rode the seas for the most part like a cork. In such a situation the great thing is to avoid a sea breaking inboard, and sometimes they pulled ahead, and sometimes backed astern, so that when a heavy sea did break it did so to windward or to loo'ard of them. And yet a hundred times in the dreadful full minutes that it took them to get down to the wreck there were moments when those in the boat and those in the *Ullswater* thought that it was all over with them.

Once a sea that no one could have avoided broke over them, and it was desperate work to bail her out. And the roar of the wind deafened them; the seas raced and hissed; they pulled or backed water with their teeth clenched. Some of them thought of nothing; others were sorry they had volunteered, and looked at the captain furiously while he whistled through his clenched teeth. One cockney swore at him horribly in a thin piping scream, and called him horrid names. For this is the strange nature of man. But he pulled as well as the others, and the skipper smiled at him as his blasphemies cut the wind. For the skipper saw a head over the rail of the wreck, and he knew that there was work to be done and that he was doing it, and that the brave fool that cursed him was a man and was doing his best. The words he spoke were such as come out of a desperate mind, and out of a man that can do things. They towed an oil-bag to windward, but there was no oil to calm the movements of the soul at such a time.

"Oh, damn you, pull!" said Amos Brown. He ceased to whistle, and cursed with a sudden and tremendous frenzy that was appalling. The cursing cockney looked up at him with open mouth.

By the "old man's" side in the stern-sheets there was a coil of rope attached to a little grapnel. If the men still alive on board the French barque were capable of motion they might be able to make a rope fast, but after hours of such a trial, while they were lashed under the weather bulwarks, it was possible that they were almost numb and helpless. Now the boat came sweeping down by the stern of the barque; they saw her smashed rudder beating to and fro, and heard the battering-ram of the southwest seas strike on her weather side.

"Back water!" roared the skipper, for astern of them a big sea roared and began to lift a dreadful lip. They held the boat, and the "old man" kept it straight on

the roaring crest, and at that moment they were lifted
high, and saw beyond the hull of the barque the white
waste of driven seas. Then they went down, down,
down; and when they were flung up again the skipper
screamed to those on board, and as he screamed he
threw the grapnel at the gear of the spanker, and as
they surged past her stern the hooks caught in the bight
of her loosened vangs. For all her gear was in a coil
and tangle, and the topping-lifts of the gaff had parted.
The men backed water hard, and the boat hung half
in the lee of the wreck, but dangerously near the wreck
of the mizzen-topmast, which had gone at the cap and
swayed in the swash of the seas. Now they saw the seamen whom they had come to save, and no man of the
boat's crew could hereafter agree as to what happened
or the order of events. The skipper called to the poor
wretches, and one cut himself adrift and slid down the
sloping deck and struck the lower rail with horrible
force. They heard him squeal, and then a sea washed
him over to them. He was insensible, and that was
lucky, for his leg was broken. Then they made out
that one of the survivors was the captain, and they saw
that he was speaking, though they heard nothing.
There were, it seemed no more than ten of the crew
left, for they counted ten with the one man that they
had. But it seemed that they moved slow, and the sea
was worse than ever. It boiled over the weather-rail
and then came over green, and all the men in the boat
yelled filthy oaths at the poor numb wretches, and
called them horrible names. The Irishman prayed
aloud to heaven and to all the saints and to the Virgin,
and then cursed so awfully that the others fell into silence.

"Jump, jump!" screamed the skipper, and another
man slid down the deck and came overboard for them.
He went under and got his head cut open on a swaying block, and knew nothing of it till he was dragged
on board. Then he wiped the blood from his eyes and

fell to weeping, whereon the swearing cockney, who had been oddly silent since his eyes had met the skipper's, cuffed him hard on the side of the head, and said, "'Old your bloody row, you bleedin' 'owler!" And then three of his mates laughed as they watched their boat and fended it off the wreck of the mizzen-mast with deadly and preoccupied energy. The cockney took out a foul handkerchief and dabbed it on the bleeding man's head, and then threw the rag at him with an oath, saying that a little blood was nothing, and that he was a blasted Dago, and, further, he'd feel sorry for him when he was on board the *Ullswater*. Then another man jumped and was swept under and past them, and just as he was going the skipper reached over and, grabbing him by the hair, got him on board in a state of unconsciousness. Then three of the poor fellows jumped at once, two being saved and the third never showing above the water again.

"As well now as wiv the rest of hus," said the cockney, who had given the Dago his "wipe," and he sniveled a little. "Hif I gets hout of this I'm for stayin' in Rovver'ive all the rest of my life."

Then they got another, and there were only the French skipper and one more man left. It was probably the mate, but he had a broken arm and moved slow. The French captain got a rope round him and slid him down to loo'ard. But when he was halfway down the old skipper (he was at any rate white-haired) lost his own hold, and came down into the swash of the lee scuppers with a run. He fell overboard, and the Irishman got him by the collar. He was lugged on board with difficulty, and lay down on the bottom boards absolutely done for. The other man didn't show up, and the men said that he must be dead. They began talking all at once, and the skipper, who was now up at the bows of the boat, turned suddenly and cuffed the Irishman hard, whereupon Mike drew his sheath-knife, saying in a squeal, "You swine, I'll kill you!"

But the bo'sun struck him with the loom of his oar under the jaw, and nearly broke it. He snatched his knife from him and threw it overboard.

Now they saw the *Ullswater* right to windward of the sinking barque, and some oil that they poured into the sea came down to them, so that the hiss of the sea was so much less that it seemed as if silence fell on them. They heard the Irishman say with difficulty as he held his jaw:

"All right, my puggy, I'll have your blood."

He had lost his oar, and the other men were wild with him. What they might have said no one knows, but the skipper turned to them, saying that he would go on board after the last man. They all said at once that he shouldn't. They gave him orders not to do it, and their eyes were wild and fierce, for they were strained and tired, and fear got hold of them, making them feel chilly in their minds. If he did not come back they would never be saved, for now the boat was heavily laden. They opened their mouths and said: "Oh please, sir," and then he jumped overboard and went hand over hand along the grapnel line and the tangle of the vangs. They groaned, and the Irishman wagged his head savagely, though no one knew what he meant, least of all himself. They saw the "old man" clamber on board as a big sea broke over her, and they lost sight of him in the smother of it. They sat in the heaving boat as if they were turned to stone, and then the Irishman saw something in the sea and grabbed for it. He hauled hard, and they cried out that the skipper mustn't try it again. But as the drowning man came to the surface they saw that it was not the skipper after all, but the French mate, and they said: "Oh, hell!" being of half a mind to let him go. But the bo'sun screamed out something, and they hung on to a dead man's legs for to the dead man's hands the skipper was clinging. They got him on board not quite insensible, and the Irishman fell to weeping over him.

"Oh, it's the brave bhoy you are," he said; and then the skipper came to and vomited some water.

"Hold on, what are you doin'?" he asked, as he saw the two cockneys trying to heave the dead man back in the sea. They said that he was dead. The bo'sun said that the deader had only half a head, and couldn't be alive in that condition. So they let the body go, and the skipper woke right up and was a man again. They hauled up to the grapnel or near it, for they were strained enough to do foolish things. Then they saw it was silly and cut the line. They drifted to loo'ard fast, and got out into the full force of the gale, which howled horribly. They saw the *Ullswater* lying to under her sturdy old main-topsail, and as soon as they saw her they were seen by the second mate, who was up aloft with his coat half torn off him. To get her off before the wind quick they showed the head of the fore-topmast-staysail, which was promptly blown out of the bolt ropes with a report they heard in the boat like the dull sound of a far-off gun. She squared away and came to the nor'east, and presently was to windward of them, and in her lee they felt very warm and almost safe, though they went up to the sky like a lark and then down as if into a grave. And then they saw their shipmates' faces, and the skipper laughed oddly. The strain had told on him, as it had on all of them, not least perhaps on some of those who had not faced the greater risks. And it seemed to the skipper that there was something very absurd in Wardle's whiskers as the wind caught them and wrapped them in a kind of hairy smear across one weather-beaten cheek. All those in the boat were now quite calm; the excitement was on board the *Ullswater,* and when the gale let them catch a word of what the mate said, as he stood on the rail with his arm about a backstay, they caught the quality of strain.

"Ould Wardle is as fidgety as a fool," said Mike the Irishman, as he still held on to his jaw. "He'll be givin' someone the oncivil word for knockin' the oar out o' me hand."

He sat with one hand to his face, with the other, as he had turned round, he helped the bo'sun.

"What about your pullin' your knife on the captain?" asked the bo'sun.

Then Micky shook his head.

"Did I now? And he struck me, and he's a brave lad," he said simply. But the hook of the davit tackle dangled overhead as they were flung skyward on a sea. There were davit ropes fitted, and one slapped the Irishman across the face.

"It's in the wars I am," he said; and then there was a wind flurry that bore the *Ullswater* almost over on them. The way was nearly off her, yet in another minute she would be right down on them.

"Now!" screamed the skipper, and they hooked on and were hauled out and up.

"Holy mother," said Mike, "and I'm not drowned this trip!"

The boat was hauled on board, and when the skipper's foot touched the deck he reeled. Humphries caught him.

"Oh, steady, sir," said Humphries, as Mike came up to them.

The captain stared at him, for he did not remember striking him.

"It's the brrave man you are," said Mike simply; "and you're the first man that I've tuk a blow from since I was the length of my arm. Oh, bhoys, it's the brrave man the skipper is."

The second mate pushed him away, and he went like a child and lent a hand to help the poor "divils of Dagoes," as he called those who had been saved. The mate came and shook hands with the captain. The tears ran down Wardle's hairy face, and he could not speak.

"I shall have another pair of binoculars over this," said Captain Amos Brown with quivering lips.

"You are a hero," bawled the mate as the wind roared again in a blinding squall with rain in it. The skipper flushed.

"Oh, it's nothin', this," he said. "Now in the Bay of Bengal—"

The wind took that story to loo'ard, and no one heard it. But they heard him wind up with "gold-mounted binoculars."

A year later he got a pair from the great French Republic. They were the first he ever got.

ANGUS MacDONALD

A few years ago the Seafarers' Education Service in London, a noble institution which does great things to bring educational facilities including libraries and courses up to university standard to merchant seamen, helped to get together a book of merchant seamen's experiences at sea in the second World War. Any who had served at sea were invited to send in simple narratives of their personal experiences—no secondhand stuff, no contrived "yarns," no matter how well written or how skillfully represented. The editor was a merchant seaman, Mr. J. Lennox Kerr, the foreword was by John Masefield, the book was called *Touching the Adventures,* and it was a considerable success. Its unvarnished narratives told of the war as the merchant seamen knew it, and some of them were very moving: none more so than Seaman Angus MacDonald's story of survival called "Ordeal."

"There is a story in this volume called 'Ordeal,'" wrote the late H. M. Tomlinson, reviewing the book for the *Seafarer* which is the official journal of the Seafarers' Education Service. "A girl the story-teller named Diana is one of the characters. To the very end, enduring rigors for long in an open boat, a length of suffering that killed most of the men, after driving some of them mad, she faced, still calm and cheerful, the operating knife of a distrusted surgeon in a German ship, and died. . . . 'Ordeal' is beyond argument. It leaves a reader dumb."

Dr. Ronald Hope, O.B.E., M.A., D.Phil., the director of the S.E.S. and the College of the Sea, told me how Angus MacDonald came to send in his story. "He saw a news item to the effect that we were collecting war stories by serving merchant seamen, and he went into our library at Liverpool, which was then at the Ocean Club in Lord Street, sat down and wrote his story. Our librarian there, a Miss Rachel Tavriger at that time, put in a few full stops and commas, and that was that. It turned out to be the story of the book, was reprinted in a couple of papers over here and turned into a broadcast feature program. . . . MacDonald had never written a word before and has never, so far as I am aware, written a word for publication since. In all my contact with him he has proved a modest and unassuming man. . . . A year or two ago, he was serving as bos'un aboard the S.S. *Carlo* of Ellerman's Wilson Line, and his home is in Liverpool."

Angus MacDonald is still at sea.

Ordeal

by ANGUS MacDONALD

The ship I served on board, the Ellerman Liner *City of Cairo*, left Bombay on the 2nd of October, 1942, homeward bound with a crew of Europeans and lascars and a hundred passengers. At 8:30 p.m. on the 6th of November, five days after leaving Cape Town, she was torpedoed by a German submarine. Three passengers and eighteen members of the crew were killed by the explosion of the torpedoes or went down with the ship.

I was a quartermaster and had charge of No. 4 lifeboat. After seeing everything in order there and the boat lowered, I went over to the starboard side of the ship to where my mate, quartermaster Bob Ironside, was having difficulty in lowering his boat. I climbed inside the boat to clear a rope fouling the lowering gear, and was standing in the boat pushing it clear of the ship's side as it was being lowered, when a second torpedo exploded right underneath and blew the boat to bits. I remember a great flash, and then felt myself flying through space, then going down and down. When I came to I was floating in the water, and could see all sorts of wreckage around me in the dark. I could not get the light on my life-jacket to work, so I swam toward the largest bit of wreckage I could see in the darkness. This turned out to be No. 1 lifeboat and it was nearly submerged, having been damaged by the second explosion. There were a few people clinging to the gunwale, which was down to water-level, and other people were sitting inside the flooded boat.

I climbed on board, and had a good look round to see if the boat was badly damaged. Some of the gear had floated away, and what was left was in a tangled mess. There were a few lascars, several women and children, and two European male passengers in the boat, and I explained to them that if some of them would go overboard and hang on to the gunwale or the wreckage near us for a few minutes we could bail out the boat and make it seaworthy. The women who were there acted immediately. They climbed outboard and, supported by the life-jackets everyone was wearing, held on to an empty tank that was floating near by. I felt very proud of these women and children. One woman (whose name, if I remember rightly, was Lady Tibbs) had three children, and the four of them were the first to swim to the tank. One young woman was left in the boat with two babies in her arms.

We men then started to bail out the water. It was a long and arduous task, as just when we had the gunwale a few inches clear, the light swell running would roll in and swamp the boat again. Eventually we managed to bail out the boat, and then we started to pick up survivors who were floating on rafts or just swimming. As we worked we could see the *City of Cairo* still afloat, but well down in the water, until we heard someone say, "There she goes." We watched her go down, stern first, her bow away up in the air, and then she went down and disappeared. There was no show of emotion, and we were all quiet. I expect the others, like myself, were wondering what would happen to us.

We picked up more survivors as the night wore on, and by the first light of dawn the boat was full. There were still people on the rafts we could see with the daylight, and in the distance were other lifeboats. We rowed about, picking up more people, among them Mr. Sydney Britt, the chief officer, and quartermaster Bob Ironside, who was in No. 3 boat with me when the second torpedo struck. Bob's back had been injured, and one of his hands had been cut rather badly. We picked up others, then rowed to the other boats to see what decision had been made about our future. Mr. Britt had, naturally, taken over command of our boat, and now he had a conference with Captain Rogerson, who was in another boat. They decided we would make for the nearest land, the island of St. Helena, lying five hundred miles due north. We transferred people from boat to boat so that families could be together. Mr. Britt suggested that, as our boat was in a bad way, with many leaks and a damaged rudder, and at least half its water-supply lost, all the children should shift to a dry boat and a few adults take their places in our boat.

When everything was settled we set sail and started on our long voyage. Our boat was now overcrowded with fifty-four persons on board—twenty-three Europeans, including three women, and thirty-one lascars. There was not enough room for everyone to sit down, so we had to take turns having a rest. The two worst injured had to lie down flat, so we made a place in the bows for Miss Taggart, a ship's stewardess, and cleared a space aft for my mate, quartermaster Bob Ironside. We did not know exactly what was wrong with Bob's back. We had a doctor in the boat, Dr. Taskar, but he was in a dazed condition and not able to attend to the injured, so we bandaged them up as best we could with the first-aid materials on hand. The youngest person among us, Miss Diana Jarman, one of the ship's passengers, and only about twenty years of age, was a great help with the first aid. She could never do enough, either in attending to the sick and injured, boat work, or even actually handling the craft. She showed up some of the men in the boat, who seemed to lose heart from the beginning.

Once we were properly under way Mr. Britt spoke to us all. He explained all the difficulties that lay ahead, and asked everyone to pull their weight in everything to do with managing the boat, such as rowing during calm periods and keeping a look-out at night. He also explained that as we had lost nearly half our drinking water we must start right away on short rations. We could get two tablespoonfuls a day per person, one in the morning and one in the evening. He told us there were no passengers in a lifeboat, and everyone would have to take turns bailing as the boat was leaking very badly.

Before noon on that first day we saw our first sharks. They were enormous, and as they glided backward and forward under the boat it seemed they would hit and capsize us. They just skimmed the boat each time they passed, and they were never to leave us all the time we were in the boat.

The first night was quiet and the weather was fine, but we didn't get much rest. A good proportion of us had to remain standing for long periods, and now and then someone would fall over in their sleep. I was in the fore-part of the boat attending to the sails and the running gear, helped by Robert Watts from Reading, whom we called "Tiny" because he was a big man. He didn't know much about seamanship, as he was an aeronautical engineer, but he said to me that first day, "If you want anything done at any time just explain the job to me and I'll do it." His help was very welcome as we did not have many of the crew available for the jobs that needed to be done. From the very beginning the lascars refused to help in any way, and just lay in the bottom of the boat, sometimes in over a foot of water.

On the second day the wind increased, and we made good speed. Sometimes the boats were close together and at other times almost out of sight of each other. Our boat seemed to sail faster than the others, so Mr. Britt had the idea that we might go ahead on our own. If we could sail faster than the others, and as we were leaking so badly, we should go ahead and when we got to St. Helena we could send help to the others. Mr. Britt had a talk with Captain Rogerson when our boats were close, and the captain said that if the mate thought that was the best plan then to go ahead. So we carried on on our own.

During the hours of darkness the wind rose stronger, and, as we could see the running gear was not in the best condition, we hove to. As it got still worse, we had to put out a sea-anchor and take turns at the steering-oar to hold the boat into the seas. We had a bad night, and two or three times seas broke over the heavily laden boat and soaked us all to the skin. It was during this night that we noticed Dr. Taskar was failing mentally. Every now and then he shouted, "Boy, bring me my coffee," or, "Boy, another beer." He had a rip in his trousers, and in the crowded boat during the night he cut a large piece out of the trousers of the ship's storekeeper, Frank Stobbart. I noticed the doctor with the knife and a piece of cloth in his hand. He was trying to fit the cloth over his own trousers. I pacified him and took his knife, a small silver knife with a whisky advertisement on the side. I had the same knife all through the years I was a prisoner in Germany, and only lost it after the war while serving in another Ellerman liner.

At noon on the third day the wind abated, and we set sails again and went on. We had lost sight of the other boats now and were on our own. We all expected to see a rescue ship or plane at any time, but nothing turned up. On the evening of the fourth day the doctor got worse, and rambled in his speech. He kept asking for water, and once Mr. Britt gave him an extra ration, although there was not much to spare. During the night the doctor slumped over beside me, and I knew he was dead. That was the first death in the boat. We cast the body overboard at dawn while Mr. Britt read a short prayer. We all felt gloomy after this first burial, and wondered who would be next.

Later in the day I crawled over to have a yarn with my mate Bob, and he said, "Do you think we have a chance, Angus?" I said, "Everything will be all right, Bob. We are bound to be picked up." Bob hadn't long been married, and he was anxious about his wife and little baby in Aberdeen. He couldn't sit up, and I was afraid his back was broken or badly damaged.

Day and night the lascars kept praying to Allah, and repeating, "Pani, sahib, pani, sahib," and they would never understand that the water was precious and had to be rationed out. On the sixth morning we found three of them dead in the bottom of the boat. The old engine-room serang read a prayer for them, and Tiny and I pushed them overboard, as the lascars never would help to bury their dead. The only two natives who helped us at any time were the old serang, a proper gentleman, and a fireman from Zanzibar, and they couldn't do enough to help.

We were getting flat calms for long periods, and we lowered the sails and used the oars. We didn't make much headway, but the work helped to keep our minds and bodies occupied. I know that doing these necessary tasks helped to keep me physically fit and able to stand up to the ordeal that lay ahead. There were a few Europeans who never gave a helping hand, and I noticed that they were the first to fail mentally. They died in the first two weeks.

I was worried about Miss Taggart's sores, as they had now festered and we had nothing to dress them with except salt water. With her lying in the same position all the time her back was a mass of sores. Tiny knew more about first aid than the rest of us, and with the aid of old life-jackets he padded her up a bit. But on the seventh night she died and slipped down from her position in the bows. As she fell she got tangled up with another passenger, a Mr. Ball from Calcutta, and when we got things straightened out they were both dead. A few more lascars died during the same night, and we had to bury them all at daybreak. The sharks were there in shoals that morning, and the water was churned up as they glided backward and forward near the bodies. Things were now getting worse on board, and a good few of the people sat all day with their heads on their chests doing and saying nothing. I talked to one young engineer, and told him to pull himself together as he was young and healthy and to take a lesson from Diana, who was always cheerful and bright. She had told us, "Please don't call me Miss Jarman; just call me Diana." The young engineer did pull himself back to normal but within two days he dropped back and gave up hope and died. As we buried the bodies the boat gradually became lighter and the worst leaks rose above the water-line, so there was not so much water to bail out, although we had still to bail day and night.

Our own ship's stewardess, Annie Crouch, died on the tenth day. She had been failing mentally and physically for a time, and persisted in sitting in the bottom of the boat. We shifted her to drier places, but she always slid back. Her feet and legs had swollen enormously. Her death left only one woman among us, Diana. She was still active and full of life, and she spent most of her time at the tiller. Mr. Britt was beginning to show signs of mental strain, and often mumbled to himself. If I asked him a question he would answer in a dazed sort of way. I worried about him a lot, for he was always a gentleman, and everyone thought the world of him. On the twelfth day he was unable to sit up or talk, so we laid him down alongside Bob Ironside, who was also failing fast. Bob called me over one day, and asked me if I thought there was still a chance. I said certainly there was, and urged him not to give up hope as he would soon be home. He said, "I can't hang on much longer, Angus. When I die, will you take off my ring and send it home if you ever get back?" There were only a few able-bodied men left among the Europeans now, and Tiny Watts, my right-hand man, died on the fourteenth morning. He hadn't complained at any time, and I was surprised when I found him dead. We buried seven bodies that morning: five lascars, Tiny, and Frank Stobbart. It took a long time to get them overboard, and I had to lie down and rest during the operation.

On the fifteenth morning at dawn both Mr. Britt and Bob were dead, also three other Europeans, and a few lascars. A few more lascars died during the day. One of the firemen said that if he couldn't get extra water he would jump overboard, and later in the day he jumped over the stern. He had forgotten to take off his life-jacket, and as we were now too weak to turn the boat round to save him, the sharks got him before he could drown. The remaining survivors voted that I should take over command. On looking through Mr. Britt's papers I could see the estimated distances for each day up to about the tenth day, but after that there were only scrawls and scribbles. When I checked up on the water I found we had enough only for a few days, so I suggested cutting down the issue to one tablespoonful a day. There were plenty of biscuits and malted-milk tablets, but without water to moisten the mouth the biscuits only went into a powder and fell out of the corner of the mouth again. Those people with false teeth had still more trouble as the malted-milk tablets went into a doughy mess and stuck to their teeth.

The boat was now much drier, and there was not so much bailing to do as we rode higher in the water and most of the leaks were above the surface. The movement, however, was not so steady as when we were heavier laden, but about the middle of the seventeenth night the boat appeared to become very steady again. I heard Diana cry out, "We're full of water," and I jumped up and found the boat half full of water. I could see the plug-hole glittering like a blue light, and I started looking for the plug. I put a spare one in place, and a few of us bailed out the water. There were two people lying near the plug-hole, and they seemed to take no interest in what was happening. About an hour later I discovered the plug gone again and water entering the boat. I put the plug back, and this time I lay down with an eye on watch. Sure enough, in less than half an hour I saw a hand over the plug pulling it out. I grasped the hand and found it belonged to a young European. He was not in his right mind, although he knew what he was doing. When I asked him why he tried to sink the boat he said, "I'm going to die, so we might as well go together." I shifted him to the fore part of the boat, and we others took turns in keeping an eye on him, but he managed to destroy all the contents of the first-aid box and throw them over the side. He died the next day, with seven or eight lascars, and a banker from Edinburgh, a Mr. Crichton. Mr. Crichton had a patent waistcoat fitted with small pockets, and the valuables we found there we put with rings and other things in Diana's handbag. Among Mr. Crichton's possessions were the three wise monkeys in jade and a silver brandy flask that was empty.

At the end of the third week there were only eight of us left alive in the boat: the old engine-room serang, the fireman from Zanzibar, myself, Diana, Jack Edmead, the steward, Joe Green from Wigan, Jack Oakie from Birmingham, and a friend of his Jack Little. Two of them had been engineers working on the new Howrah bridge at Calcutta.

There was still no rain. We had not had a single

shower since we started our boat voyage, and the water was nearly finished. Only a few drops were left on the bottom of the tank. About the middle of the fourth week I was lying down dozing in the middle of the night when the boat started to rattle and shake. I jumped up, thinking we had grounded on an island. Then I discovered a large fish had jumped into the boat and was thrashing about wildly. I grabbed an ax that was lying handy, and hit the fish a few hard cracks. The ax bounded off it like rubber, and it was a while before I made any impression, but when it did quieten down I tied a piece of rope round the tail and hung the fish on the mast. It took me all my time to lift the fish, as it was about three feet long and quite heavy. I lay down again, and at daybreak examined the fish closer. It was a dog-fish. During the struggle with it I had gashed a finger against its teeth, and as we now had no bandages or medicine all I could do was wash the cut in sea water before I proceeded to cut up the fish. I had heard and read about people drinking blood, and I thought that I could get some blood from the carcass for drinking. I had a tough job cutting up the fish with my knife, and only managed to get a few teaspoonfuls of dirty, reddish-black blood. I cut the liver and heart out, and sliced some of the flesh off. By this time all hands were awake, although everyone was feeling weak. I gave the first spoonful of blood to Diana to taste, but she spat it out and said it was horrible. I tried everyone with a taste, but nobody could swallow the vile stuff. I tried it myself, but couldn't get it down. It seemed to swell the tongue. We tried eating the fish, but that was also a failure. I chewed and chewed at my piece, but couldn't swallow any and eventually spat it into the sea.

The day following my encounter with the big dog-fish my hand and arm swelled up, and Diana said I had blood-poisoning. The following day it was much worse, and throbbed painfully. I asked Diana if she could do anything for it, as we had no medical supplies left. She advised me to let the hand drag in the water, and later in the day she squeezed the sore, and all sorts of matter came out. I then put my hand back in the water, and that seemed to draw out more poison. At intervals Diana squeezed the arm from the shoulder downward, and gradually got rid of the swelling, althought the sore didn't heal for months, and the scar remains to this day.

There was no water left now, and Jack Oakie, Jack Little, and the Zanzibar fireman all died during the one night. It took the remainder of us nearly a whole day to lift them from the bottom of the boat and roll them overboard. The serang was now unconscious and Joe Green was rambling in his speech. There were a few low clouds drifting over us, but no sign of rain, and I had lost count of the days. I had written up Mr. Britt's log-book to the end of the fourth week, but after that day and night seemed to be all the same. Diana had the sickness that nearly everyone in turn had suffered: a sore throat and a thick yellow phlegm oozing from the mouth. I think it was due to us lying in the dampness all the time and never getting properly dry. The sails were now down and spread across the boat as I was too feeble to do anything in the way of running the boat. Against all advice, I often threw small quantities of sea water down my throat, and it didn't seem to make me any worse, although I never overdid it.

One night Joe Green would not lie in the bottom of the boat in comfort, but lay on the after end in an uncomfortable position. When I tried to get him to lie down with us he said, "I won't last out the night, and if I lie down there you will never be able to lift me up and get me over the side." The next morning he was dead. So was the serang. Two grand old men, though of different races. There were only three of us left now. Jack Edmead was pretty bad by now, and Diana still had the sore throat. But we managed to get the bodies over the side. The serang by this time was very thin and wasted, and if he had been any heavier we would not have managed to get him over.

By this time we were only drifting about on the ocean. I had put the jib up a couple of times, but discovered we drifted in circles, so I took it down again. One day I had a very clear dream as I lay there in the bottom of the boat. I dreamed that the three of us were walking up the pierhead at Liverpool, and the dream was so clear that I really believed it would happen. I told Diana and Jack about the dream, and said I was sure we would be picked up. There wasn't a drop of water in the boat now, and the three of us just lay there dreaming of water in all sorts of ways. Sometimes it was about a stream that ran past our house when I was a child, another time I would be holding a hose and spraying water all round, but it was always about water. Jack was getting worse, and was laid out in the stern, while Diana was forward where it was drier. Sick as she was, she always used to smile and say, "We still have a chance if we could only get some rain."

Then one night rain came. I was lying down half asleep when I felt the rain falling on my face. I jumped up shouting, "Rain, rain," but Jack wasn't able to get up and help me. Diana was in pretty bad condition, but she managed to crawl along and help me spread the main sail to catch the water. It was a short sharp shower and didn't last long, but we collected a few pints in the sail and odd corners of the boat. We didn't waste a drop, and after pouring it carefully into the tank we sucked the raindrops from the woodwork and everywhere possible. Diana had trouble swallowing anything as her throat was swollen and raw, but I mixed some pemmican with water, and we had a few spoonfuls each. The water was very bitter as the sail had been soaked in salt water for weeks, but it tasted good to us. We all felt better after our drink, and I sat down in the well of the boat that day and poured can after can of sea water over myself, and gave Diana a bit of a wash. She was in good spirits now, although she could only speak in whispers. She told me about her home in the South of England: I think she said it was Windsor, on the Thames. She was very fond of horses and tennis and other sports, and she said, "You must come and visit us when we get home," which showed that like myself she had a firm conviction that we would get picked up.

The three days after the rain were uneventful. Diana was a bit better, but Jack was in a bad way, and lying down in the stern end. On the third day I had another shower-bath sitting down in the boat, as it had livened me up a lot the last time. Afterward I set the jib and tried to handle the main sail, but couldn't make it, so I spread the sail and used it as a bed. I had the best sleep in weeks. In the early hours of the morning Diana shook me, and said excitedly, "Can you hear a plane?" I listened, and heard what sounded like a plane in the distance, so I dashed aft and grabbed one of the red flares and tried to light it. It didn't go off, so I struck one of the lifeboat matches. It ignited at once, and I held it up as high as I could, and immediately a voice shouted, "All right, put that light out." It was still dark, but on looking in the direction of the voice we could see the dim outline of a ship, and hear the sound of her diesel engines. The same voice shouted, "Can you come alongside?" God knows how we managed, but manage it we did. Even Jack found enough strength to give a hand, and with Diana at the tiller he and I rowed the boat alongside the ship. A line was thrown to us, and I made it fast. A pilot ladder was dropped, and two men came down to help us on board. They tied a rope round Diana, and with the help of others on the ship hauled her on board. I climbed up unaided, and the men helped Jack. The first thing I asked for was a drink, and we sat on a hatch waiting to see what would happen. We thought we were on a Swedish ship at first, but I saw a Dutch flag painted across the hatch. Then I heard a couple of men talking, and I knew then we were on a German ship, as I had a slight knowledge of the language. I told the other two, and Diana said, "It doesn't matter what nationality it is as long as it is a ship."

A man came to us soon and asked us to go with him and meet the captain. Two of the crew helped Diana and Jack, and we were taken amidships to the doctor's room, where a couch had been prepared for Diana. The captain arrived, and asked us about our trip in the boat and inquired how long we had been in it. I told him our ship had been torpedoed on the 6th of November, and that I lost count of the days. He said this was the 12th of December, and that we were on board the German ship *Rhakotis,* and we should be well looked after. I remembered the bag of valuables in the boat, and told the captain where Diana's bag was. The bag was found and passed up, and given into the captain's charge. It was probably lost when the ship was sunk three weeks later. The lifeboat was stripped and sunk before the ship got under way again.

We were given cups of coffee, but were told that the doctor's orders were for us not to drink much at a time, and only eat or drink what he ordered. Diana was lying on the doctor's couch, and when the three of us were left alone for a while she bounced up and down on the springs and said, "This is better than lying in that wet boat." Later Jack and I were given a hot bath by a medical attendant, and my hand was bandaged, as it was still festering. We were taken aft to a cabin, and Diana was left in the doctor's room. The crew had orders not to bother us and to leave us on our own, as we had to rest as much as possible. When I looked at myself in the mirror I didn't recognize myself with a red beard and haggard appearance. There didn't seem to be any flesh left on my body, only a bag of bones. Jack looked even worse with his black beard and hollow cheeks.

We had been given some tablets and injected, and were now told to go to bed. Before I did so I asked one of the crew to fetch me a bottle of water. Although this was against the doctor's orders the man did so, and I hid the bottle under my pillow. Then I asked another man to bring me a bottle of water, and in this way I collected a few bottles and I drank the lot. Jack was already asleep when I turned in after drinking the water, and I turned in on the bunk above him. We slept for hours and when I awoke I found I had soaked the bedding. Later I discovered I had soaked Jack's bed too. He was still asleep. I wakened him and apologized, but he only laughed. The steward brought us coffee at 7 a.m., and when I told him about my bladder weakness he didn't seem annoyed, but took the bedclothes away to be changed. It was a year before I was able to hold any liquid for more than an hour or so.

We were well looked after and well fed on the German ship, and from the first day I walked round the decks as I liked. Jack was confined to bed for a few days. We were not allowed to visit Diana, but the captain came aft and gave us any news concerning her. She couldn't swallow any food, and was being fed by injections. When we had been five days on the ship the doctor and the captain came along to our cabin, and I could see they were worried. The captain did the talking, and said that as the English girl still hadn't been able to eat, and couldn't go on living on injections, the doctor wanted to operate on her throat and clear the inflammation. But first of all he wanted our permission. I had never liked the doctor and had discovered he was disliked by nearly everyone on board, but still, he was the doctor, and should know more about what was good for Diana than I could. So I told the captain that if the doctor thought it was necessary to operate he had my permission as I wanted to see Diana well again. Jack said almost the same, and the captain asked if we would like to see her. We jumped at the chance, and went with the doctor. She seemed quite happy, and looked well, except for being thin. Her hair had been washed and set, and she said she was being well looked after. We never mentioned the operation to her, but noticed she could still talk only in whispers.

That evening at seven o'clock the captain came to us, and I could see that something was wrong. He said, "I have bad news for you. The English girl has died. Will you follow me, please?" We went along, neither of us able to say a word. We were taken to the doctor's room where she lay with a bandage round her throat. You would never know she was dead, she looked so peaceful. The doctor spoke, and said in broken English that the operation was a success, but the girl's heart was not strong enough to stand the anesthetic. I couldn't speak, and turned away broken-hearted. Jack and I went aft again, and I turned into my bunk and lay crying like a baby nearly all night. It was the first time I had broken down and cried, and I think Jack was the same. The funeral was the next day, and when the time came we went along to the foredeck where the ship's crew were all lined up wearing uniforms and the body was in a coffin covered by the Union Jack. The captain made a speech in German, and then spoke in English for our benefit. There were tears in the eyes of many of the Germans, as they had all taken an interest in the English girl. The ship was stopped, and after the captain had said a prayer, the coffin slid slowly down the slipway into the sea. It had been weighted, and sank slowly. The crew stood to attention bareheaded until the coffin disappeared. It was an impressive scene, and a gallant end to a brave and noble girl. We had been through so much together, and I knew I would never forget her.

The *Rhakotis* was bound for Bordeaux, and was due there about New Year's Day. We had a good Christmas at sea, with all sorts of food, and as I had regained my normal appetite by then I was able to take my share of everything. The butcher had killed two pigs, and we had as much roast pork as we could eat. I am sure we got a better Christmas as prisoners on the *Rhakotis* than many seamen had on British ships.

There was great excitement on board on the 31st of December, and word got round that we had a rendezvous with four U-boats who would escort us into port. We stopped at 7 p.m. that evening, and within a few minutes the subs came close alongside out of the darkness. Nobody stopped us looking over the side at them, and we saw a couple of officers come aboard and meet the captain. They didn't stay long, and within half an hour we were on our way again. The subs disappeared, but they must have been somewhere in the vicinity. At 4 a.m. on New Year's Day Jack woke me up and said, "Look at the yellow light out on deck." The whole ship was lit up, and when I went outside I saw a flare floating above the ship. Then I heard the drone of a plane, and the anti-aircraft guns opened up. The plane dropped a load of incendiaries and some bombs. A few incendiaries landed on the ship amidships, but I don't think they did much damage. After a time all went quiet again, and we turned in. Jack remarked that this was a good beginning to the New Year.

We were having a special dinner that afternoon at 4:30 p.m., when I heard an explosion I guessed was gunfire. Immediately loud alarm bells sounded, and armed guards appeared at the door. I asked one of them what was the matter, and he said simply, "English cruiser." We could hear the gunfire plainer now, and then we felt the ship being hit. The noise was terrific, and there were loud crashes not far from where we waited. An armed guard ran down the alleyway calling out, "To the boats." Others were unwinding a coil of electric flex and setting a box against the ship's side. This was a time-bomb to scuttle the ship after we got clear, but it was not required as the ship was on fire all over and badly damaged by direct hits. I didn't know from which side the shells were coming, so I picked the port-side boat, and no sooner got there than I saw the British cruiser a good way off on the port side. She was firing salvoes, and I could see the flashes and hear the shells screaming past. The weather was bad at the time, and a large swell was running, so it wasn't easy getting the boats away. I slid down a lifeline into the boat, and was no sooner in it than a large sea came along and partly submerged the boat. I had nothing to do with the handling of the boat as the Germans were all at their proper stations, but I helped to push it clear with a boathook. We were just clear when there was a shout from the *Rhakotis,* and we could see two men waving and shouting for us to come back. The ship had a big list, and was a mass of flames from stem to stern, but the boat was turned back, and the two men jumped into the water, and were dragged into the boat. Shells were exploding all around, and I expected any minute the boat would be hit. The cruiser kept firing until the *Rhakotis* was on her beam ends, then turned and went full speed away. She must have known there were U-boats in the vicinity. I was very disappointed, as I was so sure they would have picked us up. As their ship rolled over and went down slowly the Germans took off their caps and gave her three cheers.

We were now alone in the Bay of Biscay, and in darkness. The starboard boat was not in sight, and it was many years before I learned that Jack Edmead was in her, and that she managed to reach Spain. From there poor Jack was sent home, only to join a ship that was later torpedoed. There were thirty-five of us in the port boat, including a few prisoners. I was the only Britisher. Sitting beside me were two young Danish boys, only fifteen years of age, whose ship had been captured in the Indian Ocean. These boys had been good to Jack and me on the German ship, and they turned up at the prisoner-of-war camp where I was placed. After their release they sent me a few welcome parcels of food.

The boat was in good condition and well stocked with water and large biscuits. Although there was a tremendous sea running, she was fairly steady, and only once or twice did she take any water on board during that wild night. I had no hat on, and as it was New Year's Day and cold I looked round for something to put on my head. I could see a beret sticking out of one of the German's pockets, so I quietly drew it out and put it on. He was wearing a sou'wester and did not miss the beret.

The following morning the wind had died down a bit, but there was still a big sea running. The officer in charge took a chance and set sail for the nearest land on the French coast. We each had a handful of biscuits and a glass of water for breakfast, and we were quite happy. About eleven o'clock some one shouted out, "U-boat," and I could see the periscope coming up out of the water close to us. The conning-tower appeared, and then the sub itself showed up. The hatch opened, and the commander shouted to the officer in charge of our boat, giving instructions on how we were to transfer to the submarine. We took the boat as close as we dared without touching the sub, as bumping would have capsized us, and as the nose of the sub rose to the sea one man at a time grabbed a wire and was pulled on board. It took a long time to get us all transferred, and once on the sub we all threw our life-jackets away and went below. It was only a small submarine, returning to port after fourteen days hunting the Atlantic convoys when it was ordered by radio to find the two boats from the *Rhakotis*. As soon as we got below each man was given a large mug of steaming coffee laced with rum, then shown to a spot where he had to lie. The submarine was cramped enough with its own crew, and now with thirty-five extra men it was like a sardine-tin.

We were only submerged fifteen minutes when a harsh alarm bell rang, and the nose of the sub dipped as she crash-dived. A few seconds later there were three tremendous explosions. The first shook us, the second was worse, and the third must have been very close, for the whole sub shook, and we were thrown about. I fell off the bunk I shared with another man and landed on the two spare torpedoes on the deck. The engines were stopped, and we were ordered not to speak or move. The sub was now on an even keel, and there didn't seem to be anything seriously wrong. Later we were to learn that a British plane on anti-submarine patrol had sighted us from a distance, and dropped depth-charges over the spot where we had been. After lying motionless for about an hour the engines throbbed again, and we went on our way. One of the crew told me we were bound for Bordeaux.

The air was getting very foul, and we were told that as we wouldn't surface until after dark we must lie still and keep quiet, as the air was used up by unnecessary movement. We had a good meal of bread, cheese, and coffee during the afternoon, and then lay down to await night and fresh air. During the afternoon a voice speaking English came through the loudspeaker, saying that anyone caught touching any of the machinery would be thrown overboard. As I had no wish to stay longer in the submarine than I had to, I had no intention of doing it any damage. The order to keep still was very hard on me as my bladder was still very weak, so I asked one of the officers if I could speak to the commander. On explaining my predicament he took me amidships, and I had a talk with the commander. He was only about twenty-five, though he was the oldest member of the ship's company, and he, like the rest of the crew, had a beard. He spoke perfect English, and had a talk with me about the trip in the boat. He told me that as Bordeaux was blockaded by British planes he had decided to carry on to Saint-Nazaire, and we should be there in a couple of days. He said that as the midships portion of the submarine was too crowded to let me relieve myself he would give me a case of empty beer bottles to use.

We surfaced soon after this, and we could hear the mechanism of the sub working as we rose. After assuring themselves that the coast was clear the Germans opened up the conning-tower, and fresh air poured in. Air was pumped all through the vessel, and the diesel engine started up and kept going until nearly daybreak. The cook set his fire going, and made a hot meal for all hands, which he couldn't do when the sub was submerged. It was much more comfortable now with the fresh air, and everyone was happy and looking forward to going on shore. In the early morning we submerged again, and the submarine ran on batteries. It wasn't too bad, as occasionally, if the coast was clear, the commander would surface for short periods, and we could get fresh air.

About noon on the third day of January the warning bell went again, and the Germans dashed to their stations. I was lying alongside the spare torpedoes and quite close to the torpedo-tubes, and could watch the men waiting for orders. The sub would rise a few inches at a time, then submerge a bit, and it sounded just like being in a lift on shore. This went on for a while, and I asked one of the Germans what was going on. He said it was a British destroyer. You can imagine how I felt lying there and knowing we were stalking one of our own destroyers. Everything was deadly quiet, and then all of a sudden the alarm bell clanged out harshly. Immediately the nose of the sub went down at a terrific speed as she crash-dived. She seemed to be standing on her head. The suspense was terrible, and I could see that even the men standing by the torpedo-tubes were looking a bit drawn, as though waiting for something. Then came the first depth-charge, and the sub shook with the force of the explosion. We were still going down, but the angle was not so steep, and gradually the submarine came to an even keel. Then came the second and third explosions, and we were thrown all over the place. The sub seemed to jump and then rolled from side to side.

The lights went out, and all the escape hatches were closed. She seemed to bump a bit a few seconds later, and I could only guess that we had hit the sea bottom. We could hear depth-charges going off, but they seemed to be farther away each time. There wasn't a sound now in our compartment, and I thought to myself that after coming through what I had I was to finish up like this, suffocating in a submarine at the bottom of the sea. A voice in the darkness told us to lie still and not move from where we were, which was rather hard to obey as we were all lying over each other. I lay across the spare torpedoes with a big German lying on my legs. Nobody in our compartment knew what damage had been done, but no water was coming in at our end. No orders were coming through, so we could only guess something had gone wrong amidships or aft. We lay for hours, the air getting foul, and drops of moisture falling on us from the deck head. I was choking and could hear the heavy breathing of others, and knew they were suffering as much as I was. The under-officer with us warned us not to speak or move as we would use up what air was left. I didn't think I should last long the way we were, and just lay feeling the drops of moisture dripping down in the darkness.

It seemed hours later when we heard a tapping from the other side of the bulkhead. Someone on our side tapped back an answer. They must have had some sort of code worked out beforehand, for the tapping went on for some time, until eventually the watertight door was opened, and one of the crew came through with a torch and some small square boxes which he placed on the deck. One of the men told me this was a way to test the condition of the air. I could hear a lot of hammering going on in the after section of the submarine, and a few men were working by torchlight on some mechanism in our compartment. It was early morning before the lights came on again, and the commander spoke through the loudspeaker and told everyone to stay calm, and the damage to the after end would be repaired. We were all gasping for air, as the thirty-five extra men had used up the air sooner than would the normal crew.

The submarine got under way about daybreak and rose slowly to the surface. The hatches opened, and fresh air gushed in. We had no more incidents during the trip to Saint-Nazaire, which we reached about noon on the 4th of January. We slid slowly into the submarine pens, and the Germans all went ashore where a military band played on the quay and a number of high-ranking officers welcomed them. The remainder of us, all prisoners, stood on the deck watching everything, and wondering what was going to happen to us. Later in the afternoon I was taken on shore for interrogation, and then placed in a cell on my own. I remained there until the following day, when a guard came to take me to a truck bound for Nantes, and the train to Wilhelmshaven and captivity. I was sent to the Merchant Navy prison camp at Milag Nord, where I remained until the British Army arrived to free us in May 1945.

SIR ERNEST SHACKLETON

Sir Ernest Shackleton (1874–1922) is remembered among the pioneer South Polar explorers, one of that splendid band who slogged south on their feet with dogs and sledges. Amundsen beat him to the Pole and so did Captain Scott, but Shackleton was within less than a hundred miles of that now well-frequented spot by 1909. He commanded the first trans-Antarctic expedition which set out in the *Endurance* in 1914, over thirty years before that staggering land-passage was first made (by Sir Vivian Fuchs, a scientist, who was not a sailor at all). The crushing of the *Endurance* in the Weddell Sea ice in 1916 led to Shackleton's classic voyage in an open boat, from Elephant Island in the Antarctic to the windswept island of South Georgia.

Compared with this boat journey, Bligh's run across the South Seas after the seizure of the *Bounty* may almost be regarded as a pleasant romp. After all, it was a tropic run in a fair wind, made in a good long-boat with men who were all used to naval discipline at its most rigid. Since Bligh—and before—there have been many stirring and courageous open-boat journeys necessarily made at sea, but that made by the former merchant seaman Shackleton is outstanding. To battle through those dreadful seas and in that foul, depressing climate, in a bit of a canvas-covered lifeboat with only a handful of men, setting out poorly equipped from a desolate island to sail through ghastly gales over the worst stretch of sea in the world to another island almost equally desolate—to do these things cheerfully and competently, and then to march with his little band across mountainous South Georgia in the end: even after the array of wonderful boat passages of both World Wars the feat remains staggering, incredible, magnificent.

Shackleton was trained to be a merchant service officer, from early boyhood. At sixteen he was an apprentice in the usual Limejuice style aboard the full-rigged ship *Hoghton Tower,* which he joined in Liverpool at almost the same time that Masefield was first trudging up the gangplank of the *Conway* close by. The *Hoghton Tower* flew the White Star house flag and, during Shackleton's first voyage in her, battled her way to the west'ard round the Horn in the teeth of a series of Antarctic blizzards. These ought to have been enough to put any boy off both Poles for life, but young Shackleton delighted in it all. The *Hoghton Tower* was a three-master built in 1869, just on 1,600 tons register and 247 feet on the waterline. She had once romped from Liverpool to Melbourne in sixty-eight days, pilot-to-pilot, but that was before Shackleton was born. She had been on her beam ends with her cargo shifted off the Horn too, in a violent gale of wind, as the ill-fated *Pamir* was in 1957 but, unlike the *Pamir,* she came up again and sailed on. She was a good ship for a bold spirit, and Shackleton did well in her.

He continued to do well when he passed on to steam. As an officer in the Cape-trading Union Castle Line, he attracted the favorable attention of an outstanding judge of tough men named Scott, Lieutenant Robert Falcon Scott, R.N., and Shackleton soon afterward was appointed to the National Antarctic Expedition which Scott was then organizing. He was with Scott on the *Discovery* expedition, 1901–1903 and, though he had no prior experience of exploring, he was chosen to accompany Scott on his sledge journey across the Ross shelf ice toward the Pole. After that, he led his own expeditions.

Shackleton is not a writer. Here, he is narrating a personal experience which was stirring and memorable, the very stuff of high adventure. In such a case straightforward narration is the best kind of writing. The voyage of the *James Caird* is a classic of its kind.

Shackleton died in 1922 while on a further polar voyage in a little thing called the *Quest*. He is buried at South Georgia.

The Boat Journey

by SIR ERNEST SHACKLETON

The increasing sea made it necessary for us to drag the boats further up the beach. This was a task for all hands, and after much labor we got the boats into safe positions among the rocks and made fast the painters to big boulders. Then I discussed with Wild and Worsley the chances of reaching South Georgia before the winter locked the seas against us. Some effort had to be made to secure relief. Privation and exposure had left their mark on the party, and the health and mental condition of several men were causing me serious anxiety. Blackborrow's feet, which had been frost-bitten during the boat journey, were in a bad way, and the two doctors feared that an operation would be necessary. They told me that the toes would have to be amputated unless animation could be restored within a short period. Then the food-supply was a vital consideration. We had left ten cases of provisions in the crevice of the rocks at our first camping-place on the island. An examination of our stores showed that we had full rations for the whole party for a period of five weeks. The rations could be spread over three months on a reduced allowance and probably would be supplemented by seals and sea-elephants to some extent. I did not dare to count with full confidence on supplies of meat and blubber, for the animals seemed to have deserted the beach and the winter was near. Our stocks included three seals and two and a half skins (with

From *South* by Sir Ernest Shackleton.

blubber attached). We were mainly dependent on the blubber for fuel, and, after making a preliminary survey of the situation, I decided that the party must be limited to one hot meal a day.

A boat journey in search of relief was necessary and must not be delayed. That conclusion was forced upon me. The nearest port where assistance could certainly be secured was Port Stanley, in the Falkland Islands, 540 miles away, but we could scarcely hope to beat up against the prevailing northwesterly wind in a frail and weakened boat with a small sail area. South Georgia was over 800 miles away, but lay in the area of the west winds, and I could count upon finding whalers at any of the whaling-stations on the east coast. A boat party might make the voyage and be back with relief within a month, provided that the sea was clear of ice and the boat survived the great seas. It was not difficult to decide that South Georgia must be the objective, and I proceeded to plan ways and means. The hazards of a boat journey across 800 miles of stormy sub-Antarctic Ocean were obvious, but I calculated that at worst the venture would add nothing to the risks of the men left on the island. There would be fewer mouths to feed during the winter and the boat would not require to take more than one month's provisions for six men, for if we did not make South Georgia in that time we were sure to go under. A consideration that had weight with me was that there was no chance at all of any search being made for us on Elephant Island.

The case required to be argued in some detail, since all hands knew that the perils of the proposed journey were extreme. The risk was justified solely by our urgent need of assistance. The ocean south of Cape Horn in the middle of May is known to be the most tempestuous storm-swept area of water in the world. The weather then is unsettled, the skies are dull and overcast, and the gales are almost unceasing. We had to face these conditions in a small and weather-beaten boat, already strained by the work of the months that had passed. Worsley and Wild realized that the attempt must be made, and they both asked to be allowed to accompany me on the voyage. I told Wild at once that he would have to stay behind. I relied upon him to hold the party together while I was away and to make the best of his way to Deception Island with the men in the spring in the event of our failure to bring help. Worsley I would take with me, for I had a very high opinion of his accuracy and quickness as a navigator, and especially in the snapping and working out of positions in difficult circumstances—an opinion that was only enhanced during the actual journey. Four other men would be required, and I decided to call for volunteers, although, as a matter of fact, I pretty well knew which of the people I would select. Crean I proposed to leave on the island as a right-hand man for Wild, but he begged so hard to be allowed to come in the boat that, after consultation with Wild, I promised to take him. I called the men together, explained my plan, and asked for volunteers. Many came forward at once. Some were not fit enough for the work that would have to be done, and others would not have been much use in the boat since they were not seasoned sailors, though the experiences of recent months entitled them to some consideration as seafaring men. McIlroy and Macklin were both anxious to go but realized that their duty lay on the island with the sick men. They suggested that I should take Blackborrow in order that he might have shelter and warmth as quickly as possible, but I had to veto this idea. It would be hard enough for fit men to live in the boat. Indeed, I did not see how a sick man, lying helpless in the bottom of the boat, could possibly survive in the heavy weather we were sure to encounter. I finally selected McNeish, McCarthy, and Vincent in addition to Worsley and Crean. The crew seemed a strong one, and as I looked at the men I felt confidence increasing.

The decision made, I walked through the blizzard

with Worsley and Wild to examine the *James Caird*. The 20-ft. boat had never looked big; she appeared to have shrunk in some mysterious way when I viewed her in the light of our new undertaking. She was an ordinary ship's whaler, fairly strong, but showing signs of the strains she had endured since the crushing of the *Endurance*. Where she was holed in leaving the pack was, fortunately, about the water-line and easily patched. Standing beside her, we glanced at the fringe of the storm-swept, tumultuous sea that formed our path. Clearly, our voyage would be a big adventure. I called the carpenter and asked him if he could do anything to make the boat more seaworthy. He first inquired if he was to go with me, and seemed quite pleased when I said "Yes." He was over fifty years of age and not altogether fit, but he had a good knowledge of sailing-boats and was very quick. McCarthy said that he could contrive some sort of covering for the *James Caird* if he might use the lids of the cases and the four sledge-runners that we had lashed inside the boat for use in the event of a landing on Graham Land at Wilhelmina Bay. This bay, at one time the goal of our desire, had been left behind in the course of our drift, but we had retained the runners. The carpenter proposed to complete the covering with some of our canvas, and he set about making his plans at once.

Noon had passed and the gale was more severe than ever. We could not proceed with our preparations that day. The tents were suffering in the wind and the sea was rising. We made our way to the snow-slope at the shoreward end of the spit, with the intention of digging a hole in the snow large enough to provide shelter for the party. I had an idea that Wild and his men might camp there during my absence, since it seemed impossible that the tents could hold together for many more days against the attacks of the wind; but an examination of the spot indicated that any hole we could dig probably would be filled quickly by the drift. At dark, about 5 p.m., we all turned in, after a supper consisting of a pannikin of hot milk, one of our precious biscuits, and a cold penguin leg each.

The gale was stronger than ever on the following morning (April 20). No work could be done. Blizzard and snow, snow and blizzard, sudden lulls and fierce returns. During the lulls we could see on the far horizon to the northeast bergs of all shapes and sizes driving along before the gale, and the sinister appearance of the swift-moving masses made us thankful indeed that, instead of battling with the storm amid the ice, we were required only to face the drift from the glaciers and the inland heights. The gusts might throw us off our feet, but at least we fell on solid ground and not on the rocking floes. Two seals came up on the beach that day, one of them within ten yards of my tent. So urgent was our need of food and blubber that I called all hands and organized a line of beaters instead of simply walking up to the seal and hitting it on the nose. We were prepared to fall upon this seal *en masse* if it attempted to escape. The kill was made with a pick-handle, and in a few minutes five days' food and six days' fuel were stowed in a place of safety among the boulders above high-water mark. During this day the cook, who had worked well on the floe and throughout the boat journey, suddenly collapsed. I happened to be at the galley at the moment and saw him fall. I pulled him down the slope to his tent and pushed him into its shelter with orders to his tent-mates to keep him in his sleeping-bag until I allowed him to come out or the doctors said he was fit enough. Then I took out to replace the cook one of the men who had expressed a desire to lie down and die. The task of keeping the galley fire alight was both difficult and strenuous, and it took his thoughts away from the chances of immediate dissolution. In fact, I found him a little later gravely concerned over the drying of a naturally not over-clean pair of socks which were hung up in close proximity to our evening milk. Occupation had brought his thoughts back to the ordinary cares of life.

There was a lull in the bad weather on April 21, and the carpenter started to collect material for the decking of the *James Caird*. He fitted the mast of the *Stancomb Wills* fore and aft inside the *James Caird* as a hog-back and thus strengthened the keel with the object of preventing our boat "hogging"—that is, buckling in heavy seas. He had not sufficient wood to provide a deck, but by using the sledge-runners and box-lids he made a framework extending from the forecastle aft to a well. It was a patched-up affair, but it provided a base for a canvas covering. We had a bolt of canvas frozen stiff, and this material had to be cut and then thawed out over the blubber-stove, foot by foot, in order that it might be sewn into the form of a cover. When it had been nailed and screwed into position it certainly gave an appearance of safety to the boat, though I had an uneasy feeling that it bore a strong likeness to stage scenery, which may look like a granite wall and is in fact nothing better than canvas and lath. As events proved, the covering served its purpose well. We certainly could not have lived through the voyage without it.

Another fierce gale was blowing on April 22, interfering with our preparations for the voyage. The cooker from No. 5 tent came adrift in a gust, and, although it was chased to the water's edge, it disappeared for good. Blackborrow's feet were giving him much pain, and McIlroy and Macklin thought it would be necessary for them to operate soon. They were under the impression that they had no chloroform, but they found some subsequently in the medicine-chest after we had left. Some cases of stores left on a rock off the spit on the day of our arrival were retrieved during this day. We were setting aside stores for the boat journey and choosing the essential equipment from the scanty stock at our disposal. Two ten-gallon casks had to be filled with water melted down from ice collected at the foot of the glacier. This was a rather slow business. The blubber-stove was kept going all night, and the watchmen emptied the water into casks from the pot in which the ice was melted. A working party started to dig a hole in the snow-slope about forty-feet above sea-level with the object of providing a site for a camp. They made fairly good progress at first, but the snow drifted down unceasingly from the inland ice, and in the end the party had to give up the project.

The weather was fine on April 23, and we hurried forward our preparations. It was on this day I decided finally that the crew for the *James Caird* should consist of Worsley, Crean, McNeish, McCarthy, Vincent, and myself. A storm came on about noon, with driving snow and heavy squalls. Occasionally the air would clear for a few minutes, and we could see a line of pack-ice, five miles out, driving across from west to east. This sight increased my anxiety to get away quickly. Winter was advancing, and soon the pack might close completely round the island and stay our departure for days or even for weeks. I did not think that ice would remain around Elephant Island continuously during the winter, since the strong winds and fast currents would keep it in motion. We had noticed ice and bergs going past at the rate of four or five knots. A certain amount of ice was held up about the end of our spit, but the sea was clear where the boat would have to be launched.

Worsley, Wild, and I climbed to the summit of the seaward rocks and examined the ice from a better vantage-point than the beach offered. The belt of pack outside appeared to be sufficiently broken for our purposes, and I decided that, unless the conditions forbade it, we would make a start in the *James Caird* on the following morning. Obviously the pack might close at any time. This decision made, I spent the rest of the day looking over the boat, gear, and stores, and discussing plans with Worsley and Wild.

Our last night on the solid ground of Elephant Island was cold and uncomfortable. We turned out at dawn and had breakfast. Then we launched the *Stancomb Wills* and loaded her with stores, gear, and ballast, which would be transferred to the *James Caird* when the heavier boat had been launched. The ballast consisted of bags made from blankets and filled with sand, making a total weight of about 1,000 lbs. In addition we had gathered a number of boulders and about 250 lbs. of ice, which would supplement our two casks of water.

The stores taken in the *James Caird,* which would last six men for one month, were as follows:

> 30 boxes of matches.
> 6½ gallons paraffin.
> 1 tin methylated spirit.
> 10 boxes of flamers.
> 1 box of blue lights.
> 2 Primus stoves with spare parts and prickers.
> 1 Nansen aluminum cooker.
> 6 sleeping bags.
> A few spare socks.
> Few candles and some blubber-oil in an oil bag.

Food:

> 3 cases sledging rations.
> 2 cases nut food.
> 2 cases biscuits.
> 1 case lump sugar.
> 30 packets of Trumilk.
> 1 tin of Bovril cubes.
> 1 tin of Cerebos salt.
> 36 gallons of water.
> 250 lbs. of ice.

Instruments:

Sextant.	Sea-anchor.
Binoculars.	Charts.
Prismatic compass.	Aneroid.

The swell was slight when the *Stancomb Wills* was launched and the boat got under way without any difficulty; but half an hour later, when we were pulling down the *James Caird,* the swell increased suddenly. Apparently the movement of the ice outside had made an opening and allowed the sea to run in without being blanketed by the line of pack. The swell made things difficult. Many of us got wet to the waist while dragging the boat out—a serious matter in that climate. When the *James Caird* was afloat in the surf she nearly capsized among the rocks before we could get her clear, and Vincent and the carpenter, who were on the deck, were thrown into the water. This was really bad luck, for the two men would have small chance of drying their clothes after we had got under way. Hurley, who had the eye of the professional photographer for "incidents," secured a picture of the upset, and I firmly believe that he would have liked the two unfortunate men to remain in the water until he could get a "snap" at close quarters; but we hauled them out immediately, regardless of his feelings.

The *James Caird* was soon clear of the breakers. We used all the available ropes as a long painter to prevent her drifting away to the northeast, and then the *Stancomb Wills* came alongside, transferred her load, and went back to the shore for more. As she was being beached this time the sea took her stern and half filled her with water. She had to be turned over and emptied before the return journey could be made. Every member of the crew of the *Stancomb Wills* was wet to the skin. The water-casks were towed behind the *Stancomb Wills* on this second journey, and the swell, which was increasing rapidly, drove the boat on to the rocks, where one of the casks was slightly stove in. This accident proved later to be a serious one, since some seawater had entered the cask and the contents were now brackish.

By midday the *James Caird* was ready for the voyage. Vincent and the carpenter had secured some dry clothes by exchange with members of the shore party (I heard afterwards that it was a full fortnight before the soaked garments were finally dried), and the boat's crew was standing by waiting for the order to cast off. A moderate westerly breeze was blowing. I went ashore in the *Stancomb Wills* and had a last word with Wild, who was remaining in full command, with directions as to his course of action in the event of our failure to bring relief, but I practically left the whole situation and scope of action and decision to his own judgment, secure in the knowledge that he would act wisely. I told him that I trusted the party to him and said good-by to the men. Then we pushed off for the last time, and within a few minutes I was aboard the *James Caird*. The crew of the *Stancomb Wills* shook hands with us as the boats bumped together and offered us the last good wishes. Then, setting our jib, we cut the painter and moved away to the northeast. The men who were staying behind made a pathetic little group on the beach, with the grim heights of the island behind them and the sea seething at their feet, but they waved to us and gave three hearty cheers. There was hope in their hearts and they trusted us to bring the help that they needed.

I had all sails set, and the *James Caird* quickly dipped the beach and its line of dark figures. The westerly wind took us rapidly to the line of pack, and as we entered it I stood up with my arm around the mast, directing the steering, so as to avoid the great lumps of ice that were flung about in the heave of the sea. The pack thickened and we were forced to turn almost due east, running before the wind toward a gap I had seen in the morning from the high ground. I could not see the gap now, but we had come out on its bearing and I was prepared to find that it had been influenced by the easterly drift. At four o'clock in the afternoon we found the channel, much narrower than it had seemed in the morning but still navigable. Dropping sail, we rowed through without touching the ice anywhere, and by 5:30 p.m. we were clear of the pack with open water before us. We passed one more piece of ice in the darkness an hour later, but the pack lay behind, and with a fair wind swelling the sails we steered our little craft through the night, our hopes centered on our distant goal. The swell was very heavy now, and when the time came for our first evening meal we found great difficulty in keeping the Primus lamp alight and preventing the hoosh splashing out of the pot. Three men were needed to attend to the cooking, one man holding the lamp and two men guarding the aluminum cooking-pot, which had to be lifted clear of the Primus whenever the movement of the boat threatened to cause a disaster. Then the lamp had to be protected from water, for sprays were coming over the bows and our flimsy decking was by no means water-tight. All these operations were conducted in the confined space under the decking, where the men lay or knelt and adjusted themselves as best they could to the angles of our cases and ballast. It was uncomfortable, but we found consolation in the reflection that without the decking we could not have used the cooker at all.

The tale of the next sixteen days is one of supreme strife amid heaving waters. The sub-Antarctic Ocean lived up to its evil winter reputation. I decided to run north for at least two days while the wind held and so get into warmer weather before turning to the east and laying a course for South Georgia. We took two-hourly spells at the tiller. The men who were not on watch crawled into the sodden sleeping-bags and tried to forget their troubles for a period; but there was no comfort in the boat. The bags and cases seemed to be alive in the unfailing knack of presenting their most uncomfortable angles to our rest-seeking bodies. A man might imagine for a moment that he had found a position of ease, but always discovered quickly that some unyielding point was impinging on muscle or bone. The first night aboard the boat was one of acute discomfort for us all, and we were heartily glad when the dawn came and we could set about the preparation of a hot breakfast.

This record of the voyage to South Georgia is based upon scanty notes made day by day. The notes dealt usually with the bare facts of distances, positions, and weather, but our memories retained the incidents of the passing days in a period never to be forgotten. By running north for the first two days I hoped to get warmer weather and also to avoid lines of pack that might be extending beyond the main body. We needed all the advantage that we could obtain from the higher latitude for sailing on the great circle, but we had to be cautious regarding possible ice-streams. Cramped in our narrow quarters and continually wet by the spray, we suffered severely from cold throughout the journey. We fought the seas and the winds and at the same time had a daily struggle to keep ourselves alive. At times we were in dire peril. Generally we were upheld by the knowledge that we were making progress toward the land where we would be, but there were days and nights when we lay hove to, drifting across the storm-whitened seas and watching with eyes interested rather than apprehensive the uprearing masses of water, flung to and fro by Nature in the pride of her strength. Deep seemed the valleys when we lay between the reeling seas. High were the hills when we perched momentarily on the tops of giant combers. Nearly always there were gales. So small was our boat and so great were the seas that often our sail flapped idly in the calm between the crests of two waves. Then we would climb the next slope and catch the full fury of the gale where the wool-like whiteness of the breaking water surged around us. We had our moments of laughter—rare, it is true, but hearty enough. Even when cracked lips and swollen mouths checked the outward and visible signs of amusement we could see a joke of the primitive kind. Man's sense of humor is always most easily stirred by the petty misfortunes of his neighbors, and

I shall never forget Worsley's efforts on one occasion to place the hot aluminum stand on top of the Primus stove after it had fallen off in an extra heavy roll. With his frost-bitten fingers he picked it up, dropped it, picked it up again, and toyed with it gingerly as though it were some fragile article of lady's wear. We laughed, or rather gurgled with laughter.

The wind came up strong and worked into a gale from the northwest on the third day out. We stood away to the east. The increasing seas discovered the weaknesses of our decking. The continuous blows shifted the box-lids and sledge-runners so that the canvas sagged down and accumulated water. Then icy trickles, distinct from the driving sprays, poured fore and aft into the boat. The nails that the carpenter had extracted from cases at Elephant Island and used to fasten down the battens were too short to make firm the decking. We did what we could to secure it, but our means were very limited, and the water continued to enter the boat at a dozen points. Much bailing was necessary, and nothing that we could do prevented our gear from becoming sodden. The searching runnels from the canvas were really more unpleasant than the sudden definite douches of the sprays. Lying under the thwarts during watches below, we tried vainly to avoid them. There were no dry places in the boat, and at last we simply covered our heads with our Burberrys and endured the all-pervading water. The bailing was work for the watch. Real rest we had none. The perpetual motion of the boat made repose impossible; we were cold, sore, and anxious. We moved on hands and knees in the semi-darkness of the day under the decking. The darkness was complete by 6 p.m., and not until 7 a.m. of the following day could we see one another under the thwarts. We had a few scraps of candle, and they were preserved carefully in order that we might have light at meal-times. There was one fairly dry spot in the boat, under the solid original decking at the bows, and we managed to protect some of our biscuit from the salt water; but I do not think any of us got the taste of salt out of our mouths during the voyage.

The difficulty of movement in the boat would have had its humorous side if it had not involved us in so many aches and pains. We had to crawl under the thwarts in order to move along the boat, and our knees suffered considerably. When a watch turned out it was necessary for me to direct each man by name when and where to move, since if all hands had crawled about at the same time the result would have been dire confusion and many bruises. Then there was the trim of the boat to be considered. The order of the watch was four hours on and four hours off, three men to the watch. One man had the tiller-ropes, the second man attended to the sail, and the third bailed for all he was worth. Sometimes when the water in the boat had been reduced to reasonable proportions, our pump could be used. This pump, which Hurley had made from the Flinder's bar case of our ship's standard compass, was quite effective, though its capacity was not large. The man who was attending the sail could pump into the big outer cooker, which was lifted and emptied overboard when filled. We had a device by which the water could go direct from the pump into the sea through a hole in the gunwale, but this hole had to be blocked at an early stage of the voyage, since we found that it admitted water when the boat rolled.

While a new watch was shivering in the wind and spray, the men who had been relieved groped hurriedly among the soaked sleeping-bags and tried to steal a little of the warmth created by the last occupants; but it was not always possible for us to find even this comfort when we went off watch. The boulders that we had taken aboard for ballast had to be shifted continually in order to trim the boat and give access to the pump, which became choked with hairs from the moulting sleeping-bags and finneskoe. The four reindeer-skin sleeping-bags shed their hair freely owing to the continuous wetting, and soon became quite bald in appearance. The moving of the boulders was weary and painful work. We came to know every one of the stones by sight and touch, and I have vivid memories of their angular peculiarities even today. They might have been of considerable interest as geological specimens to a scientific man under happier conditions. As ballast they were useful. As weights to be moved about in cramped quarters they were simply appalling. They spared no portion of our poor bodies. Another of our troubles, worth mention here, was the chafing of our legs by our wet clothes, which had not been changed now for seven months. The insides of our thighs were rubbed raw, and the one tube of Hazeline cream in our medicine-chest did not go far in alleviating our pain, which was increased by the bite of the salt water. We thought at the time that we never slept. The fact was that we would doze off uncomfortably, to be aroused quickly by some new ache or another call to effort. My own share of the general unpleasantness was accentuated by a finely developed bout of sciatica. I had become possessor of this originally on the floe several months earlier.

Our meals were regular in spite of the gales. Attention to this point was essential, since the conditions of the voyage made increasing calls upon our vitality. Breakfast, at 8 a.m., consisted of a pannikin of hot hoosh made from Bovril sledging ration, two biscuits, and some lumps of sugar. Lunch came at 1 p.m., and comprised Bovril sledging ration, eaten raw, and a pannikin of hot milk for each man. Tea, at 5 p.m., had the same menu. Then during the night we had a hot drink, generally of milk. The meals were the bright beacons in those cold and stormy days. The glow of warmth and comfort produced by the food and drink made optimists of us all. We had two tins of Virol, which we were keeping for an emergency; but, finding ourselves in need of an oil-lamp to eke out our supply of candles, we emptied one of the tins in the manner that most appealed to us, and fitted it with a wick made by shredding a bit of canvas. When this lamp was filled with oil it gave a certain amount of light, though it was easily blown out, and was of great assistance to us at night. We were fairly well off as regarded fuel, since we had 6½ gallons of petroleum.

A severe southwesterly gale on the fourth day out forced us to heave to. I would have liked to have run before the wind, but the sea was very high and the *James Caird* was in danger of broaching to and swamping. The delay was vexatious, since up to that time we had been making sixty or seventy miles a day, good going with our limited sail area. We hove to under double-reefed mainsail and our little jigger, and waited for the gale to blow itself out. During that afternoon we saw bits of wreckage, the remains probably of some unfortunate vessel that had failed to weather the strong gales south of Cape Horn. The weather conditions did not improve, and on the fifth day out the gale was so fierce that we were compelled to take in the double-reefed mainsail and hoist our small jib instead. We put out a sea-anchor to keep the *James Caird's* head up to the sea. This anchor consisted of a triangular canvas bag fastened to the end of the painter and allowed to stream out from the bows. The boat was high enough to catch the wind, and, as she drifted to leeward, the drag of the anchor kept her head to windward. Thus our boat took most of the seas more or less end on. Even then the crests of the waves often would curl right over us and we shipped a great deal of water, which necessitated unceasing bailing and pumping. Looking out abeam, we would see a hollow like a tunnel formed as the crest of a big wave toppled over on to the swelling body of water. A thousand times it appeared as though the *James Caird* must be engulfed; but the boat lived. The southwesterly gale had its birthplace above the Antarctic Continent, and its freezing breath lowered the temperature far toward zero. The spray froze upon the boat and gave bows, sides, and decking a heavy coat of mail. This accumulation of ice reduced the buoyancy of the boat, and to that extent was an added peril; but it possessed a notable advantage from one point of view. The water ceased to drop and trickle from the canvas, and the spray came in solely at the well in the after part of the boat. We could not allow the load of ice to grow beyond a certain point, and in turns we crawled about the decking forward, chipping and picking at it with the available tools.

When daylight came on the morning of the sixth day out we saw and felt that the *James Caird* had lost her resiliency. She was not rising to the oncoming seas. The weight of the ice that had formed in her and upon her during the night was having its effect, and she was becoming more like a log than a boat. The situation called for immediate action. We first broke away the spare oars, which were encased in ice and frozen to the sides of the boat, and threw them overboard. We retained two oars for use when we got inshore. Two of the fur sleeping-bags went over the side; they were thoroughly wet, weighing probably 40 lbs. each, and they had frozen stiff during the night. Three men constituted the watch below, and when a man went down it was better to turn into the wet bag just vacated by another man than to thaw out a frozen bag with the heat of his unfortunate body. We now had four bags, three in use and one for emergency use in case a member of the party should break down permanently. The reduction of weight relieved the boat to some extent, and vigorous chipping and scraping did more. We had to be very careful not to put ax or knife through the frozen canvas of the decking as we crawled over it, but gradually we got rid of a lot of ice. The *James Caird* lifted to the endless waves as though she lived again.

About 11 a.m. the boat suddenly fell off into the trough of the sea. The painter had parted and the sea-anchor had gone. This was serious. The *James Caird* went away to leeward, and we had no chance at all of recovering the anchor and our valuable rope, which had been our only means of keeping the boat's head up to the seas without the risk of hoisting sail in a gale. Now we had to set the sail and trust to its holding. While the *James Caird* rolled heavily in the trough, we beat the frozen canvas until the bulk of the ice had cracked off it and then hoisted it. The frozen gear worked protestingly, but after a struggle our little craft came up to the wind again, and we breathed more freely. Skin frost-bites were troubling us, and we had developed large blisters on our fingers and hands. I shall always carry the scar of one of these frost-bites on my left hand, which became badly inflamed after the skin had burst and the cold had bitten deeply.

We held the boat up to the gale during that day, enduring as best we could discomforts that amounted to pain. The boat tossed interminably on the big waves under gray, threatening skies. Our thoughts did not embrace much more than the necessities of the hour. Every surge of the sea was an enemy to be watched and circumvented. We ate our scanty meals, treated our frost-bites, and hoped for the improved conditions that the morrow might bring. Night fell early, and in the lagging hours of darkness we were cheered by a change for the better in the weather. The wind dropped, the snow-squalls became less frequent, and the sea moderated. When the morning of the seventh day dawned there was not much wind. We shook the reef out of the sail and laid our course once more for South Georgia. The sun came out bright and clear, and presently Worsley got a snap for longitude. We hoped that the sky would remain clear until noon, so that we could get the latitude. We had been six days out without an observation, and our dead reckoning naturally was uncertain. The boat must have presented a strange appearance that morning. All hands basked in the sun. We hung our sleeping-bags to the mast and spread our socks and other gear all over the deck. Some of the ice had melted off the *James Caird* in the early morning after the gale began to slacken, and dry patches were appearing in the decking. Porpoises came blowing round the boat, and Cape pigeons wheeled and swooped within a few feet of us. These little black-and-white birds have an air of friendliness that is not possessed by the great circling albatross. They had looked gray against the swaying sea during the storm as they darted about over our heads and uttered their plaintive cries. The albatrosses, of the black or sooty variety, had watched with hard, bright eyes, and seemed to have a quite impersonal interest in our struggle to keep afloat amid the battering seas. In addition to the Cape pigeons an occasional stormy petrel flashed overhead. Then there was a small bird, unknown to me, that appeared always to be in a fussy, bustling state, quite out of keeping with the surroundings. It irritated me. It had practically no tail, and it flitted about vaguely as though in search of the lost member. I used to find myself wishing it would find its tail and have done with the silly fluttering.

We reveled in the warmth of the sun that day. Life was not so bad, after all. We felt we were well on our way. Our gear was drying, and we could have a hot meal in comparative comfort. The swell was still heavy, but it was not breaking and the boat rode easily. At noon Worsley balanced himself on the gunwale and clung with one hand to the stay of the mainmast while he got a snap of the sun. The result was more than encouraging. We had done over 380 miles and were getting on for halfway to South Georgia. It looked as though we were going to get through.

The wind freshened to a good stiff breeze during that afternoon, and the *James Caird* made satisfactory progress. I had not realized until the sunlight came how small our boat really was. There was some influence in the light and warmth, some hint of happier days, that made us revive memories of other voyages, when we had stout decks beneath our feet, unlimited food at our command, and pleasant cabins for our ease. Now we clung to a battered little boat, "alone, alone—

all, all alone; alone on a wide, wide sea." So low in the water were we that each succeeding swell cut off our view of the sky-line. We were a tiny speck in the vast vista of the sea—the ocean that is open to all and merciful to none, that threatens even when it seems to yield, and that is pitiless always to weakness. For a moment the consciousness of the forces arrayed against us would be almost overwhelming. Then hope and confidence would rise again as our boat rose to a wave and tossed aside the crest in a sparkling shower like the play of prismatic colors at the foot of a waterfall. My double-barreled gun and some cartridges had been stowed aboard the boat as an emergency precaution against a shortage of food, but we were not disposed to destroy our little neighbors, the Cape pigeons, even for the sake of fresh meat. We might have shot an albatross, but the wandering king of the ocean aroused in us something of the feeling that inspired, too late, the Ancient Mariner. So the gun remained among the stores and sleeping-bags in the narrow quarters beneath our leaking deck, and the birds followed us unmolested.

The eighth, ninth, and tenth days of the voyage had few features worthy of special note. The wind blew hard during those days, and the strain of navigating the boat was unceasing; but always we made some advance toward our goal. No bergs showed on our horizon, and we knew that we were clear of the ice-fields. Each day brought its little round of troubles, but also compensation in the form of food and growing hope. We felt that we were going to succeed. The odds against us had been great, but we were winning through. We still suffered severely from the cold, for, though the temperature was rising, our vitality was declining owing to shortage of food, exposure, and the necessity of maintaining our cramped positions day and night. I found that it was now absolutely necessary to prepare hot milk for all hands during the night, in order to sustain life till dawn. This meant lighting the Primus lamp in the darkness and involved an increased drain on our small store of matches. It was the rule that one match must serve when the Primus was being lit. We had no lamp for the compass and during the early days of the voyage we would strike a match when the steersman wanted to see the course at night; but later the necessity for strict economy impressed itself upon us, and the practice of striking matches at night was stopped. We had one water-tight tin of matches. I had stowed away in a pocket, in readiness for a sunny day, a lens from one of the telescopes, but this was of no use during the voyage. The sun seldom shone upon us. The glass of the compass got broken one night, and we contrived to mend it with adhesive tape from the medicine-chest. One of the memories that comes to me from those days is of Crean singing at the tiller. He always sang while he was steering, and nobody ever discovered what the song was. It was devoid of tune and as monotonous as the chanting of a Buddhist monk at his prayers; yet somehow it was cheerful. In moments of inspiration Crean would attempt "The Wearing of the Green."

On the tenth night Worsley could not straighten his body after his spell at the tiller. He was thoroughly cramped, and we had to drag him beneath the decking and massage him before he could unbend himself and get into a sleeping-bag. A hard northwesterly gale came up on the eleventh day (May 5) and shifted to the southwest in the late afternoon. The sky was overcast and occasional snow-squalls added to the discomfort produced by a tremendous cross-sea—the worst, I thought, that we had experienced. At midnight I was at the tiller and suddenly noticed a line of clear sky between the south and southwest. I called to the other men that the sky was clearing, and then a moment later I realized that what I had seen was not a rift in the clouds but the white crest of an enormous wave. During twenty-six years' experience of the ocean in all its moods I had not encountered a wave so gigantic. It was a mighty upheaval of the ocean, a thing quite apart from the big white-capped seas that had been our tireless enemies for many days. I shouted, "For God's sake, hold on! It's got us." Then came a moment of suspense that seemed drawn out into hours. White surged the foam of the breaking sea around us. We felt our boat lifted and flung forward like a cork in breaking surf. We were in a seething chaos of tortured water; but somehow the boat lived through it, half full of water, sagging to the dead weight and shuddering under the blow. We bailed with the energy of men fighting for life, flinging the water over the sides with every receptacle that came to our hands, and after ten minutes of uncertainty we felt the boat renew her life beneath us. She floated again and ceased to lurch drunkenly as though dazed by the attack of the sea. Earnestly we hoped that never again would we encounter such a wave.

The conditions in the boat, uncomfortable before, had been made worse by the deluge of water. All our gear was thoroughly wet again. Our cooking-stove had been floating about in the bottom of the boat, and portions of our last hoosh seemed to have permeated everything. Not until 3 a.m., when we were all chilled almost to the limit of endurance, did we manage to get the stove alight and make ourselves hot drinks. The carpenter was suffering particularly, but he showed grit and spirit. Vincent had for the past week ceased to be an active member of the crew, and I could not easily account for his collapse. Physically he was one of the strongest men in the boat. He was a young man, he had served on North Sea trawlers, and he should have been able to bear hardships better than McCarthy, who, not so strong, was always happy.

The weather was better on the following day (May 6), and we got a glimpse of the sun. Worsley's observation showed that we were not more than a hundred miles from the northwest corner of South Georgia. Two more days with a favorable wind and we would sight the promised land. I hoped that there would be no delay, for our supply of water was running very low. The hot drink at night was essential, but I decided that the daily allowance of water must be cut down to half a pint per man. The lumps of ice we had taken aboard had gone long ago. We were dependent upon the water we had brought from Elephant Island, and our thirst was increased by the fact that we were now using the brackish water in the breaker that had been slightly stove in in the surf when the boat was being loaded. Some sea-water had entered at that time.

Thirst took possession of us. I dared not permit the allowance of water to be increased since an unfavorable wind might drive us away from the island and lengthen our voyage by many days. Lack of water is always the most severe privation that men can be condemned to endure, and we found, as during our earlier boat voyage, that the salt water in our clothing and the salt spray that lashed our faces made our thirst grow quickly to a burning pain. I had to be very firm in refusing to allow anyone to anticipate the morrow's allowance, which I was sometimes begged to do. We did the necessary work dully and hoped for the land. I had altered the course to the east so as to make sure of our striking the island, which would have been impossible to regain if we had run past the northern end. The course was laid on our scrap of chart for a point some thirty miles down the coast. That day and the following day passed for us in a sort of nightmare. Our mouths were dry and our tongues were swollen. The wind was still strong and the heavy sea forced us to navigate carefully, but any thought of our peril from the waves was buried beneath the consciousness of our raging thirst. The bright moments were those when we each received our one mug of hot milk during the long, bitter watches of the night. Things were bad for us in those days, but the end was coming. The morning of May 8 broke thick and stormy, with squalls from the northwest. We searched the waters ahead for a sign of land, and though we could see nothing more than had met our eyes for many days, we were cheered by a sense that the goal was near at hand. About ten o'clock that morning we passed a little bit of kelp, a glad signal of the proximity of land. An hour later we saw two shags sitting on a big mass of kelp, and knew then that we must be within ten or fifteen miles of the shore. These birds are as sure an indication of the proximity of land as a lighthouse is, for they never venture far to sea. We gazed ahead with increasing eagerness, and at 12:30 p.m., through a rift in the clouds, McCarthy caught a glimpse of the black cliffs of South Georgia, just fourteen days after our departure from Elephant Island. It was a glad moment. Thirst-ridden, chilled, and weak as we were, happiness irradiated us. The job was nearly done.

We stood in toward the shore to look for a landing-place, and presently we could see the green tussock-grass on the ledges above the surf-beaten rocks. Ahead of us and to the south, blind rollers showed the presence of uncharted reefs along the coast. Here and there the hungry rocks were close to the surface, and over them the great waves broke, swirling viciously and spouting thirty and forty feet into the air. The rocky coast appeared to descend sheer to the sea. Our need of water and rest was well-nigh desperate, but to have attempted a landing at that time would have been suicidal. Night was drawing near, and the weather indications were not favorable. There was nothing for it but to haul off till the following morning, so we stood away on the starboard tack until we had made what appeared to be a safe offing. Then we hove to in the high westerly swell. The hours passed slowly as we waited the dawn, which would herald, we fondly hoped, the last stage of our journey. Our thirst was a torment and we could scarcely touch our food; the cold seemed to strike right through our weakened bodies. At 5 a.m. the wind shifted to the northwest and quickly increased to one of the worst hurricanes any of us had ever experienced. A great cross-sea was running, and

the wind simply shrieked as it tore the tops off the
waves and converted the whole seascape into a haze of
driving spray. Down into valleys, up to tossing heights,
straining until her seams opened, swung our little boat,
brave still but laboring heavily. We knew that the wind
and set of the sea was driving us ashore, but we could
do nothing. The dawn showed us a storm-torn ocean,
and the morning passed without bringing us a sight
of the land; but at 1 p.m., through a rift in the flying
mists, we got a glimpse of the huge crags of the island
and realized that our position had become desperate.
We were on a dead lee shore, and we could gauge our
approach to the unseen cliffs by the roar of the breakers against the sheer walls of rock. I ordered the double-
reefed mainsail to be set in the hope that we might
claw off, and this attempt increased the strain upon the
boat. The *Caird* was bumping heavily, and the water
was pouring in everywhere. Our thirst was forgotten in
the realization of our imminent danger, as we bailed
unceasingly, and adjusted our weights from time to
time; occasional glimpses showed that the shore was
nearer. I knew that Annewkow Island lay to the south
of us, but our small and badly marked chart showed
uncertain reefs in the passage between the island and
the mainland, and I dared not trust it, though as a last
resort we could try to lie under the lee of the island.
The afternoon wore away as we edged down the coast,
with the thunder of the breakers in our ears. The approach of evening found us still some distance from
Annewkow Island, and, dimly in the twilight, we could
see a snow-capped mountain looming above us. The
chance of surviving the night, with the driving gale
and the implacable sea forcing us on to the lee shore,
seemed small. I think most of us had a feeling that the
end was very near. Just after 6 p.m., in the dark, as the
boat was in the yeasty backwash from the seas flung
from this iron-bound coast, then, just when things
looked their worst, they changed for the best. I have
marveled often at the thin line that divides success

from failure and the sudden turn that leads from apparently certain disaster to comparative safety. The wind suddenly shifted, and we were free once more to make an offing. Almost as soon as the gale eased, the pin that locked the mast to the thwart fell out. It must have been on the point of doing this throughout the hurricane, and if it had gone nothing could have saved us; the mast would have snapped like a carrot. Our backstays had carried away once before when iced up and were not too strongly fastened now. We were thankful indeed for the mercy that had held that pin in its place throughout the hurricane.

We stood off shore again, tired almost to the point of apathy. Our water had long been finished. The last was about a pint of hairy liquid, which we strained through a bit of gauze from the medicine-chest. The pangs of thirst attacked us with redoubled intensity, and I felt that we must make a landing on the following day at almost any hazard. The night wore on. We were very tired. We longed for day. When at last the dawn came on the morning of May 10 there was practically no wind, but a high cross-sea was running. We made slow progress toward the shore. About 8 a.m. the wind backed to the northwest and threatened another blow. We had sighted in the meantime a big indentation which I thought must be King Haakon Bay, and I decided that we must land there. We set the bows of the boat toward the bay and ran before the freshening gale. Soon we had angry reefs on either side. Great glaciers came down to the sea and offered no landing-place. The sea spouted on the reefs and thundered against the shore. About noon we sighted a line of jagged reef, like blackened teeth, that seemed to bar the entrance to the bay. Inside, comparatively smooth water stretched eight or nine miles to the head of the bay. A gap in the reef appeared, and we made for it. But the fates had another rebuff for us. The wind shifted and blew from the east right out of the bay. We could see the way through the reef, but we could not approach it directly. That afternoon we bore up, tacking five times in the strong wind. The last tack enabled us to get through, and at last we were in the wide mouth of the bay. Dusk was approaching. A small cove, with a boulder-strewn beach guarded by a reef, made a break in the cliffs on the south side of the bay, and we turned in that direction. I stood in the bows directing the steering as we ran through the kelp and made the passage of the reef. The entrance was so narrow that we had to take in the oars, and the swell was piling itself right over the reef into the cove; but in a minute or two we were inside, and in the gathering darkness the *James Caird* ran in on a swell and touched the beach. I sprang ashore with the short painter and held on when the boat went out with the backward surge. When the *James Caird* came in again three of the men got ashore, and they held the painter while I climbed some rocks with another line. A slip on the wet rocks twenty feet up nearly closed my part of the story just at the moment when we were achieving safety. A jagged piece of rock held me and at the same time bruised me sorely. However, I made fast the line, and in a few minutes we were all safe on the beach, with the boat floating in the surging water just off the shore. We heard a gurgling sound that was sweet music in our ears, and, peering around, found a stream of fresh water almost at our feet. A moment later we were down on our knees drinking the pure ice-cold water in long draughts that put new life into us. It was a splendid moment.

The next thing was to get the stores and ballast out of the boat, in order that we might secure her for the night. We carried the stores and gear above high-water mark and threw out the bags of sand and the boulders that we knew so well. Then we attempted to pull the empty boat up the beach, and discovered by this effort how weak we had become. Our united strength was not sufficient to get the *James Caird* clear of the water. Time after time we pulled together, but without avail.

I saw that it would be necessary to have food and rest before we beached the boat. We made fast a line to a heavy boulder and set a watch to fend the *James Caird* off the rocks of the beach. Then I sent Crean round to the left side of the cove, about thirty yards away, where I had noticed a little cave as we were running in. He could not see much in the darkness, but reported that the place certainly promised some shelter. We carried the sleeping-bags round and found a mere hollow in the rock-face, with a shingle-floor sloping at a steep angle to the sea. There we prepared a hot meal, and when the food was finished I ordered the men to turn in. The time was now about 8 p.m., and I took the first watch beside the *James Caird,* which was still afloat in the tossing water just off the beach.

Fending the *James Caird* off the rocks in the darkness was awkward work. The boat would have bumped dangerously if allowed to ride in with the waves that drove into the cove. I found a flat rock for my feet, which were in a bad way owing to the cold, wetness, and lack of exercise in the boat, and during the next few hours I labored to keep the *James Caird* clear of the beach. Occasionally I had to rush into the seething water. Then, as a wave receded, I let the boat out on the alpine rope so as to avoid a sudden jerk. The heavy painter had been lost when the sea-anchor went adrift. The *James Caird* could be seen but dimly in the cove, where the high black cliffs made the darkness almost complete, and the strain upon one's attention was great. After several hours had passed I found that my desire for sleep was becoming irresistible, and at 1 a.m. I called Crean. I could hear him groaning as he stumbled over the sharp rocks on his way down the beach. While he was taking charge of the *James Caird* she got adrift, and we had some anxious moments. Fortunately, she went across toward the cave and we secured her unharmed. The loss or destruction of the boat at this stage would have been a very serious matter, since we probably would have found it impossible to leave the cove except by sea. The cliffs and glaciers around offered no practicable path toward the head of the bay. I arranged for one-hour watches during the remainder of the night and then took Crean's place among the sleeping men and got some sleep before the dawn came.

The sea went down in the early hours of the morning (May 11), and after sunrise we were able to set about getting the boat ashore, first bracing ourselves for the task with another meal. We were all weak still. We cut off the topsides and took out all the movable gear. Then we waited for Byron's "great ninth wave," and when it lifted the *James Caird* in we held her and, by dint of great exertion, worked her round broadside to the sea. Inch by inch we dragged her up until we reached the fringe of the tussock-grass and knew that the boat was above high-water mark. The rise of the tide was about five feet, and at spring tide the water must have reached almost to the edge of the tussock-grass. The completion of this job removed our immediate anxieties, and we were free to examine our surroundings and plan the next move. The day was bright and clear.

King Haakon Bay is an eight-mile sound penetrating the coast of South Georgia in an easterly direction. We had noticed that the northern and southern sides of the sound were formed by steep mountain-ranges, their flanks furrowed by mighty glaciers, the outlets of the great ice-sheet of the interior. It was obvious that these glaciers and the precipitous slopes of the mountains barred our way inland from the cove. We must sail to the head of the sound. Swirling clouds and mist-wreaths had obscured our view of the sound when we were entering, but glimpses of snow-slopes had given us hope that an overland journey could be begun from that point. A few patches of very rough tussocky land, dotted with little tarns, lay between the glaciers along the foot of the mountains, which were heavily scarred with scree-slopes. Several magnificent peaks and crags gazed out across their snowy domains to the sparkling waters of the sound.

Our cove lay a little inside the southern headland of King Haakon Bay. A narrow break in the cliffs, which were about a hundred feet high at this point, formed the entrance to the cove. The cliffs continued inside the cove on each side and merged into a hill which descended at a steep slope to the boulder-beach. The slope, which carried tussock-grass, was not continuous. It eased at two points into little peaty swamp terraces dotted with frozen pools and drained by two small streams. Our cave was a recess in the cliff on the left-hand end of the beach. The rocky face of the cliff was undercut at this point, and the shingle thrown up by the waves formed a steep slope, which we reduced to about one in six by scraping the stones away from the inside. Later we strewed the rough floor with the dead, nearly dry, underleaves of the tussock-grass, so as to form a slightly soft bed for our sleeping-bags. Water had trickled down the face of the cliff and formed long icicles, which hung down in front of the cave to the length of about fifteen feet. These icicles provided shelter, and when we had spread our sails below them, with the assistance of oars, we had quarters that, in the circumstances, had to be regarded as reasonably comfortable. The camp at least was dry, and we moved our gear there with confidence. We built a fireplace and arranged our sleeping-bags and blankets around it. The cave was about 8 ft. deep and 12 ft. wide at the entrance.

While the camp was being arranged Crean and I climbed the tussock slope behind the beach and reached the top of a headland overlooking the sound. There we found the nests of albatrosses, and, much to our delight, the nests contained young birds. The fledglings were fat and lusty, and we had no hesitation about deciding that they were destined to die at an early age. Our most pressing anxiety at this stage was a shortage of fuel for the cooker. We had rations for ten more days, and we knew now that we could get birds for food; but if we were to have hot meals we must secure fuel. The store of petroleum carried in the boat was running very low, and it seemed necessary to keep some quantity for use on the overland journey that lay ahead of us. A sea-elephant or a seal would have provided fuel as well as food, but we could see none in the neighborhood. During the morning we started a fire in the cave with wood from the topsides of the boat, and though the dense smoke from the damp sticks inflamed our tired eyes, the warmth and the prospect of hot food were ample compensation. Crean was cook that day, and I suggested to him that he should wear his goggles, which he happened to have brought with him. The goggles helped him a great deal as he bent over the fire and tended the stew. And what a stew it was! The young albatrosses weighed about fourteen pounds each, fresh killed, and we estimated that they weighed at least six pounds each when cleaned and dressed for the pot. Four birds went into the pot for six men, with a Bovril ration for thickening. The flesh was white and succulent, and the bones, not fully formed, almost melted in our mouths. That was a memorable meal. When we had eaten our fill, we dried our tobacco in the embers of the fire and smoked contentedly. We made an attempt to dry our clothes, which were soaked with salt water, but did not meet with much success. We could not afford to have a fire except for cooking purposes until blubber or driftwood had come our way.

The final stage of the journey had still to be attempted. I realized that the condition of the party generally, and particularly of McNeish and Vincent, would prevent us putting to sea again except under pressure of dire necessity. Our boat, moreover, had been weakened by the cutting away of the topsides, and I doubted if we could weather the island. We were still 150 miles away from Stromness whaling-station by sea.

The alternative was to attempt the crossing of the island. If we could not get over, then we must try to secure enough food and fuel to keep us alive through the winter, but this possibility was scarcely thinkable. Over on Elephant Island twenty-two men were waiting for the relief that we alone could secure for them. Their plight was worse than ours. We must push on somehow. Several days must elapse before our strength would be sufficiently recovered to allow us to row or sail the last nine miles up to the head of the bay. In the meantime we could make what preparations were possible and dry our clothes by taking advantage of every scrap of heat from the fires we lit for the cooking of our meals. We turned in early that night, and I remember that I dreamed of the great wave and aroused my companions with a shout of warning as I saw with half-awakened eyes the towering cliff on the opposite side of the cove.

Shortly before midnight a gale sprang up suddenly from the northeast with rain and sleet showers. It brought quantities of glacier-ice into the cove, and by 2 a.m. (May 12) our little harbor was filled with ice, which surged to and fro in the swell and pushed its way on to the beach. We had solid rock beneath our feet and could watch without anxiety. When daylight came rain was falling heavily, and the temperature was the highest we had experienced for many months. The icicles overhanging our cave were melting down in streams, and we had to move smartly when passing in and out lest we should be struck by falling lumps. A fragment weighing fifteen or twenty pounds crashed down while we were having breakfast. We found that a big hole had been burned in the bottom of Worsley's reindeer sleeping-bag during the night. Worsley had been awakened by a burning sensation in his feet, and asked the men near him if his bag was all right; they looked and could see nothing wrong. We were all superficially frost-bitten about the feet, and this condition caused the extremities to burn painfully, while at the same time sensation was lost in the skin. Worsley thought that the uncomfortable heat of his feet was due to the frost-bites, and he stayed in his bag and presently went to sleep again. He discovered when he turned out in the morning that the tussock-grass which we had laid on the floor of the cave had smoldered outwards from the fire and had actually burned a large hole in the bag beneath his feet. Fortunately, his feet were not harmed.

Our party spent a quiet day, attending to clothing and gear, checking stores, eating and resting. Some more of the young albatrosses made a noble end in our pot. The birds were nesting on a small plateau above the right-hand end of our beach. We had previously discovered that when we were landing from the boat on the night of May 10 we had lost the rudder. The *James Caird* had been bumping heavily astern as we were scrambling ashore, and evidently the rudder was then knocked off. A careful search of the beach and the rocks within our reach failed to reveal the missing article. This was a serious loss, even if the voyage to the head of the sound could be made in good weather. At dusk the ice in the cove was rearing and crashing on the beach. It had forced up a ridge of stones close to where the *James Caird* lay at the edge of the tussock-grass. Some pieces of ice were driven right up to the canvas wall at the front of our cave. Fragments lodged within two feet of Vincent, who had the lowest sleeping-place, and within four feet of our fire. Crean and McCarthy had brought down six more of the young albatrosses in the afternoon, so we were well supplied with fresh food. The air temperature that night probably was not lower than 38° or 40° Fahr., and we were rendered uncomfortable in our cramped sleeping quarters by the unaccustomed warmth. Our feelings toward our neighbors underwent a change. When the temperature was below 20° Fahr. we could not get too close to one another—every man wanted to cuddle against his neighbor; but let the temperature rise a few degrees and the warmth of another man's body ceased to be a blessing. The ice and the waves had a voice of menace that night, but I heard it only in my dreams.

The bay was still filled with ice on the morning of Saturday, May 13, but the tide took it all away in the afternoon. Then a strange thing happened. The rudder, with all the broad Atlantic to sail in and the coasts of two continents to search for a resting-place, came bobbing back into our cove. With anxious eyes we watched it as it advanced, receded again, and then advanced once more under the capricious influence of wind and wave. Nearer and nearer it came as we waited on the shore, oars in hand, and at last we were able to seize it. Surely a remarkable salvage! The day was bright and clear; our clothes were drying and our strength was returning. Running water made a musical sound down the tussock slope and among the boulders. We carried our blankets up the hill and tried to dry them in the breeze 300 ft. above sea-level. In the afternoon we began to prepare the *James Caird* for the journey to the head of King Haakon Bay. A noon observation on this day gave our latitude as 54° 10′ 47″ S., but according to the German chart the position should have been 54° 12′ S. Probably Worsley's observation was the more accurate. We were able to keep the fire alight until we went to sleep that night, for while climbing the rocks above the cove I had seen at the foot of a cliff a broken spar, which had been thrown up by the waves. We could reach this spar by climbing down the cliff, and with a reserve supply of fuel thus in sight we could afford to burn the fragments of the *James Caird*'s topsides more freely.

During the morning of this day (May 13) Worsley and I tramped across the hills in a northeasterly direction with the object of getting a view of the sound and possibly gathering some information that would be useful to us in the next stage of our journey. It was exhausting work, but after covering about 2½ miles in two hours, we were able to look east, up the bay. We could not see very much of the country that we would have to cross in order to reach the whaling-station on the other side of the island. We had passed several brooks and frozen tarns, and at a point where we had to take to the beach on the shore of the sound we found some wreckage—an 18-ft. pine-spar (probably part of a ship's topmast), several pieces of timber, and a little model of a ship's hull, evidently a child's toy. We wondered what tragedy that pitiful little plaything indicated. We encountered also some gentoo penguins and a young sea-elephant, which Worsley killed.

When we got back to the cave at 3 p.m., tired, hungry, but rather pleased with ourselves, we found a splendid meal of stewed albatross chicken waiting for us. We had carried a quantity of blubber and the sea-elephant's liver in our blouses, and we produced our treasures as a surprise for the men. Rough climbing on the way back to camp had nearly persuaded us to throw the stuff away, but we had held on (regardless of the condition of our already sorely tried clothing), and had our reward at the camp. The long bay had been a magnificent sight, even to eyes that had dwelt on grandeur long enough and were hungry for the simple, familiar things of everyday life. Its green-blue waters were being beaten to fury by the northwesterly gale. The mountains, "stern peaks that dared the stars," peered through the mists, and between them huge glaciers poured down from the great ice-slopes and fields that lay behind. We counted twelve glaciers and heard every few minutes the reverberating roar caused by masses of ice calving from the parent streams.

On May 14 we made our preparations for an early start on the following day if the weather held fair. We expected to be able to pick up the remains of the sea-elephant on our way up the sound. All hands were recovering from the chafing caused by our wet clothes during the boat journey. The insides of our legs had suffered severely, and for some time after landing in the cove we found movement extremely uncomfortable. We paid our last visit to the nests of the albatrosses, which were situated on a little undulating plateau above the cave amid tussocks, snow-patches, and little frozen tarns. Each nest consisted of a mound over a foot high of tussock-grass, roots, and a little earth. The albatross lays one egg and very rarely two. The chicks, which are hatched in January, are fed on the nest by the parent birds for almost seven months before they take to the sea and fend for themselves. Up to four months of age the chicks are beautiful white masses of downy fluff, but when we arrived on the scene their plumage was almost complete. Very often one of the parent birds was on guard near the nest. We did not enjoy attacking these birds, but our hunger knew no law. They tasted so very good and assisted our recuperation to such an extent that each time we killed one of them we felt a little less remorseful.

May 15 was a great day. We made our hoosh at 7:30 a.m. Then we loaded up the boat and gave her a flying launch down the steep beach into the surf. Heavy rain had fallen in the night and a gusty northwesterly wind was now blowing, with misty showers. The *James Caird* headed to the sea as if anxious to face the battle of the waves once more. We passed through the narrow mouth of the cove with the ugly rocks and waving kelp close on either side, turned to the east, and sailed merrily up the bay as the sun broke through the mists and made the tossing waters sparkle around us. We were a curious-looking party on that bright morning, but we were feeling happy. We even broke into song, and, but for our Robinson Crusoe appearance, a casual observer might have taken us for a picnic party sailing in a Norwegian fiord or one of the beautiful sounds of the west coast of New Zealand. The wind blew fresh and strong, and a small sea broke on the coast as we advanced. The surf was sufficient to have endangered the boat if we had attempted to land where the carcass of the sea-elephant was lying, so we decided to go on to the head of the bay without risking anything, particularly as we were likely to find sea-elephants on the upper beaches. The big creatures have a habit of seeking peaceful quarters protected from the waves. We had hopes, too, of finding penguins. Our expectation as far as the sea-elephants were concerned was not at fault. We heard the roar of the bulls as we neared the head of the bay, and soon afterwards saw the great unwieldy forms of the beasts lying on a shelving beach toward the bay-head. We rounded a high, glacier-worn bluff on the north side, and at 12:30 p.m. we ran the boat ashore on a low beach of sand and pebbles, with tussock growing above high-water mark. There were hundreds of sea-elephants lying about, and our anxieties with regard to food disappeared. Meat and blubber enough to feed our party for years was in sight. Our landing-place was about a mile and a half west of the northeast corner of the bay. Just east of us was a glacier-snout ending on the beach but giving a passage toward the head of the bay except at high water or when a very heavy surf was running. A cold, drizzling rain had begun to fall, and we provided ourselves with shelter as quickly as possible. We hauled the *James Caird* up above high-water mark and turned her over just to the lee or east side of the bluff. The spot was separated from the mountain-side by a low morainic bank, rising twenty or thirty feet above sea-level. Soon we had converted the boot into a very comfortable cabin *à la* Peggotty, turfing it round with tussocks, which we dug up with knives. One side of the *James Caird* rested on stones so as to afford a low entrance, and when we had finished she looked as though she had grown there. McCarthy entered into this work with great spirit. A sea-elephant provided us with fuel and meat, and that evening found a well-fed and fairly contented party at rest in Peggotty Camp.

Our camp, as I have said, lay on the north side of King Haakon Bay near the head. Our path toward the whaling-stations led round the seaward end of the snouted glacier on the east side of the camp and up a snow-slope that appeared to lead to a pass in the great Allardyce Range, which runs northwest and southeast and forms the main backbone of South Georgia. The range dipped opposite the bay into a well-defined pass from east to west. An ice-sheet covered most of the interior, filling the valleys and disguising the configuration of the land, which, indeed, showed only in big rocky ridges, peaks, and nunataks. When we looked up the pass from Peggotty Camp the country to the left appeared to offer two easy paths through to the opposite coast, but we knew that the island was uninhabited at that point (Possession Bay). We had to turn our attention further east, and it was impossible from the camp to learn much of the conditions that would confront us on the overland journey. I planned to climb to the pass and then be guided by the configuration of the country in the selection of a route eastward to Stromness Bay, where the whaling-stations were established in the minor bays, Leith, Huvik, and Stromness. A range of mountains with precipitous slopes, forbidding peaks, and large glaciers, lay immediately to the south of King Haakon Bay and seemed to form a continuation of the main range. Between this secondary range and the pass above our camp a great snow-upland sloped up to the inland ice-sheet and reached a rocky ridge that stretched athwart our path and seemed to bar the way. This ridge was a right-angled offshoot from the main ridge. Its chief features were four rocky peaks with spaces between that looked from a distance as though they might prove to be passes.

The weather was bad on Tuesday, May 16, and we stayed under the boat nearly all day. The quarters were cramped but gave full protection from the weather, and we regarded our little cabin with a great deal of satisfaction. Abundant meals of sea-elephant steak and liver increased our contentment. McNeish reported during the day that he had seen rats feeding on the scraps, but this interesting statement was not verified. One would not expect to find rats at such a spot, but there was a bare possibility that they had landed from a wreck and managed to survive the very rigorous conditions.

A fresh west-southwesterly breeze was blowing on the following morning (Wednesday, May 17), with misty squalls, sleet, and rain. I took Worsley with me on a pioneer journey to the west with the object of examining the country to be traversed at the beginning of the overland journey. We went round the seaward end of the snouted glacier, and after tramping about a mile over stony ground and snow-coated debris, we crossed some big ridges of scree and moraines. We found that there was good going for a sledge as far as the northeast corner of the bay, but did not get much information regarding the conditions further on owing to the view becoming obscured by a snow-squall. We waited a quarter of an hour for the weather to clear but were forced to turn back without having seen more of the country. I had satisfied myself, however, that we could reach a good snow-slope leading apparently to the inland ice. Worsley reckoned from the chart that the distance from our camp to Huvik, on an east magnetic course, was seventeen geographical miles, but we could not expect to follow a direct line. The carpenter started making a sledge for use on the overland journey. The materials at his disposal were limited in quantity and scarcely suitable in quality.

We overhauled our gear on Thursday, May 18, and hauled our sledge to the lower edge of the snouted glacier. The vehicle proved heavy and cumbrous. We had to lift it empty over bare patches of rock along the shore, and I realized that it would be too heavy for three men to manage amid the snow-plains, glaciers, and peaks of the interior. Worsley and Crean were coming with me, and after consultation we decided to leave the sleeping-bags behind us and make the journey in very light marching order. We would take three days' provisions for each man in the form of sledging ration and biscuit. The food was to be packed in three socks, so that each member of the party could carry his own supply. Then we were to take the Primus lamp filled with oil, the small cooker, the carpenter's adze (for use as an ice-ax), and the alpine rope, which made a total length of fifty feet when knotted. We might have to lower ourselves down steep slopes or cross crevassed glaciers. The filled lamp would provide six hot meals, which would consist of sledging ration boiled up with biscuit. There were two boxes of matches left, one full and the other partially used. We left the full box with the men at the camp and took the second box, which contained forty-eight matches. I was unfortunate as regarded footgear, since I had given away my heavy Burberry boots on the floe, and had now a comparatively light pair in poor condition. The carpenter assisted me by putting several screws in the sole of each boot with the object of providing a grip on the ice. The screws came out of the *James Caird*.

We turned in early that night, but sleep did not come to me. My mind was busy with the task of the following day. The weather was clear and the outlook for an early start in the morning was good. We were going to leave a weak party behind us in the camp. Vincent was still in the same condition, and he could not march. McNeish was pretty well broken up. The two men were not capable of managing for themselves and McCarthy must stay to look after them. He might have a difficult task if we failed to reach the whaling-station. The distance to Huvik, according to the chart, was no more than seventeen geographical miles in a direct line, but we had very scanty knowledge of the conditions of the interior. No man had ever penetrated a mile from the coast of South Georgia at any point, and the whalers, I knew, regarded the country as inaccessible. During the day, while we were walking to the snouted glacier, we had seen three wild ducks flying toward the head of the bay from the eastward. I hoped that the presence of these birds indicated tussock-land and not snow-fields and glaciers in the interior, but the hope was not a very bright one.

We turned out at 2 a.m. on the Friday morning and had our hoosh ready an hour later. The full moon was shining in a practically cloudless sky, its rays reflected gloriously from the pinnacles and crevassed ice of the adjacent glaciers. The huge peaks of the mountains stood in bold relief against the sky and threw dark shadows on the waters of the sound. There was no need for delay, and we made a start as soon as we had eaten our meal. McNeish walked about 200 yds. with us; he could do no more. Then we said good-by and he turned back to the camp. The first task was to get round the edge of the snouted glacier, which had points like fingers projecting toward the sea. The waves were reaching the points of these fingers, and we had to rush from one recess to another when the waters receded. We soon reached the east side of the glacier and noticed its great activity at this point. Changes had occurred within the preceding twenty-four hours. Some huge pieces had broken off, and the masses of mud and stone that were being driven before the advancing ice showed movement. The glacier was like a gigantic plow driving irresistibly toward the sea.

Lying on the beach beyond the glacier was wreckage that told of many ill-fated ships. We noticed stanchions of teakwood, liberally carved, that must have come from ships of the older type; iron-bound timbers with the iron almost rusted through; battered barrels, and all the usual debris of the ocean. We had difficulties and anxieties of our own, but as we passed that grave-yard of the sea we thought of the many tragedies written in the wave-worn fragments of lost vessels. We did not pause, and soon we were ascending a snow-slope, headed due east on the last lap of our long trail.

The snow-surface was disappointing. Two days before we had been able to move rapidly on hard, packed snow; now we sank over our ankles at each step and progress was slow. After two hours' steady climbing we were 2,500 ft. above sea-level. The weather continued fine and calm, and as the ridges drew nearer and the western coast of the island spread out below, the bright moonlight showed us that the interior was broken tremendously. High peaks, impassable cliffs, steep snow-slopes, and sharply descending glaciers were prominent features in all directions, with stretches of snow-plain overlaying the ice-sheet of the interior. The slope we were ascending mounted to a ridge and our course lay direct to the top. The moon, which proved a good friend during this journey, threw a long shadow at one point and told us that the surface was broken in our path. Warned in time, we avoided a huge hole capable of swallowing an army. The bay was now about three miles away, and the continued roaring of a big glacier at the head of the bay came to our ears. This glacier, which we had noticed during the stay at Peggotty Camp, seemed to be calving almost continuously.

I had hoped to get a view of the country ahead of us from the top of the slope, but as the surface became more level beneath our feet, a thick fog drifted down. The moon became obscured and produced a diffused light that was more trying than darkness, since it illuminated the fog without guiding our steps. We roped ourselves together as a precaution against holes, crevasses, and precipices, and I broke trail through the soft snow. With almost the full length of the rope between myself and the last man we were able to steer an approximately straight course, since, if I veered to the right or the left when marching into the blank wall of the fog, the last man on the rope could shout a direction. So, like a ship with its "port," "starboard," "steady," we tramped through the fog for the next two hours.

Then, as daylight came, the fog thinned and lifted, and from an elevation of about 3,000 ft. we looked down on what seemed to be a huge frozen lake with its further shores still obscured by the fog. We halted there to eat a bit of biscuit while we discussed whether we would go down and cross the flat surface of the lake, or keep on the ridge we had already reached. I decided to go down, since the lake lay on our course. After an hour of comparatively easy travel through the snow we noticed the thin beginnings of crevasses. Soon they were increasing in size and showing fractures, indicating that we were traveling on a glacier. As the daylight brightened the fog dissipated; the lake could be seen more clearly, but still we could not discover its east shore. A little later the fog lifted completely, and then we saw that our lake stretched to the horizon, and realized suddenly that we were looking down upon the open sea on the east coast of the island. The slight pulsation at the shore showed that the sea was not even frozen; it was the bad light that had deceived us. Evidently we were at the top of Possession Bay, and the island at that point could not be more than five miles across from the head of King Haakon Bay. Our rough chart was inaccurate. There was nothing for it but to start up the glacier again. That was about seven o'clock in the morning, and by nine o'clock we had more than recovered our lost ground. We regained the ridge and then struck south-east, for the chart showed that two more bays indented the coast before Stromness. It was comforting to realize that we would have the eastern water in sight during our journey, although we could see there was no way around the shore-line owing to steep cliffs and glaciers. Men lived in houses lit by electric light on the east coast. News of the outside world waited us there, and, above all, the east coast meant for us the means of rescuing the twenty-two men we had left on Elephant Island.

CAPTAIN ALAN VILLIERS

Apart from the occasional letter home, I had no intention of writing anything when I went off to sea. I was almost sixteen, and I had been at a pre-sea training school on the Albert Park Lake in Melbourne then for the best part of a year. It was a weekend-and-one-night-a-week place, run by old sailing-ship sailors for young such. If you did not intend to become a regular square-rigger man, it was no place to go. It suited me, and I was delighted to get a berth, in my turn, in the half-deck of an old Scots barque, the *Rothesay Bay*. For the next three or four years my letters home were few and far between, but usually I did keep some sort of private log. Write anything? It seemed to me if ever I thought about the subject (and I don't recall that I ever did, then) that all the good sea books had been written. I was brought up on Conrad, Bullen, Masefield, Dana, Melville, Marryat, and the rest. They had said it all, surely, and said it very well. My plan was to become master of a deepsea square-rigged sailing-ship, the sooner the better.

But I was a little late. In the end, my promotion came through writing, long after it was hopeless otherwise. The sailing-ships were on the way out, finally. I bought a full-rigger with the proceeds of some books, which I had written only because an American publisher had asked me to. Well, I'm glad he did: but it was the profession of sailing deepsea ships which first attracted me, and still does. The writing is on the side.

I have tried to sail in many different kinds of vessels, from an Arab Indian Ocean dhow to a late-sixteenth-century barque of sorts, a copy of the *Mayflower*, from a Cape Horn full-rigged ship to a rebuilt *Bon Homme Richard*, and to *sail* them, too—not only *in* them. I tried to write of what I know. Though I have never been a professional fisherman, much less a doryman, I was six months in the Portuguese dory-fishing schooner *Argus,* out of Lisbon to the Banks and Greenland, learning about that arduous, strange, and most courageous life. I left the *Argus* with the greatest respect for those cod-banging shipmasters and for their dorymen.

The Captains from Ilhavo

by CAPTAIN ALAN VILLIERS

The valiant Portingalls that plow the Main.

For the thirtieth time that morning, Captain Silvio Ramalheira of the motor-ship *Elisabeth* paced impatiently the weather wing of his minute bridge, his blue eyes roving intently over the wide seascape, from the dark mass of the West Greenland shore way to the eastward, round the assembled schooners of the Portuguese hand-lining fleet, over the sea and sky. What was the weather going to do? That was the problem. That was always the problem; and a man could guess no better at the answer, here in Davis Straits, after a dozen or more voyages. He had launched his fifty-five dories a little after four that morning, as all the other captains had done, doubtfully indeed, for the weather was far from settled. But if they kept the dories nested whenever there was doubt, they would never fill with fish. The dorymen had gone cheerfully.

The dorymen went at the captain's bidding: their lives were in his hands. He sent them; he had to get them back. Captain Silvio had an excellent crowd of

From *The Quest of the Schooner Argus* by Alan Villiers.

dorymen and, like all the other captains, he felt very keenly the responsibility for their lives. Like most of the other captains, too, he had lost some lives. It was no fault of his but it distressed him profoundly. His eyes fell upon the white speck of a small sailing-ship with square yards, far off by the Greenland mountains. He knew that speck well. That was the barquentine *Gazela*. Captain Silvio had been a deckboy in her on his first Grand Banks voyage almost forty years before, though he was still a man on the right side of fifty. He had been mate in the *Gazela* and had been several years in command of her, later. In her, he remembered —he could never forget—he had lost two dorymen.

He was fishing that day in July, 1932, off Holsteinsborg Bay, in the treacherous currents there, where a master had to be doubly careful. A sudden southerly wind, springing out of a clear sky on what had been a lovely day of good weather and good fishing, brought up a breaking sea. The *Gazela* had not then made many Greenland voyages, and neither had her youthful master. The barquentine had no power in those days: he could not weigh at once when he saw bad weather approaching, or when it was suddenly upon him, as it was that day, without giving any sign of its approach. He could not drift down among his dorymen to pick them up and save them the dangerous battle back to wind'ard to regain the ship. He could do nothing. The *Gazela* was securely anchored to a long scope of cable and there she had to stay, for it took at least four hours for all hands to weigh her great Banks anchor, and she had only the cook and a few deckboys aboard. It was not in Captain Silvio's character to do nothing. In those days, if the ship herself could not reach her dorymen, it was the custom to float back a long grass line to them, over the stern of the anchored ship. This line was generally buoyed on an empty dory. The dory was launched, the grass line attached, and away drove the dory astern carried by wind and tide and taking the line with it, out to its utmost length. Then the dorymen made for the grass line and, once with a turn of their painters on that, they could be hauled up to the ship. It was primitive, but it was all that could be done and it was usually effective.

Captain Silvio went in the dory himself that day, taking the line. He took a second dory too, and in this he rowed and sailed to his distressed dories until he had found and succoured all that he could see, towing the heavily laden, encouraging the disheartened. He had thirty-one dories out that day. Twenty-nine he found: the other two never came. The wind screamed at the little barquentine, roaring in her square rigging, and the sea leaped at her exultantly. Hour after hour, Captain Silvio in his dory fought wind and sea to save his fishermen. But the lost two did not come. A deck-boy said afterwards that he had seen one overturn near the ship, quite close by; but there was no other dory there just then, and the doryman did not rise again. Next day, when the *Gazela* was miles from there, that dory returned to her and gently bumped her stem; and in the afternoon, the lost doryman's dinner-pail drifted slowly by.

Many dorymen were drowned that day, from many ships. The dangers of the sudden southerlies were not then fully appreciated. They had been, ever since. Was the infernal weather going to do the same sort of thing again? It might. The only certainty, indeed, was that sooner or later, it would. But when? Captain Silvio knew he had ample power under his sea-booted feet now. Gone were the days of drifting back grass lines. He could have warning of southerlies, too, from captains further to the south than himself. But he needed good warning. Fifty-five dories, each two miles and more from the ship, each with at least a 600-hook long-line down in twenty fathoms of turbulent water, needed time to recover their gear, return to the ship, gaff up their fish into the pounds, and be hoisted aboard. He looked at the narrow platform across the main deck on the fore part of his bridge, where the six nests of dories had to be stacked: he looked and he hated it, for he knew that the curse of the motor-ships was that they could not always recover their dories quickly in a sudden blow.

Away on the southern horizon, he could see the four masts of a big steel schooner and, not so far away, another of the same sort. These were the *Argus* and the *Creoula,* and their captains, the brothers Paião, would be as worried about the weather and their dorymen as he was. He knew that. He had spoken to them both, over his microphone, six times that morning already. Adolfo in the *Argus* was not always strictly accurate in his reports about his fish; but he was a good fisherman, an experienced Greenlands campaigner, and a good weather-guesser. So was his younger brother. They were still fishing and did not think of hoisting the recall just yet. But they could hoist dories inboard all along their low main decks. If necessary, they could sail them inboard, take them over the side as the schooners rolled. Motor-ships were short and stumpy compared with schooners. The schooners were long and lean, to sail well: the motor-ship needed no such provision. So her short main-deck had room only for her pounds and the fish-cleaning gear, and the dories had to be stacked on a false deck above, and wherever they could be fitted round the funnel and the engine-casing.

There was much to be said for the schooner. Captain Silvio knew this well, for he had been in many of them and had been part-owner of his last. He had been years in the old tops'l schooner *Creoula,* forerunner of the graceful four-master which now bore that name, in the swift *Neptuno* and the *Gamo* as well as in the *Gazela.* And the *Maria da Gloria*—ah, the *Maria da Gloria!* He had not been in a schooner since the U-boat had shelled her. He hated to think of it, even now. The *Maria da Gloria* was a lovely three-master, a wooden schooner, graceful and able. His life savings were in her, and he loved that ship. During the 1939–1945 war, she continued to fish on the Grand Banks and in Davis

Straits. One day, out of a clear sky, shells suddenly began to burst round her, coming apparently from nowhere. He had thought at first that he had failed to notice some gray wolf of a warship signaling him to heave-to for the usual wartime identification, a Britisher, or a Canadian, to check that he was no Graf Felix von Luckner, and the *Maria da Gloria* no new *Seeadler,* or lesser *Graf Spee* in disguise. But the horizon disclosed no warship, though the visibility was good.

Then the shells began to burst aboard. Several dorymen were killed. A shell struck the jib-boom, bringing down the foremast. Some nests of dories began to burn. Some of the shells were "anti-personnel," designed to kill his people rather than to damage the ship. She, unfortunately, was already damaged enough, afire and sinking. He gave the order to abandon ship. Nine dories got away with the survivors. Then he saw what was attacking him. A big submarine, which had been shelling from the surface, came closer to finish off the *Maria da Gloria,* and did so. They clearly saw the German submarine which, when it had sunk his schooner, turned its attention to the surviving dories and began to shell them. A shell burst in the middle of the nine dories, and Captain Silvio was among those gravely wounded by its flying fragments. The submarine then went away. Almost immediately, the wind and sea got up, from the southwest. Within an hour it was blowing a gale. The dories were secured together and tried to ride to sea anchors, but some had their gear, and others had not, for they had had to be launched quickly from the nests. Since the schooner was on passage to new grounds at the time they were not all rigged for fishing. The weather and the high sea caused some of the dories to break adrift and these were not seen again. Many men were badly wounded. Some died. Some went mad from their sufferings. They had no food and no water, and the gale blew for four days. During this time Captain Silvio, just sufficiently conscious to keep control, shaped a course toward the coast of Labrador or northern Newfoundland, crossing the tracks of the Greenland-bound schooners which, he hoped against hope, might pick them up. But they saw no schooners.

On the fifth day, only three dories remained. Meanwhile, Captain Silvio's condition was rapidly worsening. His dorymen thought it best to put him in the mate's dory, which was still in company, and so they did. That night, they were lost, and only the mate's dory was left. After nine days, an aircraft on anti-submarine patrol sighted them and dropped canisters of flares and food. Two days later, these flares lighted the American auxiliary *Sea Cloud* to the last dory. There were only six survivors, and it was many months before Captain Silvio could walk. When he could, he went to sea again. Thirty-six men had died with the *Maria da Gloria*.

Captain Silvio did not know it at the time, but it was the misfortune of his schooner that she was across the probable track of the fleeing *Bismarck,* and so she had to go. He did not see the *Bismarck,* and did not even know that the big German had broken out.

He shuddered now as he thought of it, and his scars hurt. They always hurt in Davis Straits. The doctor said it was imagination, but the doctor had not been eleven days adrift in a dory.

Captain Silvio grasped his microphone, threw the switch, and began to call young Captain Leite in the *Gazela,* nearer inshore, and Captain Adolfo in the *Argus.*

"*Elisabeth* calling *Gazela* and *Argus,*" he began, in his strong voice. "*Elisabeth* calling *Gazela* and *Argus. Elisabeth* calling . . ." From the microphone on the bridge, he could see out over the fore-deck where his cousin the mate, Elmano Ramalheira, was superintending the work. There were many Ramalheiras of Ilhavo with the codfishing fleet. Another cousin, Manuel, was in command of the schooner *Infante de Sagres.* Yet another cousin, João Pereira Ramalheira called Vitorino, had the hospitalship *Gil Eanes,* which should soon be arriving. Anibal Ramalheira, brother to Vitorino and Elmano, and Silvio's cousin, was marine superintendent for the Bensaude line ashore at Lisbon, after a long and distinguished career in command of the schooners. It was this Anibal who had first tried out the revolutionary *Argus* and *Creoula* and who, with the dynamic Vasco Bensaude to back him, was largely responsible for many of the innovations which had been made. Radio telephony, for example: only a few years before, the old die-hards of the last generation of Ilhavo Banks masters had been sworn opponents of the very idea. What! Talk about fishing over the free air, for all men to listen? Tell the fleet when you were on fish, and bring the hungry lot of them to spoil the ground? Not likely! They had managed a few hundred years without such new-fangled things as pieces of black plastic called microphones to help them to bridge the gap across the miles of sea. They did not at first realize the life-saving value of the innovation. But the Bensaudes and the Ramalheiras went ahead. They had gone ahead, too, with the long-line, with echo-sounding, with contracts for the supply of refrigerated bait. And they had supported the Gremio in many of the ideas which owners, captains, and dorymen alike opposed, excellent as the ideas later turned out to be.

How long the Ramalheiras have been going to the Banks no man can say with certainty, for there are no early records of Banking crews at Ilhavo. Many a ship hailing from the neighboring port of Aveiro had been manned by mariners and masters from Ilhavo. Ilhavo has almost a monopoly in providing masters for the Banking schooners; and the Ramalheiras have been in the trade as long as any. The men of Ilhavo have always followed the sea. There is little choice for them, indeed, for the arable land has long been parceled out until most inheritances mean nothing. A man cannot hope for land enough to provide his family with a liv-

ing. The arms of the sea running inland from Aveiro,
and the open Atlantic so near, provide a perfect training ground for boys destined for the sea. To this day
craft strongly reminiscent of the slow-moving, lovely
vessels of the ancient Phoenicians move quietly and
with grace through the waters of the estuary, still pro-
pelled by sails. On the Douro, not far away, the wine
boats make their seasonal passages under sail. The sail
is still accepted there as the ideal means of imparting
movement to anything waterborne.

The mariners of Ilhavo sailed many a deepsea
schooner and square-rigged ship, until the day of such
ships was done. Now they sail about their estuary in
their distinctive small craft; in coastal and Mediterranean schooners, in the Grand Banks and Greenland
fleet. The Monicas at Gafanha, their yards in sight of
the Aveiro bar, built lovely schooners, brigantines, and
barquentines for generations. There were others before them. Ilhavo is a town of ships and shipping—almost the last place in Europe where a barquentine
could be manned for a voyage to the Banks or a run to
Rio; where a brig could be fitted out for a treasure
hunt to the Cocos Islands, and sailed there. Sail-makers,
shipwrights of the old school, rope makers, builders of
schooners and of dories, all flourish in the area, their
skills now centered on the Arctic sailing fleet. Not only
the great majority of the schooner captains but also a
large proportion of the trawler masters hail from Ilhavo. The Portuguese merchant service draws many of
its best recruits from this strange old town, whose foun-
dation legend ascribes to the Greeks. Ships, ships, ships,
sailors, sailors, sailors—Ilhavo's history is their history.
In the sixteenth century, Aveiro—which the Ilhavo
mariners considered a suburb of their town—sent more
than sixty ships to the Banks, and had another hundred and fifty in general trade. Aveiro was one of the
pioneer ports in the Newfoundland fishery.

Perhaps some of these things flashed through Captain Silvio's mind as he waited for Captain Leite to

come to the microphone. He had an abiding interest in the maritime history of his country, especially in the history of its Transatlantic fisheries. The fisheries at Gloucester, in Massachusetts, were an offshoot from those of Ilhavo and the Algarve, in the days when Portuguese money was current in much of New England and the Portuguese language was spoken in many places where it is now heard no longer, or only rarely. Those days are gone. Not many Portuguese now cross the North Atlantic to fish from Gloucester, as whole families did in his youth. Young Leite's grandfather was drowned in command of a Gloucester schooner on the Banks: his widow took the children back to Ilhavo and the boys were reared to become Bankers out of there. It might as easily have been Gloucester. Indeed, several of them went back to Gloucester, to fish from there, Leite's father among them, and English was spoken in the Leite home almost as well as their native Portuguese.

Young Captain Leite was typical of the modern Ilhavo Banks masters. Nowadays, instead of beginning as a deckboy and graduating as a doryman, the aspirant to command has a long period of more academic instruction, perhaps more theoretical than practical. But Captain Leite was still a Banks master in the old tradition, though he was not then twenty-five. He could handle the *Gazela* and get good speed out of her, though the only other square-rigged ship he had ever served in was the State's school-ship *Sagres,* a big barque in which he was but one of 300 boys.

"Elisabeth! Elisabeth! Elisabeth! Here is *Gazela!* Good morning, and good fishing, Captain Silvio."* It was the voice of young Captain Leite. He was not much worried about the weather at the moment. His fishing, he said, was bad, very bad (They all said that.) The dorymen were well away, and there was no present sign of any sudden coming of a southerly blow. But Captain Leite was worried about what he considered

his poor catch of fish, and worried, too, about the salting. Were the fish salted sufficiently, or too much? Or perhaps not enough? There was no old-timer in the barquentine's after-guard to whom he could turn for advice. A first voyage in command was a worrying experience. The optimistic note that rang in his pleasant voice across the air in part belied the real anxieties he felt. He was, in fact, worried about the weather. The previous day had been full of mirage. The Greenland coast about the mouth of the Isortok fjord was contorted wildly as if it were trying to curl up and hide, and a great tabular iceberg inshore was miraged until it looked like a five-storied castle, sinister and enormous. He did not like mirage. It was a bad sign. He did not like calm, for that was a bad sign too. What good signs were there for a harassed fishing master in Davis Straits, with thirty-one dorymen's lives in his keeping? And a six-month voyage to make, such as his father, and his grandfather, and his great-grandfather had made before him. There was strength in that thought. What they had done successfully, he could do though ships had grown considerably and difficulties had not lessened with the passage of the years. When the older dorymen first saw the *Gazela* brought into service, rebuilt at Setubal in 1900 after seventeen years as a merchant ship, they were filled with gloom. This had been before Captain Leite's time, but the dorymen still remembered the presages of disaster.

"Too big!" they had said. "Too big, and too high! Dorymen will never fill that ship with fish!" Well, they had been doing it season after season, over the intervening fifty years. José Leite stared round the little white saloon, spotless and neat, with the old-fashioned compass swung in gimbals above the captain's place, *his* place, at table so that it could be viewed from below and the captain never unmindful of the course; and the gracefully proportioned winding companionway which led to the deck. Through this there came more than a slight reminder of the Benz diesel with which the old barquentine had been fitted for the past decade. When her stern had been opened for the shaft, the timbers were as sound and as sweet as the day they were first put there. Four little cabins opened off the saloon, for the mate (aged twenty, and making his first voyage to the Banks and in a sailing-ship), the boatswain—then away in his dory—and the engineer, whose hands were full enough with the Benz, the refrigerator, and a diesel for the windlass.

Through the small skylight, Captain Leite could see the trysail set as a riding sail above the main boom. It was flapping now, for there was no wind. For how long might there be no wind? Captain Silvio had sounded anxious. He did not get anxious easily, though he was always concerned for his men. Captain Leite took his binoculars and hurried on deck. There was still no sign of any real change coming in the weather. All the dory-men he could see were fishing steadily, most of them hauling in their long-lines after the first cast of the day. He noted with regret that they did not seem to be taking many fish. Here and there, already he could see the tell-tale triangles of colored sails breaking on the morning air, speaking of dorymen dissatisfied with the results of their first cast and setting off in quest of better ground. But the dories from the *Argus* were doing well. He could see a couple of them already returning to the four-master, full. Full dories were always for other ships!

Captain Adolfo Simoes Paião, Jr., of the schooner *Argus,* was thinking the same thing. His binoculars showed him four dories making for the schooner *Condestavel* and three more for the motor-ship *Cova da Iria,* while his own most expert men had broken out their sails and were heading not for the *Argus* to gaff up a fill of fish, but for fresh ground. Captain Adolfo knew all his dorymen even at a distance of three miles and more. All dories were alive, but their rigs were not. He could distinguish minor differences in the sails: the way Senhora de Oliveira sewed a mains'l was quite different from that of any of the other Fuzeta wives, and the Azoreans' sails were distinctive enough for anyone. If the sails were not set, Captain Adolfo was still able to distinguish his dories by the men in them—all fifty-three of them. His eyes did not linger on the two dories approaching the ship. One was the Little King's, the other belonged to a doryman almost as noteworthy for his poor catches. They were coming back, doubtless, because they had lost gear—grapnels, lines, hooks, bait. Always lost gear! One of the curses of the long-line fishing was that, when gear was lost, it was a costly loss. When a dory overturned, the financial loss might be considerable even if the doryman survived. In the old days, a doryman had his jiggers and his hand-lines, his personal pail, and the bait of his own catching, and that was all. But he did not go to Greenland then.

Captain Adolfo walked the confines of his short quarterdeck, dodging to avoid the skylights, the standard and the steering compasses, Setter, the bad-tempered water-dog, and Bobby, the yellow mongrel which was forever round his feet, to say nothing of a couple of spare dories and a large salt-bin which the first and second mates were building on the starboard side to house salt from the hold and make room for more fish down there. More fish! More fish was what he wanted, what they all wanted. More fish, more fish, more fish! And here came the Little King, prince of bait-wasters, obviously to moan about lost grapnel and strong tides, and half his long-line lying off Holsteinsborg Bay.

During long years Captain Adolfo had acquired a good stock of patience. He had been in sailing-ships since he was eight years old, for his father had taken him as cabin-boy in the big wooden full-rigged ship *America,* at that age, and he had been a deckboy, not with his father, at nine. A cabin-boy from Ilhavo, with his father or not, had a hard life. Not only did he keep all the cabins in the poop spotlessly clean and tend the meals, but he had to help on deck too, and steer all day when the ship was in the trade winds and his elders at work. The *America* had a small crew. She leaked. She was old, and bits of her tophamper came adrift from time to time. She was in the trade between Oporto and the Gulf of Mexico; they were generally about two months from New Orleans back to Portugal. Before he was nine years old, he could take in a royal by himself in any but really bad weather, and he could patch old sails and splice small wire. Adolfo was one of five brothers who all became shipmasters, most of them in sail; but they scarcely knew one another, except when they were on the Banks together in their schooners. They had begun at sea at different ages, some with their father, others not. Once they went to sea, the separation was complete, though they continued to have homes at Ilhavo, and the Bankers among them were usually able to spend a few months each year there. The oldest brother, Manuel, had gone in the merchant service and had command of a deepsea steamer, and so was rarely home. Another brother had command of a Banks trawler which was at sea ten months of the year. The youngest brother, Julio, had died while in command of the Banks schooner *Cruz de Malta* a year or two before, leaving only Adolfo and his brother Francisco (called Almeida) of the *Creoula,* still with the sailing Bankers. Neither Adolfo nor Francisco had spent a summer at home, or any part of a summer at home for more than thirty years. They saw one another occasionally, at the blessing service, at St. John's and at North Sydney, for a few weeks before Christmas at Ilhavo. For the rest, their converse was by the radio telephone.

Well, that was the sailor's life. The seafaring man from Ilhavo was still a man cut off from shore pursuits, as the traditional seaman had always been but now was trying hard not to be, in so many merchant services. In Ilhavo he accepted the fact. The presence in the little town of so many deepsea shipmasters, officers, and men, and the acceptance by their womenfolk of their lot, was in many ways a source of strength to the Bankers, for they and their womenfolk were always among their own kind. Men had always gone to sea from Ilhavo: no girl really hoped to marry a stay-at-home. If she saw her man for three months of the year she was doing well. Even when they were at home, most of the men tended to keep to each other's company, talking about ships or looking at ships, down at Gafanha. A woman's business was to rear more sailors and properly to sustain those already at sea, though she was no longer expected to send her children away in ships at the age of eight. There were no more full-rigged ships and big wooden barques for them to go in, and the Gremio, among its many activities, kept a watchful eye on juvenile recruitment for the Bankers.

It was a long haul from the ship *America* and the barque *Clara* in the Rio trade to command of the steel schooner *Argus* in Davis Straits, and from the ancient two-masters of the old fishing fleet to the stately and powerful big schooners and motor-ships which came with the renascence of the industry. Captain Adolfo's lifetime spanned both phases, though he was a man only just past fifty. When he was a boy in the deepsea square-riggers, his father and his uncle did not go to the Banks. Banks fishing from Portugal was in a temporary decline and, moreover, the first World War had provided much employment for the mariners of Ilhavo, both under their own flag and that of Brazil. Many of them held licenses as Brazilian master mariners, as well as Portuguese. It was not until 1919 that Captain Adolfo first made a Banks voyage. He was twenty-two years old when he first signed on as mate of the fishing schooner *Vencedor* but he had been at sea continuously for fourteen years. The *Vencedor* did poorly, taking less than one-and-a-half thousand quintals of cod; the life was incredibly hard, and the rewards poor. But the impetus given to the industry by the Government in the early 1930's and its reorganization under the Gremio, made a great difference. The men of Ilhavo flocked back into the Bankers, and they have been there ever since. Captain Adolfo, who in the interval had spent a few years in merchant schooners, was standing by the beautiful new *Hortense* on the stocks at Gafanha by 1930, to go out with her on her maiden voyage as mate. The *Hortense* was then the pride of the Bensaude fleet, and her first master was the famous Anibal Ramalheira. Anibal Ramalheira knew a born seaman and a natural codhunter when he met one: Adolfo Paião was both these things. From the *Hortense* he never looked back. His next ship was the shapely *Gamo*—another of the older Bensaude fleet, now gone—as mate; then the swift *Neptuno* in command. After her, *Hortense* in command, then *Creoula* and finally *Argus*, the commodore's ship. He had not lost a ship and, by the mercy of God, very few dorymen. It had been his good fortune, since joining the Bensaude line, to serve always in vessels of distinction: he had served them well.

But it was a strain on a man, a constant, nagging strain. Six solid months cooped up in a steel schooner—or a wooden one—year after year, tethered by the nose on the shallow, dangerous Banks, always with the lives of half a hundred men in his hands, required to fill the ship: his the decision which committed the dorymen, day after day; his the business of out-guessing the weather, of never being caught by the murderous sudden gusts of wild south wind . . . it *was* a strain. But it was his life. It was a man's life. Though they talked a lot about it, he did not think that many of the masters would change their fishing schooners for a more comfortable berth in the merchant service. Most had tried both. Almost any of them could go in merchant ships if they liked, and come Banking no more.

But year after year, the captains from Ilhavo sailed with the ships, bound out for the Banks. Year after year, anxious day after anxious day, they walked the small poops of their crowded schooners or strode the bridges of their motor-ships, worried about the lives of their dorymen, as he was doing now. His brother Francisco was doing the same thing in the *Creoula;* and so were Silvio Ramalheira in the *Elisabeth,* Armando Ramalheira in the *San Jacinto,* Manuel Ramalheira in the *Infante de Sagres,* and all the rest of them. All from Ilhavo. Men cut off from the land and its pastimes, on the Banks their only interest is cod. To them the world is the Arctic and the Grand Banks fishing grounds, and the very word "fish" means cod. The only ships are fishing ships, the only news of interest concerns these ships and the cod they hunt. Ilhavo is a place far away, from which they set out upon their fishing voyages. They rarely listen to world news for the radio is eternally tuned in to the discourse of their brother captains, and this is invariably of cod—of cod and bait and sudden blows, and dorymen and illnesses aboard and lamentations about the weather and the paucity of cod.

Aye, men cut off. The captains from Ilhavo were severed from the land far more completely than any doryman was. The doryman, year after year, retained his intense interest in his home and family and the things of the shore. To him the campaign was a necessary interlude, for his bread and butter. But for the captains, as the years passed it tended more and more to become their lives, almost their whole lives. A doryman's heart was always ashore, and there was no doubt about that. But a captain's loyalties had to be divided. In the end, in a good many cases, the ship won—the ship, the codfish, and the sea. There were old captains with the fleet who had come back again after retiring, for they found they could no longer live ashore. The doryman went over the side, but the captain, to a great degree, carried the real burden.

And now those two dories came back to the *Argus,* the dory of the Little King and his consort, and to the astonishment of all aboard and not least of the Little King himself, they were full. Not a Laurencinha full, it is true: but full enough. The Little King gaffed up his fish with an air of great superiority, called for more bait and a drink of cold water, and was gone for a second load, while Azoreans with full dories began to approach the ship from all directions and not an Algarvian was in sight.

"Ah, miséria!" Captain Silvio moaned, watching the scene through binoculars. "The *Argus* on fish again, and only a miserable few dories coming back here!"

Captain Adolfo, for the moment, held his peace. So did the south wind, and that was more important than the strange freak of luck which had put the Little King and a few Azoreans for once on fish.

SIR JAMES BISSET

Ex-Commodore of the Cunard Line and former wartime master of both the wonderful *Queens,* Sir James Bisset's status in the maritime profession is unquestioned. Commodore of Cunard is generally recognized as tops, even internationally and the lofty status of this maritime high executive among high executives is approached today by only one other seafarer upon earth, the Commodore-master of the mighty *United States.*

Sir James Bisset, K.B., C.B.E., R.D., R.N.R., LL.D. (Cantab.), Commander of the Legion of Merit, was at sea from the age of fifteen when he shipped away as apprentice in a Limejuice Cape Horning square-rigger, until his sixty-fifth year when he retired from Cunard. Since then, wise man, he has made his home at Sydney, Australia, where he wrote *Sail-Ho!* the story of his early years at sea. Sir James Bisset is not the only Cunard commodore to produce a book, but his is the best.

His first ship was the tough Welsh barque *County of Pembroke* which registered a little over a thousand tons, and *Sail-Ho!* deals mainly with his experiences in her and in another Welshman, the *County of Cardigan*—four circumnavigations, with plenty of the toughest kind of seafaring on all of them. Those Welsh ships were hard, and their masters were sometimes inclined to be none too friendly toward young officers appointed to their ships. Young Bisset was only nineteen when he was appointed second mate of the heavy full-rigger *County of Cardigan.* Here he writes of his welcome.

A Frigid Reception

by SIR JAMES BISSET

A few days later, I called at the Board of Trade office and was handed my certificate on parchment.

With this in hand I wasted no time, and, going to the office of William Thomas & Co., Ltd., I asked for an interview with Mr. Thomas.

The millionaire greeted me cordially and, after a glance at my certificate, said, "Now, Mister Bisset, what age are you?"

"I'll be twenty in less than two months from now, sir!"

"Well," he commented, "that means you're only nineteen now! Do you feel capable of taking on a job as Second Mate of a large sailing-ship?"

My heart stood still for a moment, but on a sound impulse I did not falter as I looked him straight in the eye and said slowly and deliberately, "That was my intention, sir, when I went up for my examination!"

"Yes, yes," he said testily, "but you look so young! Do you think you will be able to control the men and make them obey your orders?"

My pride was nettled. "I served my full time in the *County of Pembroke,* and five months after that in her as an A.B.," I said. "I've been three times round Cape Horn, and I was in that barque when she took a purler over the stern, and when she was dismasted, and when she went over on her beam ends, and—"

"Yes, yes!" he interrupted. "And you were in her on that last voyage when Captain Hughes neglected to pro-

From *Sail-Ho!* by Sir James Bisset.

vision her, which got him and us into so much trouble! Don't tell me what I already know, young man! I don't doubt your ability, especially as you have your ticket as Second Mate. I can see for myself that you are strong and healthy, stockily built, and as hard as nails, eh?"

"Yes, sir," I said firmly, "I'm fit! If you give me a job as Second Mate, I'll see that the men do as I tell them!"

"Good! Good!" said Mr. Thomas. "Do you know our ship, *County of Cardigan,* now in the Salthouse Dock?"

"I've seen her there, and also at Newcastle in New South Wales, and at Callao!"

"Well, Mister Bisset, we'll give you a chance to go as Second Mate in her. She'll be going presently to Fremantle in Western Australia. Captain William Roberts is in command of her, and Mr. John Kinley is her First Mate. I'll give you a note to take down to the Captain. You can start work next week, and help to get her ready for sea."

"What will be my pay, sir?"

"Ah, yes, your pay! Well, as you are only nineteen, Mister Bisset, and this your first appointment, you should be well satisfied with four pounds a month, eh?"

I felt like telling the old skinflint to keep his job, as Second Mates were usually paid five pounds and upward a month, and I realized that he was taking advantage of my youth and inexperience to save expense; but, on the other hand, it was a big chance to go as Second Mate in a full-rigged ship.

"Thank you, sir," I said. "I'll sign on at that."

The millionaire stood up and patted me on the back with a skinny hand, as I too rose and stood with my mind in a whirl. "Indeed to goodness," he said, "and I'm sure you'll do well, Mister Bisset!"

With a note from the manager of the company, Mr. Evans, I went straight down to the Salthouse Dock, entered the gates, rounded the wharf shed, then stood for several minutes carefully examining the *County of Cardigan* and quelling the tumult of my feelings. She lay on the other side of the dock and had been lying there for several weeks, after discharging a cargo of grain from San Francisco. She looked forlorn. Her sides were scarred with rust and the white paint on her masts and yards was grimed by the soot of the city. Aloft, she had been stripped to a gantline, and several fag ends of gaskets and "Irish pennants" were whipping untidily in the breeze.

The *County of Cardigan* was a three-masted full-rigged ship, of 1,323 tons gross (1,245 tons net), built in Liverpool by R. & J. Evans, and launched in 1887. She had a steel hull, steel masts and yards, and planked decks. She was 229 feet long, 37 feet beam, and 22 to 27 feet deep. She was therefore somewhat bigger than the *County of Pembroke* and could carry a cargo of 2,000 tons. Though not one of the most famous flyers of her day, she had made some remarkably smart passages to Australia and around the Horn. Her hull had trim lines, with a clipper bow and a low monkey poop, but to my eyes she seemed heavily sparred and clumsy aloft. This extra strength in the masts would enable her to carry a press of sail which might have dismasted a more lightly sparred vessel; but I could see at a glance that she would be a heavy ship to work.

She had five yards crossed on each of her three masts. The yards of the "courses"—the foresail, mainsail and "Cro'jick" or mizzen sail—were fully sixty feet long and projected well out over the sides. They were of hollow steel, ten inches thick in the middle, and tapering to seven inches at the yardarms. The lower and upper topsail yards were also of steel, slightly shorter and smaller than the yards of the courses, but heavy as compared with those in other ships of similar tonnage. The courses and topsails were crossed on the steel masts below the usual height, giving her a squat but very sturdy appearance aloft. Above the topmasts were wooden masts for the topgallant sails and royals, with wooden yards crossed on them. The truck of the mainmast was one hundred and twenty feet above the deck, and the cap of the topmast ninety feet.

The running rigging, to control fifteen square sails (as compared with ten square sails in a three-masted barque) was necessarily more complicated than I had been accustomed to in the *County of Pembroke,* but I knew that I would soon become familiar with it. Walking around the end of the dock, I had a nearer view and was disgusted at the dirty condition she had been allowed to fall into. The only sign of life was a sailmaker seated in the waist, sewing a staysail. I mounted the rickety gangway and jumped down on to her main deck. She had not been washed down for weeks. The remains of her grain cargo were strewn, damp and moldy, around the hatches. I made a mental note that there would be much hard work to be done to get her ready for sea.

"Is the Captain aboard?" I asked the sailmaker.

He glanced at me and said, "He's in his cabin under the poop, if you know where that is."

"Look here, Sails," I said. "I'm to be Second Mate in this ship!"

Leaving him to ponder on that remark, I sprang up to the poop and called down the companionway to the cabin, "Is Captain Roberts there?"

A voice growled, "What do you want?" and a thin, wiry, tall, tough-looking man, thirty years of age, emerged from the cabin. I sensed correctly that he was the First Mate, John Kinley. He was from the Isle of Man.

"To see the Captain," I said. "I have a letter for him, from Mr. Evans, of the owner's office."

"Come below," a gruff voice boomed from inside the saloon. I entered. Captain William Roberts, a Welshman, middle-aged, of burly build, with a leathery, wrinkled countenance and steely gray eyes, was seated at his table. He took the letter from me, opened it, read it in grim silence, looked at me with undisguised hostility, then handed the letter to the Mate, saying, "Shiver my timbers! Read that, Mister Mate!"

The Mate did so, then remarked, as though I were not there, "He looks rather young!"

"Young?" the Captain growled. "He looks like a boy, just out of his time!" Then he turned to me, and asked, "Ever been Second Mate before?"

I recited my history, in brief. It didn't please either of them. Ignoring my presence again, the Captain said complainingly to the Mate, "I asked the owners particularly to send me an experienced officer because this ship is a heavy ship to work, and they send me a beardless youth!"

"Yes," the Mate agreed. "I should advise him to get a job in a smaller ship for a voyage or two, until he grows up and gains experience."

They both looked at me hopefully, expecting that I would back out; but I stood my ground and had the sense not to argue with them. I remained silent and listened while they discussed me for a few minutes more, in total disregard of my feelings. I was duly qualified and appointed to this ship, so why shouldn't I have the job? The thought of tramping the docks looking for a chance in a small ship did not appeal to me.

At last the Captain said, "I suppose we'll have to put up with him!" Then he turned to me and said, "Very well, Mister, start on Monday morning, and we'll soon see what you're made of. The riggers are coming then to bend sail, and we'll be taking in the cargo, too. Show the Second Mate his cabin, Mister Mate!"

The Mate led me to a cabin next to his, on the port side under the poop. It was a small compartment, with two bunks, one above the other. "That's yours," said the Mate, bitterly. "All on your own! I hope you're not frightened of work, for there's a hell of a lot to be done to get this grimy old hooker ready for sea. You'll have the four apprentices to clean her up, take in stores, and bend the staysails and jibs. I'll be busy keeping an eye on the riggers and stowing the cargo."

"I can handle the job, Mister Mate," I assured him.

"Time will tell," he grunted.

Going ashore, feeling very discouraged by the hostile reception I had suffered, I had vague thoughts of growing a beard and mustache to hide my youthful appearance; but there would not be time to do that before Monday morning. However, I went and bought a peaked badge cap, of rakish design, with a patent-leather strap over the top, and wore it well on the side of my head, in the approved fashion of smart young second mates of that period.

With my confidence thus enhanced, I was ready to begin work, come what may.

Sailing day was on Monday, 2nd June. I now learned that we were to be towed to Glasgow, with a crew of runners, to load more cargo there. On Sunday evening, after a last meal at home, I bade farewell to my family and went on board at 9 p.m. stowing my sea chest and sea bag in my cabin. During the evening the apprentices, a cook, a carpenter, and four Welsh seamen moved into their quarters—quietly, since the pubs were closed. The Welsh seamen came from the same village as the Captain, and he could rely on them as personal acquaintances. We were to sign on another eight seamen at Glasgow.

Soon after dawn, all hands were roused out, and the stout tug *Jane Joliffe* came nosing to the river lock gate, ready to tow us from the Mersey to the Clyde, a distance of 200 miles. In these narrow and fairly sheltered waters there was little chance of breaking adrift from the tug and having to make sail to avoid running ashore, but the law required a sailing vessel to carry a full crew, in case of emergencies, when in tow.

The runners came on board, eight old shellbacks who had signed on at a contract price of one pound each, to work the ship to Glasgow. Their contract required them to do no work except that involved in handling the ship. As soon as we were safely through the river lock gates and towing downstream, they divided themselves into watches and stood by, smoking their pipes. This sight infuriated the Mate, but there was nothing he could do about it, as the men were within their rights.

The Mate and I picked watches—two Welshmen, two apprentices, and four runners each. In the circumstances, as there was no handling of sail, my first experience of watch-keeping consisted of walking up and down the poop and keeping an eye on the helmsman to see that he followed closely in the tug's wake.

The Captain and the Mate maintained an attitude of resentment to me and had no word of encouragement, even though they had not been able to find fault with my part of the work of getting the ship ready for sea. It was estimated that the tow to Glasgow would take two days.

On the first morning out, I was on watch from four to eight. At 6:30 a.m. a fog set in and thickened. It was unseasonable in the summer weather, but anything can happen in the Irish Sea and the North Channel. I called the Captain. He came on deck in a vile temper, looked around and growled at me, "You must be the Jonah in this ship!"

Thinking that the remark was intended to be a joke, I replied flippantly, "Jonah came out all right!"

The Captain's face darkened with rage as he snarled, "Keep a good lookout there. If there's any more backchat from you, I'll log you for insolence, and put you ashore at Glasgow as unsuitable!"

This taught me my first useful lesson as an officer: never adopt a familiar attitude with the Captain. I have never forgotten it. He held all the high cards in the game. Without a good reference from him at the end of the voyage, I would not be able to sit for my First Mate's examination. If he chose to treat me as a boy rather than an officer, I would have to knuckle under. Perhaps he thought he was giving me good training. I will admit that his methods taught me to control my feelings.

FELIX RIESENBERG

Felix Riesenberg (1879–1939) had a remarkable career. Born in Wisconsin far from the sea, he became a sailing-ship sailor in a big Down-Easter named the *A. J. Fuller* and in the New York state sailing-school-ship, a Polar explorer with the Wellman expedition, navigator of a North-Pole-bound airship as far back as 1907, and a shore-side civil engineer with a considerable practice in New York for something like thirty years. He was also a prolific and able writer of books to do with the sea, none better (in my opinion) than his *Under Sail*. This is the story of his voyage in the *A. J. Fuller*, made when Yankee sailing-ships were still an important and colorful part of the world's merchant service. Riesenberg was in time to catch the last of them, before their decline in the face of Europe's effective steam competition, and it was his ambition that they should not be allowed to disappear wholly unchronicled.

I knew Felix Riesenberg fairly well, as one gets to know people around a sprawling seaport like New York. I met him first when he was, with Christopher Morley, one of the organizers of the Three Hours for Lunch Club, aboard the old full-rigged ship *Inverglas* which was then bought to the American flag, renamed *Tusitala* for Robert Louis Stevenson, and used as clubhouse by as convivial and talented a group of seafaring writers and their friends as one could hope to meet. The *Tusitala*, as a club, failed to outlive the depression, and was put to the Hawaiian trade by Mr. Farrell, under sail again. I met Riesenberg frequently at places such as the South Street Seamen's Mission, on 25 South (where he was interested in the Conrad Library) and the New York Athletic Club. Here other stalwarts from the days of sail in general and the New York state sailing-school-ships *St. Mary's* and *Newport* in particular, used to get to-gether for a yarn. Riesenberg was a quiet chap with reflec-tive blue eyes, and a way of sitting back and summing things up as if he were figuring the probable next move of some Cape Horn gale. He was back aboard the *A. J. Ful-ler* with a meal of salt horse and hard tack, though we might be sitting in a splendid restaurant overlooking Cen-tral Park, with plates piled high with the best of excellent food before us. Instead of a run aloft to shake the reefs out in the tops'ls, all we had to do afterward was to ascend swiftly by some ingenious and rapid elevator to the so-larium, to stretch out in indolent and well-filled satisfac-tion—at least for a while.

The *Fuller* was a three-skys'l yarder with a crew of eight-een men, a boy, and two officers when Riesenberg was in her, and the good Yankee seamen who worked their guts out aboard were paid eighteen dollars a month. The rate of pay of the chief mate was sixty dollars a month, and "to earn his two dollars a day," writes Riesenberg, "he had to be a seaman of the highest attainments. His was a knowl-edge won only after a hard and long apprenticeship at sea. He had to have the force of character of a top executive, combined with ability and initiative. . . . In addition to this he might be as rough and as foul-mouthed as he saw fit, and some of them were very liberal in this respect."

It was a tough school, and it bred tough men.

Christmas Day on the High Seas

by FELIX RIESENBERG

Life was not always so pleasant on board the *Fuller*. Hard words were the common run of things and the most frightful and artistic profanity often punctuated the working of the ship. Given a ship's company barely strong enough to handle a two thousand five hundred ton three-skysail yarder, even had they all been seasoned able seamen, our officers had to contend with a crew over half of which rated below that of the "ordinary" classification of seamanship, thick skinned clodhoppers, all thumbs on a dark night, and for many weeks after leaving port, as useless as so much living ballast. The kicking and molding into form of this conglomerate mass of deepsea flotsam, gathered for the ship by the boarding masters, and duly signed on the ship's articles as A.B., called for all but superhuman efforts. The curse is far more potent than the gentle plea, especially when hard fists and hobnailed sea boots are backed by all of the age-old authority of the sea. To work a ship of the proportions of the *Fuller*, with seventeen hands forward, called for man driving without thought of anything but the work required.

The latter days of the sailing ship as a carrier, before invoking the aid of steam auxiliary apparatus, in the hoisting and hauling, brought forth the brute sea officer aft, and the hardened fo'c'sle crowd, half sailor and half drudge, forward. The "bucko mate" walked her decks, and the jack tar, stripped of his pigtail, his bell

From *Under Sail* by Felix Riesenberg

mouthed canvas trousers, his varnished sailor hat, and
his grog, remained in plain dungaree and cotton shirt
to work the biggest sailing craft in the history of the
world on the last hard stages of their storm tossed
voyages.

Mixed with our real sailors were the worthless (so
far as sea lore went) scrapings of the waterfront.
Shipped by the boarding masters for the benefit of
their three months' "advance," and furnished for sea
with rotten kits of dunnage, as unreliable and unfitted
for the work as the poor unfortunate dubs who were
forced by an unkind fate to wear them.

On the other hand, the real sailor men of the crew
were valued accordingly, and I can hardly remember
an instance where either one of the mates singled out
for abuse those men who had shipped as A.B. and were
so in fact. My schoolship training (*St. Mary's* '97) stood
by me, and though barely turned eighteen, I was saved
from most of the drudgery meted out to the farmers
of the watch.

After washing through the heavy seas we encountered for the first few weeks of the voyage, while beating off the coast on the long reach eastward to the
Azores, the long hard pine sweep of the main deck became slippery with a deposit of white salt-water slime.
The sheen of this scum, in the moonlight, under a
film of running water, gave the decks a ghastly "Flying
Dutchman" like appearance, and the footing became
so precarious that something had to be done.

"They have the 'bear' out," Scouse announced, as
he trudged into the fo'c'sle carrying a "kid" of cracker
hash, ditto of burgoo, a can of coffee, and a bag of hard
tack, this cargo of sustenance being our regulation
breakfast menu.

"The bear?" I asked, as we gathered about this appe-
tizing spread.

"Yes, the bear," volunteered Brenden, grinning with
the rest of the sailors. "The bear for Scouse, and Joe,
and Martin, and Fred."

At eight bells, as we mustered aft, a subdued banter went on among the men. The starboard watch were all grinning, and as they went below four sheepish looking fellows of the other side turned the "bear" over to the farmers of our watch. "Keep that jackass baby carriage moving now. D'ye hear me? Keep it moving!" bellowed the mate, for there was some reluctance in taking hold, and as Scouse and Martin tailed on, opposed to Joe and Fred, the doleful scrape of the bear mingled with the general laughter at the mate's sally.

The bear consisted of a heavy box, a thick thrum mat lashed on the bottom of it, and the inside loaded with broken holystones and charged with wet sand. Four stout rope lanyards were rigged to the corners and served to haul the thing back and forth while the sand filtered down through the mat, providing the necessary scouring agent. A day or two with the bear in constant service, both day and night, cleaned up the decks and provided us with considerable amusement, that is, those of us who were lucky enough to be kept at more dignified jobs.

Ships leaving the Atlantic Coast in the winter months bend their best suit of sails. The severe weather usually encountered in working clear of the land, and the chance of having to ratch off from a lee shore, make this precaution one of great importance. The fact that green crews are bound to be more or less slow in taking in sail during squalls may also account for the "storm suit" under which we sailed from port.

On our first night out, shortly before one bell in the mid watch, our crowd having just gone below, the fore topmast stays'l blew from the bolt ropes with the report of a cannon. We had already clambered into our bunks, dog tired, when this occurred, and muttered oaths, anticipating a call of "all hands," came from untold depths of weariness within the fo'c'sle. On deck there was the hurried tramping of feet, and the shouting of the second mate. We could hear the long wail of the men at brace and downhaul, the "Ah-hee-Oh-hee-ah-Ho!" with all of its variation as the slaves of the ropes launched their age-old complaint on the whipping winds. I lapsed into slumber with the dim consciousness that the second mate was handling the situation alone, and a heartfelt thanks for the warmth of the blankets in my narrow bunk; a foot above me the cold rain pattered against the roof of the fo'c'sle house, its music mingling with the swish of the water under the fore channels.

After three weeks of beating to the eastward, having fetched almost as far across as the Azores, and being in the region of the northern limit of the N. E. trades, the captain hauled his wind and squared away for the run through the trade wind belt to the doldrums and the line. Fine weather became the order of the day and life on board settled down to a more regular routine.

On a Saturday morning, the day having broken remarkably fine, a brilliant red sunset followed by a cold gray dawn, assuring us of the settled weather that the steady "glass" made more certain, all the world seemed ready to rejoice, for it was Christmas Day. Word was passed into the fo'c'sle by the other watch, as we turned out for our breakfast, "We shift sail today."

"All hands on deck for us, me boys!" piped Australia. "An' the first watch on deck tonight," chipped in Jimmy Marshall, "an' a hell of a Christmas Day!"

Jimmy lit his pipe for a morning puff; climbing into his bunk, he dangled his short legs over the frowsy head of big Scouse who sat with his dejected poll bent under the upper bunk board, a fair sample of the despondent crowd of farmers who faced a Christmas Day of labor.

> "A hell of a Christmas Day, boys,
>   A hell of a Christmas Day,
>   For we are bound for the bloody Horn
>   Ten thousand miles away."

Jimmy rendered this little ditty of cheerfulness as Fred picked up the breakfast kids and started for the galley, while we turned out on the sun-splashed planks as the last of eight bells vibrated over the ship. She lay still in a near calm like a scene by Turner, all of her canvas hanging in picturesque festoons from the jackstays, where the starboard watch had cast off the courses and tops'ls, leaving them depending in their gear. The decks had not been washed down, in order to keep them dry, and the mate himself had turned out at four bells to start the ball rolling.

Long bundles of the fine weather canvas were stretched on the decks ready for swaying aloft. Working like demons in the forenoon, and with all hands on deck after dinner, which was dispatched in haste, we had the courses, and in turn the tops'ls and light sails, lowered to the deck, and the gantlines rigged to hoist the summer canvas; this we sent aloft in record time. These old sails, soft and mellow, veterans of a dozen voyages, patched and repatched, with whole new cloths of a lighter grade here and there streaking the dull white-weathered surface, were as smooth and pliable as a baby's bonnet.

On some of them, the fore upper tops'l especially, we found records of the many crews who had handled them before. "James Brine, Liverpool. On his last voyage," was one inscription. I hope Brine achieved his end and stayed ashore. A date under this was hardly decipherable but may have been Jan., June, or July, the day the eighth, and the year 1893.

Bending a sail calls for the nicest knowledge; the passing of the head earing must be done in a certain manner, so the head of the sail will hold well up on the yard arm; the gear, consisting of tacks, sheets, clew garnets, and buntlines, in the case of a "course," not to mention the leechlines, and bowlines, must all be rove and rigged just so. The "robands" or pieces of rope yarn, are all looped through the "head holes" ready for bending the sail to the iron jackstay on the yard, and when a sailor does the job, all goes as smooth as a wedding when the parson knows his job.

After the labors of a busy day, the ship presented the comfortable well-patched appearance of a man in the woods, free from the stiffness of new white linen, and naturally fitting into the familiar folds of old duds, unconventional but plenty good enough. The bright spars still attested to her "smartness," but we were in easy trade wind weather and dressed accordingly. The fores'l was particularly large, with extra clothes in the leeches, made to catch and hold every breath of wind blowing over the deck.

The sail locker was re-stowed with our "best suit," and between the coils of canvas we liberally spread a bundle of old newspapers brought out by the mate. "To give the rats something to chew on," he remarked, as we ran the stiff new canvas in, tier upon tier.

One thing that Frenchy called my attention to in the stowing of the locker was the fact that the storm canvas, lower tops'ls and stays'ls, were placed handy for immediate removal, the mate assuring himself of this fact by personal supervision; indeed he knew just where each particular sail was located in the locker, and could go in and lay his hand upon it in the darkest night, as he more than once demonstrated during the course of the voyage.

That night a tired lot of men sat down to supper. The cold salt beef, the hard bread and the can of tea came from the galley in their usual order. Fred, who was mess cook for that week, went back to the galley, after depositing the regulation Saturday night grub. As he left the fo'c'sle door he turned back at us with a grin on his wide good natured face, bristling with uneven outcroppings of yellow stubble. Fred reminded me of an amiable plodder hulking out in his dungaree jacket, while the watch fell to on the beef and tack.

"I guess he forgot to thank the cook for putting so many bugs in the tea," ventured Brenden.

"Maybe he's going aft to take Christmas Dinner

with the captain in the cabin. They have a real plum pudding there; I saw it in the galley," said Joe.

Plum pudding! Christmas! The thoughts of loved ones far away, and of those distant homes that perhaps were remembering some of us out on the broad bosom of the deep waters, came as a pang. All of us, I believe, felt this. For a moment or two silence ensued, then Fred burst through the fo'c'sle door with the big surprise.

"Pie, boys! Pie!" he shouted, depositing three tin plates on the fo'c'sle deck, for we dined with the deck as a table, sitting about the kids on low benches. The precious pie was cut with the greatest regard for equality by no less an expert hand than that of Frenchy, assisted by Australia, who showed us how to cut a pie into three parts by measuring across the diameter with a knife, adding a little to this, and then this length went three times into the circumference.

Jimmy Marshall failed to agree with this theory, but was fairly beaten in the result, for Australia was right. The pie certainly was cut into three very equal parts.

"An engineer in the mines showed me this," said Australia. "He says, 'Pie times across the pie, is all the way around.' Mathematics is wot he calls this." Australia was nearly right at that, and the marks he made on the crust of the confections baked by Chow served as a reliable guide for Frenchy, also bolstering him immensely in the eyes of the more humble members of the port watch. That Australia chap certainly knew a thing or two, even if he was not the best sailor in the world.

But Jimmy Marshall's comment was simply, "Rats!"

After supper, when pipes were glowing, and most of us sought our bunks for the hour or so that remained to us in the last dog watch, a discussion arose as to what kind of pie it was. Frenchy, the great gastronomic authority, claimed it was English currant pie. "They taste so bitter, that's why I know," he added with an air of finality.

Others differed with him. Scouse said it was red crabapple pie. Martin claimed it was nothing but plum pie. I thought it tasted like cranberry, but was not sure. At last, to settle the matter, and at the earnest request of the crabbed Jimmy, Fred trudged aft to the galley to consult Chow and wind up the argument. He returned in triumph with a large tin can done up in a gaudy red label marked "Pie Fruit."

CAPTAIN JAN de HARTOG

Captain Jan de Hartog is a Hollander who began life as fisherman and sailor, and continued at sea to become shipmaster. He knows what he is writing about in both wide fields. The following little gem is taken from his most readable collection of self-contained sea essays, *A Sailor's Life,* which he says that he began as a sort of Young Sailor's Companion. It is an excellent and most pithy piece of work, of value to sailors and landsmen alike.

Skipper Next to God

by CAPTAIN JAN de HARTOG

So now you are a captain, and you are terrified. Anyone who says he isn't is either a bad captain, or like everybody else.

For years this has been your goal. You couldn't wait for it to materialize; at every opportunity you have made it discreetly known to the company that your appointment was overdue. And now you sit in the double cabin, as lonely as sin, wishing you had never gone to sea.

Even before the ship moves, the loneliness begins.

From *A Sailor's Life* by Jan de Hartog

You haven't given a single order yet, and here you are: this is the end of the messroom days, of the watches, the outings, and, most sorely missed of all, the wonderful stimulant of cursing the captain. You suddenly realize that you are the most common brand of sailor: a born mate. Your wife's delight will depress and irritate you; your colleagues, who are colleagues no longer but subordinates, have vanished behind an invisible barrier of politeness. Well: you have asked for it; here it comes.

Your first voyage starts, and instantly everybody comes to see you about something. You had never realized that when you went to see the Old Man about something in the past, you were a member of an endless procession; now, at last, you understand why he received you occasionally with a marked lack of enthusiasm. The nature of the errands will severely tax you in the beginning, and you may be tempted to drink more than is good for you. For nobody comes to ask your advice; they come for final decisions ranging from "Shall I take those stewed pears or shan't I, Captain?" to "Must I take Williams off watch because of the boil on his neck or mustn't I?" You will feel like asking both inquirers what their own opinion in the matter is, as they know more about the stewed pears and Williams' boil than you do. But the first rule to observe is: don't ever revert the responsibility to those who come in asking to be relieved of it. It doesn't matter whether the stewed pears are taken, or whether Williams can act as a look-out with a boil on his neck. The first question should be answered "No," and the second, "Yes," for it is a good practice to give those questions serial numbers and answer "Yes" to the even ones and "No" to the odd ones. By the time they get to you, their pros and cons have been weighed in the inquirer's mind to such an extent that he can no longer decide on merit; he wants someone to choose for him from two equally valid decisions. You should never betray your ignorance about either the pears or the boil, even if you feel like an impostor. In due course, you will know about those things somehow; it is only a matter of time. And it is the captain's business to wait for his own maturity as a master, not his crew's.

To help you to give orders or to lay down the law in disputed questions, there is another rule: when you arrive at a decision, stick to it. There is nothing more unnerving than a captain who has said "No," coming back five minutes later to say, "By the way, I've thought it over and I think you are right." Even if the other person were right, it should be a lesson to you, and not to him.

In good time, you will settle down, and your life will start. For this is certain: there is no fuller existence for a man than to be the captain of a ship, as soon as he has found his self-confidence. As for this self-confidence, the important thing to remember is that it will never be yours entirely. The sea is the sea, the ship is a ship, and they will never be at peace. You will find your feet quickest if you immediately start by impersonating the favorite captain of your memory. If he happened to be calm and placid, be calm and placid too, even if the sweat prickles under your hatband. If he was wiry and nervy, be wiry and nervy. For, in both cases, you will have admired him because he complemented a lack of those characteristics in yourself.

This above all: remember that the way to be a good captain is not decided between you and the crew, nor you and the ship, but between you and your empty desk.

KENNETH HARDMAN

In these days, one often wonders just what are the attractions of a seafaring career. All the sailing-ships have gone, except for some school-ships and the Portuguese Grand Banks dory-fishing schooners, and both these are somewhat specialized fields. For my own part, I would not have gone to sea if there had not been a square-rigger to go in, and a deepwaterman at that. I often get pathetic letters from youth today imploring me to tell them where they may find such a ship. Kenneth Hardman, who wrote this little piece for the annual essay competition run by the British Seafarers' Education Service—and won a prize with it too—knows his stuff. He is a working seaman, and was able-seaman in a motor-ship called the *Diplomat* when he produced this answer.

The Advantages of Seafaring

by KENNETH HARDMAN

To be brutally frank, the average modern seaman does not go to sea because he likes the feel of the "blown spume against his face"; nor does he, Masefield-like, revel in the ever-changing moods of the elements on which he sails. I doubt if anyone, a comparative handful of dedicated poets and storm-lovers apart, has ever

liked being on the sea (as distinct from being on dry
land looking at the sea) in its more violent moods.
The indefinable "call of the sea" can and does draw
hundreds of lads a year to the training establishments
and, ultimately, to the sea—but it cannot hold them
there after the first romance and adventure of the
thing have worn a trifle thin. Many of them retire, dis-
illusioned, after a few years; others, in this age of
conscription, stay on until they are no longer liable
for military service, and then slide back into a shore
job as gracefully as possible. To the not inconsiderable
remainder, the manifold advantages of a seafaring life
become more and more apparent as the years go by,
until they reach the stage where they begin to wonder
how the devil people manage to live permanently
ashore at all.

The realization is gradual and made up of small
things. At home, on leave, you notice how so-and-so,
who used to sit next to you at school, has aged so obviously that he might almost be taken for your uncle.
An isolated case, you think. Then other school-mates
and contemporaries pop up, and you see the beginnings of a sedentary paunch here and a factory or ma-
chine-shop pallor there. All this is, of course, pure personal vanity; but it is a vanity that everyone possesses
in some degree. No one likes to appear to grow old—
and it is my steadfast opinion that, as a general rule,
seamen retain their youth, both physically and mentally, far longer than their shore-bound contemporaries. I don't really know why; perhaps there's something in this "sea-air" stuff after all.

Another aspect of the personal vanity view, which
might be neither readily admitted nor discussed but
which is nevertheless still there, is this: the very fact
that one is a seaman leads others to recognize that one
is a "man of the world," a man who has been places
and seen things. An adroitly handled phrase, like
"When I passed through the Panama a month ago,"
can reduce a non-seagoing gathering to something like

awe. A man who can speak of a city at the other end of the world with the easy familiarity with which his friends speak of the neighboring town is definitely not a person to argue with about world affairs.

But these are somewhat nebulous things. The down to earth advantages of a professional sailor's lot are, to a professional sailor, so numerous that it is difficult to know where to begin.

I suppose that, in this mercenary world, the question of money must take first place. Here a seafarer has a unique advantage over a shore wage-earner in that he is practically forced to save a substantial part of his earnings—simply because there is little or no opportunity to spend money at sea. For perhaps nine months of the year, there are none of the expensive diversions of life ashore to worry him. Nor is this too much of a hardship for everyone aboard is, literally and metaphorically, in the same boat. Whilst the landsman decides to stop off at the local for a few beers, or to take the girl friend to a show, the sailor in the middle of the Atlantic blithely and inexpensively plays cribbage, smokes his duty-free cigarettes, yarns with his mates, and turns in.

There are, of course, the "subs." or advances on wages, drawn in foreign parts, but these are seldom very large; and the Old Man usually sees to it that there are not too many of them. The result is quite a substantial pay-off in the home port. Jack, when he does eventually get ashore at home, can usually afford to live at the rate of several thousands a year for the length of his leave—in fact, the rate at which some seamen spend money would probably make many a millionaire blench. There is nothing quite like the good spirits and downright jubilation—known somewhat cynically as the "Channels"—of a homeward-bound crew, with the hard-earned pay-off looming large on the horizon. Whatever trials and tribulations the trip has had to offer, you suddenly feel that it was worth it after all.

The old criticism of life at sea—poor and even bad conditions—is, in the main, no longer valid. Admittedly there are still a few of the older ships where the living accommodation leaves much to be desired, but these can't last much longer, nor will they be the subject of sentimental tears when they do finally end up at the breakers. Almost all the new ships being built now have excellent quarters for every member of the crew. Food and victualing, whilst varying greatly from ship to ship and from company to company, is on the whole pretty fair. It is to be hoped that the days of skimping and saving on ships' catering bills are on the way out.

Many years ago a certain celebrated lady politician is said to have made the statement that seamen should not require payment for their work. The joys of travel, she maintained, should be sufficient in themselves. After all, her friends paid hundreds of pounds in passage money to go to exactly those places to which the seaman went free. There was an obvious flaw in her logic; but, nevertheless, the so-called "wanderlust" has always been a powerful trait in most men. Even the most entrenched bank-clerk or civil servant must at times dream of visiting "far-away places with strange sounding names," as a recent popular song puts it. Whilst there are few romantic illusions left for the seasoned sailor—he soon discovers that places and people are much the same the world over—the old thrill of new horizons does not completely desert him. Though he may suspect that Zanzibar will turn out to be the usual conglomeration of flies, heat and stenches, he still watches it grow out of the Indian Ocean with interest. There is always the sense of "going places" about a ship and the very thought of exchanging it for an immovable office or factory is enough to send a shudder through the nautical frame.

How well married life mixes with a life at sea is always a debatable subject. So much depends on the individuals concerned that no hard and fast rule can possibly be laid down. Many men leave the sea when they marry: some through wifely pressure, others because of a natural inclination to be with their wives as much as possible. But many also stay at sea, and are apparently quite happy about it. I read an article in an illustrated magazine recently: the magazine had conducted a survey amongst wives in three classes, or income groups, to discover what job or profession was most conducive to a happy married life in each group. It was the usual hackneyed kind of thing, but the unusual point about it was that, in two of the classes, seamen romped home hands down. The wives concerned gave their reasons—and quite substantial ones they were, too. One said that every time her husband came home it was like a second honeymoon. Another maintained that in nautical marriages there was never time for the couple to get tired of each other: they always tried to look their best and be on their best behavior to each other during the husband's leaves, all of which it would be well-nigh impossible to keep up indefinitely. All things considered, I believe a seaman can have a happy married life, provided that he confines himself to comparatively short trips. Even the most amenable of wives would be likely to balk at trips lasting two years or more.

Since time immemorial, the sea has been regarded as a molder of character. Family black sheep, erring sons, and just plain ruffians, were pushed off to sea as a last resort, the theory apparently being that the sea was an almighty leveler of men, and that they would return home chastened, wiser and better beings. Nowadays the practice is not as popular as it was, but the fact remains that a few years at sea can do wonders for a lad if he has half a mind to avail himself of the unique advantages it offers in the way of self-education. I don't mean education in the scholastic sense— although that is easy enough to come by, too—but in the wider sense of the word: a breadth of mind that comes only with meeting and mingling with people of many races, understanding to the best of your ability their ways of life and viewpoints; and, above all, learning to tolerate that which you cannot agree with nor understand. I have sailed in the fo'c'sles of ships with learned men who never saw the inside of more than a primary school, but they could leave the majority of university graduates standing in their grasp of life and its implications.

So rests the case for the sea. Doubtless just as many arguments could be made out against the sea as a livelihood. I could find a few myself. It is, as all things are, a matter of personal taste; either you like it or you don't. For myself, I can make no stronger statement than this: if I had a son and he showed the slightest inclination toward a nautical life, he would go away to sea with my blessing.

HUGH POPHAM

Though he has been a lot in trawlers (he writes well of trawlermen and their hard seafaring) and once helped to get a New Zealand-bound motor fishing vessel as far as Jamaica, where the promoter of the venture ran out of cash as promoters sometimes do, Hugh Popham's professional seafaring began in the air. He was a wartime fighter pilot in the Fleet Air Arm of the Royal Navy. That is a pretty tough way to begin anything. I hand it to him that, with such a beginning, he continued to follow the sea afterward whenever he could.

In the second World War, I saw a little of these Fleet Air Arm types. Through some error somewhere I found myself once briefly in an aircraft carrier, a huge, ghastly-looking stack of a thing that had been built up on the lithe hull of a giant cruiser. *Furious* she was called, and perhaps she was furious at having been so horribly converted. She was a good ship with a grand group of fellows. Among these was "Butch" Judd, the first fighter pilot to be given a real airplane in the Fleet Air Arm, some of whose ships in th early days of the war were almost incredibly bad. Judd a brave man and a fine one. He lost his life, still f fighters, down in the Med. . . .

Here Hugh Popham writes of the moment tha staggered me when contemplating these youthful f and their skill in the air—the first deck-landing. kind of seafaring; but it belongs. The lad wl generations might have discovered his outl Horn barque's royal yard, now rides a figl the sky, and lands on carriers.

First Deck Landing

by HUGH POPHAM

Macrihanish is the Crewe Junction of the Fleet Air
Arm, the uniquely desolate station you arrive at in
the early hours of the morning, wait about at, and
finally depart from, none the wiser. I suppose Crewe
has an existence apart from the midnight fantasies of
passing travelers, a solid existence of Rotary Clubs and
Chambers of Commerce and City Fathers, just as Macrihanish has a championship golf-course and all the
long sea-coast of the Firth of Clyde; but not for me.
Supremely it is the place of departure, from which
one flies to deck-land within the shadow of Ailsa Craig;
an uneasy, queasy staging-point, a bowl in the hills of
the filthiest weather in the British Isles.

At Macrihanish the remainder of the squadron was
waiting, having flown ashore from *Furious,* and Crooky
and I met the C.O. for the first time. It was a meeting
we had anticipated with some foreboding. "Wait till
you meet the C.O.," Steve had said on more than one
occasion, and with an unpleasant relish. "You won't
get away with that with the Butcher."

"The Butcher," known familiarly as Butch—in reality, Lieutenant Commander F. E. C. Judd, R.N.—was
certainly unsettling in appearance. He was tall, perhaps six foot two, and wore a reddish beard and mustache. They require separate mention, for while his
beard was trimmed somewhat after the fashion of the
late King George V's, his mustaches were allowed to

from *Sea Flight* by Hugh Popham.

run wild. They sprang out horizontally from his upper lip, stiff, plentiful and coarse, like a couple of tarred rope's ends in need of whipping. He was forever handling them; thrusting them up away from his mouth in a pensive way when he was in good humor; grabbing and tugging at them when, as was more usual, he was angry. His temper was volcanic, and his ferocity a matter of legend.

Moose presented us to him in the wardroom anteroom the first evening. He was sitting in a corner, a glass of lemon squash in front of him, reading an ancient copy of the *Tatler* with furious concentration.

"The two new boys, sir," Moose said. "Cruickshank and Popham." Butch lowered the magazine and glared at us with small, unexpectedly mild blue eyes. Then he grunted something unintelligible, but not unfriendly.

"Done any deck landings?"

"No, sir," said Crooky quickly.

Another grunt. He regarded us for a moment longer, and it was then I noticed his eyes. They were set in skin at once sandy, softly wrinkled and almost feminine, among the surrounding hair, like two pools of shallow water in the lion-colored African bush. Lost in all that bristling masculine fur, there was something incongruous about them, a softness and uncertainty that did not tally with his manner or his reputation.

"We join the ship the day after tomorrow," he said, to Moose more than to us. His eyes flickered over us, and then he lifted the *Tatler* and went on reading.

"That was Butch," Moose said. "Have a beer."

"I think I'll have a lemon squash," Crooky said.

"And I'll have a scotch," I said. It was borne in upon me that, despite the hesitancy in Butch's eyes, there was trouble ahead.

Two days later we embarked in *Indomitable*, then the newest and largest of the Fleet Carriers afloat.

Because *Argus,* the oldest and smallest carrier afloat, and the ship that did duty as a training-carrier, had been on operations in the exigencies of the time, neither Crooky nor I had ever yet seen a deck. Landing on one was the ordeal that had lain in waiting for us for fourteen months; it was implicit in our choice of service. Without having been through it, our calling ourselves Fleet Air Arm pilots was unsubstantiated, as we had discovered before now.

"What's it like, landing on one of those aircraft carriers?" we had been asked by pretty little things, all agog for hair-crisping tales of pitching decks and hair-breadth escapes. "I can't imagine how you do it."

"Nor can we," we had murmured, truthfully; and watched the look of adoration fade.

Now we were about to find out; and our one idea when we took off and set course over the Clyde was to get it done with as quickly, and with as little fuss, as possible. In this, on our first attempt, we were frustrated by being unable to find the ship; and we returned, the two of us, to Macrihanish with our tails between our legs. Later, after some pointed inquiries from the ship, we took off again, and found her with so little difficulty we could not imagine how we had missed her the first time.

We flew over her in careful formation, and then turned and circled, waiting for the affirmative flag—the white cross on a red ground—to flutter out on the signal boom on the port side and stream aft like a board in the wind. The deck was clear, and we looked down on it incredulously. Were we really going to land on that flat, floating sheet of metal? The idea made no picture in our minds; imagination had no materials to work with beyond the picture that our eyes could see, the long, low, lopsided ship, steaming idly over a gray sea among the hissing rain-squalls.

She began to turn, and as she did so the wake boiled up astern and her speed increased. The steam-jet on the center-line wavered and began to flow aft. The batsman took his place on the port side of the after 4.5 turrets, a minute, hardly visible figure among all the detail of the ship's side, holding out his yellow bats to us in invitation as we flew past. One or two figures were still moving about on the deck; many more were grouped round the island. As we turned, we looked back. The flag was out. They were ready for us. One after the other, we dropped our hooks.

Crooky, who was leading, put his wheels down and turned across wind. I flew on for a little, and then turned after him in a wider circle; pushed back the hood; lowered my wheels—red lights on, then one reassuring click, and another, as they locked and the lights went off. Wheels down. And downwind now, and the ship in profile racing past in the opposite direction at the tip of an arrow of white water. Crooky was turning in on the last leg of his approach. I put my flaps down, re-trimmed to bring the nose up a little, pushed the mixture control to rich, airscrew into fine pitch, let the speed fall off, following a routine as habitual, as familiar, as tying a tie, yet with the familiarity undermined as in a dream. Under the shadow of this sudden, aching doubt, I began the gentle turn across wind and finally into wind, in line with the ship.

There was Crooky now, almost stationary, poised it seemed over the after end of the deck. Then, with a little bird-like motion, the tail of the aircraft tipped and dropped back. He was down. Two men ran out from each side to clear the wire from the hook, and the batsman, pausing long enough to wave me round, jumped up on to the wing of his aircraft. Words of encouragement, congratulation? Cursing, I opened up and went round again.

What was happening? They were wheeling him aft. . . . O Lord! they were making us do more than one landing. I did another circuit and aligned myself with the ship as Crooky sailed off over the bows. Checked my speed: eighty knots. Still too fast. Throttle back a bit. Seventy-five. That's better. Now, where's the batsman? For a moment I can't pick him out. Ah, yes, there he is. And his bats are held level—O.K. I don't seem to be getting any closer; of course, the ship is steaming away from me at twenty-six knots. The right bat goes up and the left one down: looking over the port side, one tends to drop that wing a little. And now, suddenly, the deck is rushing up at me; a glimpse of the thrashing white turbulence of the wake over the trailing edge of the wing; down a bit, down a bit— am I over the deck yet? A fraction of a second of blind disorientation—and the cut. I chop back the throttle, keep the stick central, we're dropping like a brick, a touch of motor, and the quick hard bounce as the wheels touch, and, at once, the jerk of the wire that throws one against one's straps, the tip of the tail, and back, with a soft little thump on to the deck.

For a second relief dizzies me. Then the aircraft is being pushed back; a Petty Officer, leaning against the wind, waves his arms for the brakes and I jam them on and lock them. Someone taps me on the shoulder; the batsman, clinging on to the side of the cockpit.

"That was all right," he shouts, "but watch that port wing. You tend to drop it. O.K.?"

"O.K."

"One more good one then."

He hops down. Quick cockpit check, and he holding up the green flag. I give him a thumb; he waves the flag; open up against the brakes; the flag drops; off brakes, and we're away up the deck, past the island, a bump as the port wheel rides over the catapult ramp, and into the air over the bows. Round again for a second landing.

This time I ended up well over on the port side and saw myself, for one breathless instant before the hook caught, going over the side. But all was well, and the Flight Deck Petty Officer signaled me up the deck and on to the for'ard lift. Switches off, magnetos, petrol, radio; unlock the straps and throw them back; snap the release box of the parachute, and step out of the harness, over the side of the cockpit on to the wing, to be almost swept away by the hard, flat blow of the wind. My rigger, who is on his way up to take my place, grabs my arm and grins.

"They was all right, sir. Mr. Cruickshank's too. Both very nice, sir."

I mutter something, and scramble down the wing on to the deck, and look round. How bare and bald it is, with the wind tearing over it, and splinters of rain and spray in the wind. There, by the door into the island, is Butch, one half of his vast mustache blowing across his face. I'd better report.

He glares at me through a screen of wind and hair with those uneasy eyes. "Feel all right?"

"Fine, sir."

A grunt. "Second one. Over to port. Must keep straight. Give you, Cruickshank, some more." He frowned and grabbed his flying mustache and with a look of indescribable ferocity muttered: "But not bad. Report to Commander Flying." And strode off down the deck.

First deck landings—but no longer do we deign to underline such red-letter days in red.

CAPTAIN JOSEPH CONRAD

Conrad began my anthology. He ends it, too, and I offer no apologies for that. In this, I am regarding only those works of Captain Conrad's which deal almost entirely with ships and the sea. Others can appraise the rest. What sort of a *man* was he, apart from seaman? You might as well ask what sort of man was Herman Melville. There were many Melvilles. I guess there were many Conrads, too, all somehow contained in the slight form and great mind of that introspective, bearded Anglo-Pole. Captain Bone knew him, and carried him across the North Atlantic once, as a passenger in the Cunard-Anchor liner *Tuscania*.

"Conrad's appearance did not agree at all with my pre-conception of a robust sailor and a gifted and successful author," he writes of their first meeting, in 1919.* "Here was a reflectively quiet man, obviously apprehensive of a public occasion . . ." for they were both invited to address a gathering of dons. Aboard the *Tuscania*, Bone showed Conrad the bridge, thinking he "would be interested in the development of shipping and seafarers, since he retired from active service in 1896, but whether the old trade secrets that he knew so well remained with him, I could not easily determine. . . . Quickly, he had understood the use and purpose of the many mechanical devices there installed, but he seemed not at all impressed by their manifest efficiency. . . . He betrayed a faint displeasure that we had come to rely upon mechanical power to do much that, in his sea days and mine, had to be manhandled by sailor stratagem and strength and resolution. . . ."

* In *Landfall at Sunset* by Sir David W. Bone, Duckworth (London).

Conrad himself once briefly summed up his views of the powered ship. "The efficiency of a steamship consists not so much in her courage as in the power she carries within herself. It beats and throbs like a pulsating heart within her iron ribs, and when it stops, the steamer, whose life is not so much a contest as the disdainful ignoring of the sea, sickens and dies upon the waves. The sailing ship, with her unthrobbing body, seemed to lead mysteriously a sort of unearthly existence, bordering upon the magic of the invisible forces, sustained by the inspiration of life-giving and death-dealing winds."

For my second Conrad selection, I choose the brief essay which he called "The Character of the Foe," in his *The Mirror of the Sea*.

The Character of the Foe

by CAPTAIN JOSEPH CONRAD

It seems to me that no man born and truthful to himself could declare that he ever saw the sea looking young as the earth looks young in spring. But some of us, regarding the ocean with understanding and affection, have seen it looking old, as if the immemorial ages had been stirred up from the undisturbed bottom of ooze. For it is a gale of wind that makes the sea look old.

From a distance of years, looking at the remembered aspects of the storms lived through, it is that impression which disengages itself clearly from the great body of impressions left by many years of intimate contact.

If you would know the age of the earth, look upon

From *The Mirror of the Sea* by Joseph Conrad.

the sea in a storm. The grayness of the whole immense surface, the wind furrows upon the faces of the waves, the great masses of foam, tossed about and waving, like matted white locks, give to the sea in a gale an appearance of hoary age, lusterless, dull, without gleams, as though it had been created before light itself.

Looking back after much love and much trouble, the instinct of primitive man, who seeks to personify the forces of Nature for his affection and for his fear, is awakened again in the breast of one civilized beyond that stage even in his infancy. One seems to have known gales as enemies, and even as enemies one embraces them in that affectionate regret which clings to the past.

Gales have their personalities, and, after all, perhaps it is not strange; for, when all is said and done, they are adversaries whose wiles you must defeat, whose violence you must resist, and yet with whom you must live in the intimacies of nights and days.

Here speaks the man of the masts and sails, to whom the sea is not a navigable element, but an intimate companion. The length of passages, the growing sense of solitude, the close dependence upon the very forces that, friendly today, without changing their nature, by the mere putting forth of their might, become dangerous tomorrow, make for that sense of fellowship which modern seamen, good men as they are, cannot hope to know. And, besides, your modern ship which is a steamship makes her passages on other principles than yielding to the weather and humoring the sea. She receives smashing blows, but she advances; it is a slogging fight, and not a scientific campaign. The machinery, the steel, the fire, the steam have stepped in between the man and the sea. A modern fleet of ships does not so much make use of the sea as exploit a highway. The modern ship is not the sport of the waves. Let us say that each of her voyages is a triumphant progress; and yet it is a question whether it is not a more subtle and more human triumph to be the sport of the waves and yet survive, achieving your end.

In his own time a man is always very modern. Whether the seamen of three hundred years hence will have the faculty of sympathy it is impossible to say. An incorrigible mankind hardens its heart in the progress of its own perfectibility. How will they feel on seeing the illustrations to the sea novels of our day, or of our yesterday? It is impossible to guess. But the seaman of the last generation, brought into sympathy with the caravels of ancient time by his sailing-ship, their lineal descendant, cannot look upon those lumbering forms navigating the naïve seas of ancient woodcuts without a feeling of surprise, of affectionate derision, envy, and admiration. For those things, whose unmanageableness, even when represented on paper makes one gasp with a sort of amused horror, were manned by men who are his direct professional ancestors.

No; the seamen of three hundred years hence will probably be neither touched nor moved to derision, affection, or admiration. They will glance at the photogravures of our nearly defunct sailing-ships with a cold, inquisitive, and indifferent eye. Our ships of yesterday will stand to their ships as no lineal ancestors, but as mere predecessors whose course will have been run and the race extinct. Whatever craft he handles with skill, the seaman of the future shall be not our descendant, but only our successor.